German aesthetic and literary criticism:
The Romantic Ironists and Goethe

German
aesthetic and literary criticism:
The Romantic Ironists and
Goethe

Edited by Kathleen M. Wheeler

Fellow of St John's College, Cambridge
and University Assistant Lecturer

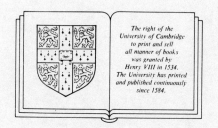

The right of the
University of Cambridge
to print and sell
all manner of books
was granted by
Henry VIII in 1534.
The University has printed
and published continuously
since 1584.

Cambridge University Press

Cambridge

London   New York   New Rochelle

Melbourne   Sydney

Published by the Press Syndicate of the University of Cambridge
The Pitt Building, Trumpington Street, Cambridge CB2 1RP
32 East 57th Street, New York, NY 10022, USA
296 Beaconsfield Parade, Middle Park, Melbourne 3206, Australia

First published 1984

Printed in Great Britain at the University Press, Cambridge

Library of Congress catalogue card number: 84-1703

British Library Cataloguing in Publication Data

German aesthetic and literary criticism.
1. Criticism—Germany—History
I. Wheeler, Kathleen M.
801′.95′0943 PN99.G4
ISBN 0 521 23631 2 hard covers
ISBN 0 521 28087 7 paperback

Contents

Preface

This volume is one of three in a series of anthologies of German aesthetic writing (in English translation) from the second half of the eighteenth and the early nineteenth century. The choice of selections was extremely difficult to make given the scope, variety, and richness of the writings of the period covered by this volume, namely the 1790s to about 1820. In a sense, there was no question of making the 'right' choice, since the appropriateness would depend upon the various and of course often irreconcilable needs and demands of different readers. So much material of great value had to be excluded that one can hope not to justify the exclusions but only that the selections presented will be found to be of value both in themselves and as indications of the individual style and wide-ranging interests of the authors represented. Similarly, the second half of the bibliography on suggested further reading should be taken in the same spirit, as an aid to introducing the interested reader to the enormous field of research that might otherwise overwhelm. The inclusion of Goethe in this volume may strike most readers as odd until it is considered that because of his stature and uniqueness, his inclusion in any of the three volumes would have been odd, but his total exclusion would have been still more awkward. Nor is his inclusion with these German romantics meant to suggest an affinity in intellectual outlook, but only to express first, that Goethe was writing at the same time as the romantics and, second, that he was, like some of these others, a creative artist and writer of literary criticism rather than a systematic philosopher.

One of the main considerations in the selection of material was to provide extracts that would be of particular interest to an English-speaking readership. The tremendous impact that Shakespeare had upon German intellectual life in the latter part of the eighteenth century is directly reflected in the writings of several of the authors included here, and should add to the interest of these selections. But the indirect impact upon the theorizing and practical criticism was incalculable, especially as it was mediated through, for example, Lessing and Herder. Shakespeare proved to be, in both England and Germany, the liberating influence that freed literary theorists and creative artists alike from Neo-classicism. This in itself is so familiar a characterization of literary history as to seem no longer enlightening. What is not yet altogether appreciated, however, is the direct line between the theorizing inspired by Shakespeare's works that broke Neo-classical constraints and that of modern critical theory today. For, as will be evident from these selections, German romanticists and romantic ironists in particular found in Shakespeare the impetus for many of their best insights. Not surprisingly, many of these insights are well-developed ideas coincident with many of the most exciting concepts of modern criticism today.

For example, in Novalis' short piece, 'Monologue', can be found the idea, inspired by Shakespeare's (and Goethe's) use of language, of language as significant by convention and difference rather than by reference to an extra-linguistic reality. Next, the fragment genre and mode of publication of the Romantics' first fragments (mixed and unidentified authorship) as well as explicit statements in Friedrich Schlegel, Novalis, Jean Paul, and others, are a challenge to conventional notions of textual unity and authorship, and reveal how the 'Romantic' concept of organic unity has been misunderstood as suggesting an absolute unity, rather than being an indication of how relative parts can be said to be related to a relative and open-ended concept of a whole. Further anticipations and concerns of modern critical issues come in Jean Paul, Friedrich Schlegel, and Novalis where we find particularly stimulating references to reading as writing, and criticism as interminable decoding and creative play. Solger's, Tieck's, and Novalis' reflections on language as symbolic, allegorical, and mystical can be seen as yet further attempts to reveal how language does not necessarily depend upon reference to reality for its significance, whether conceived as material or transcendental. Rather, language depends upon highly sophisticated and cultivated conventions and differences which have a history, are subject to alteration, and do not enjoy any existence apart from the specific circumstances and concrete, lived experience in which they occur.

'Irony' in the German Romantic sense and the correlative concept of self-criticism, express concepts, first, of the work of art as a self-consuming artifact (one, that is, which protects itself from attempts to finalize its 'meaning') and, second, of criticism as creatively destructive in the sense of dismantling the preconceptions and received opinion (whether author's or readers' or tradition's) that block fresh response and pass for the work itself or characteristics of or facts about it. The concept of irony as evolved by the Romantics also helps us to understand better how deeply rooted these ideas are in a long tradition of 'alternative' interpretation of the major figures of Western culture, a tradition running side by side with the tradition of received opinion about them, and which sporadically and vigorously asserts itself as an alternative. The relation of poetry and 'creative' writing in general to philosophy and criticism is also explored, particularly by F. Schlegel, Novalis, and Solger, and the latter two fields are suggested to be as fictional and 'creative' as their so-called opposite, poetry. Nor is science allowed to retain a privileged position as certain and objective.

Finally, implicit in the philosophical orientation of not only the theoretical but also the practical criticism of many of the authors included here is the challenge to both the empirical and the idealist (as well as the absolutist) notions of truth, knowledge, and certainty, a challenge operative in their dynamic and sophisticated relativism whose modern-day counterpart is the pragmatic approach to art, language, truth, and knowledge characteristic of such writers as Wittgenstein in his late work, John Dewey, and Heidegger, to mention only a few. It would be too much to say that German Romanticism and the related English Romanticism of, for example, Blake, Shelley, and Coleridge was the *origin* of modern critical theory. German Romanticism, like modern criticism itself, was a stage in the reinterpretation of the past that constituted a rewriting of it, based upon the contention that in such central figures as Plato, Aristotle, and Shakespeare could be found the creative affirmation of the necessity for a continuous reanalysis of received opinion ('fact' or TRUTH) and of the necessity for new and more adequate linguistic descriptions not of reality or truth, but of previous descriptions – or, as John Dewey said, interpretations of other people's interpretations.

Acknowledgments

To Joyce Crick and Mark Ogden acknowledgment is due for the translation of numerous previously untranslated essays or extracts. Mrs Crick translated Friedrich Schlegel's essay 'On Goethe's *Meister*', all the Novalis selections, Goethe's 'Aphorisms', and the Karl Solger *Erwin* extracts. Mr Ogden translated the Tieck and the Tieck–Solger correspondence. To both translators I am grateful, furthermore, for cooperation with editorial adjustments.

For permission to publish previously translated material the following publishers are gratefully acknowledged: For F. Schlegel's 'On Incomprehensibility', 'Critical Fragments', 'Athenäum Fragments', and 'Ideas': Friedrich Schlegel, translated by Peter Firchow. *'Lucinde' and the Fragments*. University of Minnesota Press, Minneapolis. Copyright © 1971 by the University of Minnesota.

For the F. Schlegel extract from *Dialogue on Poetry*, 'Letter about the Novel': the Pennsylvania State University Press, at University Park, Pa.

For the extracts from Jean Paul's *School for Aesthetics*: the Wayne State University Press at Detroit, Michigan.

To Professor Barry Nisbet I am indebted for improvements to the introduction which he kindly suggested and I am also grateful to him for other editorial advice. Terry Moore of the Cambridge University Press was extremely patient and helpful throughout all stages of the work, and was particularly generous with attention and advice in the final stages. The librarians and staff of the Cambridge University Library and of St John's College library were generous with their time and advice in helping me to track difficult references. I also owe thanks to St John's College for its generosity in numerous ways that bore both directly and indirectly upon the completion of this volume.

K.M.W.
Cambridge, 1983

Introduction

A good preface must be at once the square root and the square of its book.
(Friedrich Schlegel, *Critical Fragments*, 8)

1. Storm and Stress

In the period preceding the rise of romanticism was enacted the conflict between Neo-classicism and the Storm and Stress movement – the rejection of those 'rigid rules of reason' binding art and human experience generally. The Storm and Stress rejection of reason for the emotional, mystical side of human nature gained strength first from Neo-Platonic speculations mediated by Shaftesbury* in the early eighteenth century, from Leibniz's philosophy, and from the pietistic strain in the German tradition. Johann Georg Hamann and Johann Gottfried Herder both drew upon these sources for their inspirational revival of German mysticism into a philosophy of feeling opposed to the tyranny of reason that was stifling, as they thought, the deepest creative and artistic impulses in man, impulses coming not from the faculty of reason but from the irrational and the unconscious. Like the Romanticism superseding it, Storm and Stress rejected rigid adherence to formal conventions derived from literal interpretations of Aristotle. It strove to replace objective representation of nature with subjective representation of feeling, and the simplicity of ancient art (with its emphasis on representation of the visual aspects of the natural world) with the complexity and turmoil of the inner world of feelings, intuitions, and the unconscious. But the emphasis on feeling and the rejection of reason for emotion was the great weakness of the Storm and Stress movement in its struggle against Neo-classicism and rationalism; Storm and Stress was superseded by Romanticism as the major spokesman against the advocates of dogmatic rationalism.

Romanticism attacked the leaders of Storm and Stress, such as Hamann, Herder, and the young Goethe, for rejecting reason. The romantics insisted that

---

* Shaftesbury, Anthony Ashley Cooper, 3rd Earl of (1671–1713), whose *Characteristics of Man, Manners, Opinions, Times* (1711) had an incalculable influence upon the eighteenth century both in England and abroad. The dialogue form typical of the treatises in *Characteristics* was modelled after Plato's method of leading the learner (and, analogously, the reader) from confused opinion to subject that received opinion to analysis and liberate the mind from pseudo-knowledge.

their common goal, of a striving toward knowledge of the infinite, was a
rational, not a merely irrational, striving. As Kant had taught the young
romantics, it was a postulate of reason itself to seek for the eternal, the infinite,
the final cause. Friedrich Schlegel, basing his philosophy of the synthesis of
reason and emotions firmly upon Kant's faith in reason, sought to overthrow
the extremism of Storm and Stress, and sought to prove to adherents of the
philosophy of feeling, such as Herder and August Wilhelm Schlegel, that they
too, unaware perhaps, were using their reason to formulate irrationalism and to
set feeling up to dominate over reason. Friedrich Schlegel, along with Friedrich
Schleiermacher and Friedrich Schelling, insisted upon the necessity to
synthesize these two only apparently conflicting sides of man's nature, if
knowledge of the sort they sought was to be gained. While Kant's earlier
Humean scepticism may have been the grounds for Hamann and Herder's
rejection of reason as incapable of handling the deeper and the most pressing of
human questions, his own later development of a transcendental metaphysic
provided the new basis needed for the early romantic challenge to extremist
emotionalism, and also provided grounds for their insistence upon a philosophy
of art, religion, and man that involved the synthesis of these several faculties
into a single, powerful, and integrated tool for probing the essence of existence.
The romantics learned from Kant that reason could be an ally of the sublime
and inspirational in man's spirit. They learned from him that feelings could be
articulated into conceptions and related to thought so as to become knowledge.
But they went beyond Kant (at least beyond the literal position of his published
writings) in asserting that man could achieve his highest spiritual knowledge
and perfection not merely by means of the reason articulating emotions,
feelings, and intuitions into conceptions and ideas. Reasoning alone, even
about feeling, could never lead man to the knowledge of himself that he was
really capable of unless, in addition to reasoning, he united his reason with the
education of his aesthetic and moral spirit.

From this rejection of Kant's Stoic ethics (derived solely from reasoning and
a sense of duty) arose once again the idea of the aesthetic education of man as
central to his moral and intellectual development, an idea elaborated by
Schiller, Schelling and later by Karl Solger, and inspired perhaps by
Shaftesbury's much earlier speculations. Man's delight in beauty and the
gradual refinement of his taste was seen not only as a worthy end in itself, but
also as a means of inspiring him to knowledge of his transcendental self and
thereby to knowledge of reality. Love of beauty led naturally to love of the good,
so that the harsh demands of Kant's Stoic duty were replaced by an emotional
yearning to live morally – an inner drive, rather than duty imposed from
without and performed without the desire to do the good.

2. Ancient and modern literature

Romanticism sought, then, to integrate the two opposing forces in Neo-
classicism and Storm and Stress. In reuniting reason and feeling in philosophy,

the Romantic was still, however, confronted on the aesthetic side by the same basic conflict, the conflict between ancient and modern literature. All the writers represented here were deeply interested in trying to grasp and articulate the distinction between ancient and modern literature, as expressive of the principles of art and of a theory of literature that could account for the value and aesthetic validity of modern literature in spite of its glaring divergence from the classical aesthetic. The concept of romantic irony first arose from the efforts to define the essentially modern in literature, but later came to be recognized as a principle essential to all art. Ludwig Tieck explained that 'Romantisch' refers not to a particular type (*Gattung*) of poetry: rather, 'Classic and romantic are not opposites, because poetry is everywhere the same essentially, whether called romantic or classical. Indeed all poetry is in itself romantic; in this sense there is nothing but romantic poetry' (Köpke, *Nachgelassene Schriften*, II, 237). Nevertheless, the word 'romantic' retained the historical reference from which it originated even after its significance was broadened to include not just modern but all great art. This ambivalence reflects more the development and articulation of the concept than any contradiction in the theory itself.

The word 'Romantisch', used to signify the distinguishing characteristic of modern literature, originated from a family of terms, including 'Roman' (meaning only very roughly 'novel' and including romance and related prose narratives), the adjective 'Roman' (meaning Roman civilization), 'Romanze' (referring to medieval romances and ballads), and 'romantic' (suggesting love, the sentimental, the exotic, and the fantastic). All these elements contributed to the acceptance of 'Romantisch' as the adjective used to describe the essentially modern. To identify any single element as the predominant source would seem to be reductive (but see Lovejoy (1916 and 1917), and Eichner's response (1956), both efforts to identify such a predominant source). Friedrich Schlegel was the most forward of the young writers of the circle of Romantics in expounding a theory of 'Romantische Poesie', and was probably catalysed into articulating his position by Friedrich Schiller's article 'Über naive und sentimentalische Dichtung' in *Die Horen* of December 1795. Schlegel's reading of J. G. Herder would already have prepared him to receive this decisive influence from Schiller. Herder, as Jean Paul Richter of all the Romantics was most vividly aware, had, some twenty years earlier, expressed many of the ideas which were to become the starting points for romantic theory, scattering them throughout his innovative and influential writings on Shakespeare (the dramatist who was to be seen as the 'centre of romantic poetry': see especially 'Shakespeare' in *Von Deutscher Art und Kunst*), his work on the origins of modern poetry in the Middle Ages, and his discussions on the relation of ancient and modern literature. Herder explicitly identified the characteristically modern or post-classical genre as originating in the 'Mischung' of the Middle Ages, and as being itself a mixed genre, or 'Mischgedicht', as Friedrich Schlegel was later to name it (see *Critical Fragments*, 4). Herder identified the essentially modern genre as the *Roman* (using the term very broadly) or the *Abenteuer*, and characterized it as having a marvellous, all-encompassing content (*Sämtliche*

Werke, ed. B. Suphan, 33 vols. (Berlin, 1877–1913), xviii, 59f., 107–9). Herder also identified Shakespeare's plays as the central examples of *Romane* and as the link between medieval and modern literature. He further anticipated Friedrich Schlegel's account of the essentially modern literary form when he insisted that the *Roman* had become more and more philosophical, that it was poetry in prose, and contained all genres and types of poetry while including criticism, philosophy, theory of art, history, and science. Goethe shared some of these ideas of Herder's; in his 'Aphorisms on Art and Art History' he emphasized the need for artists and critics to unite artistic and philosophic realms: 'if you would write, and certainly if you would dispute, about art today, you should at least have some inkling of the continuing achievements of philosophy in our time'. In the same group of aphorisms, Goethe maintained the need for modern art forms to be many-sided and miscellaneous, including both the 'highest' and the 'lowest', the former for the sake of seriousness, the latter for fun (but see headnote to Goethe for an account of his early hostility to Romanticism). In this he continues Herder's *Mischung* concept, and also expresses the romantic concept of the necessity for seriousness and play, tragedy and comedy, positive and negative to be united in art.

   Roman, then, did not have a genre meaning, as, for example, 'novel' does; rather, it indicated a *tendency* in modern literature away from classical styles and toward prose of an intensely poetic type, encompassing a wide range of content and styles as well as genre, a *Mischgedicht*. As a tendency, the word *Roman* included not only *Romane* and *Novellen*, but also the plays of Shakespeare, medieval romances, and the writings of Cervantes, Dante and others. As Friedrich Schlegel explained in the 'Letter on the Novel' (in this volume), 'Romantic is not so much a literary genre as an element of poetry which may be more or less dominant or recessive, but never entirely absent . . . I postulate that all poetry should be Romantic and . . . I detest the novel as far as it wants to be a separate genre' (*Dialogue on Poetry*, 101 and below, p. 78). However, Goethe, in his letters and conversations with Schiller, insisted that the novel was an inferior form (to the lyric, drama, and verse-epic). He and Schiller stoutly defended the traditional genres in the face of romantic syncretism. Schlegel saw the tendency of modern art to be toward firstly a fusion of genres into an all-embracing art form; secondly a fusion of poetry and prose into a 'poetic prose', that is, a prose highly concentrated and compressed, a prose that also included passages of poetry; and finally a fusion of the separate realms of philosophy, art, religion, and criticism that would reveal their intrinsic interdependence. Jean Paul shared this view, regarding all genre classification with scepticism and demanding from the highest poetry a fusion of all literary forms. Only through such a fusion would each part find its richest, most adequate expression. The preoccupation with the *Roman* did not indicate a preference for prose over poetry; rather it indicated that the tendency of modern literature was away from 'pure' classical norms and genres, towards *Mischung*. The *Roman* was the poetic form in which 'all the faculties are in bloom at once' and which most aptly represented the nature of genius; it was the 'poetic encyclopedia, a poetic licence to use every poetic licence' (Jean Paul, *School for Aesthetics*, 35, 180 and below, p. 167).

In the context of Lessing (whom the Schlegels and Jean Paul praised for his ironic style in spite of his classicism), Herder, and finally Schiller's and Goethe's renewal and development of earlier Neo-classical theories of art and criticism, under the influence of Winckelmann's classical researches, and in relation to the philosophical developments of Kant, Schelling, and Fichte, the romantics brought about a transition in criticism that forms the basis of modern critical thought today. While Schiller, along with Goethe, was the impetus for freeing the romantics from an aesthetic of objectivity and the superiority of classical over modern literature, Kant's *practical* philosophy (that is, an action can be permissible for me only if it is permissible for anyone *in my situation* – the last three words constitute the sense of relativism as applied to Kant) on which the *Critique of Practical Reason* was grounded, along with Herder's aesthetic of historical relativism (expressed, for example, in his essay 'Shakespeare', in *Von Deutscher Art und Kunst*), had pointed the way for a revolution in criticism. A respect for the relativism of beauty was the analogue to Kant's moral relativism and made it possible for the young romantics to embrace both ancient and modern types of art as good art, since each was representative of the different culture from which it emerged, and since art, according to the new philosophy, need not be judged by pure or absolute laws but rather by relative ones representing evolving conceptions of beauty and worth. Dialectical oppositions between perfection or completion and a striving or progression toward unattainable perfection came to represent the distinction between classical and modern art. Nevertheless, while relativism pointed the way toward a liberation from Neo-classical criticism, the new criticism tended to establish romantic irony as a principle expressive of the essentially aesthetic in *all* great art, though irony certainly began as the concept characteristic of post-classical literature as distinct from ancient art. The Aristotelian Neo-classical canon, then, was for the romantics simply false as characterizing the essential in art, whether Greek or modern; it only described the accidents of ancient art. Like Kant, romantic theorists achieved a balancing act between relativism and absolutism that reflected the awareness of a need to recognize a family resemblance amongst aesthetic objects without, however, postulating a shared essence and without losing sight of the limitations of cultural and intellectual perspective.

While the term *Romantisch* is closely related to Schiller's *sentimentalisch* in that both represent the tendency in much modern or post-classical art towards the progressive and infinite (as distinct from the alleged perfection of classical art through limitation and cyclic rather than progressive movement), the difference between the two terms becomes immediately apparent when Schiller judges Shakespeare to be *naiv*, not *sentimentalisch*, and categorizes him with Homer; by contrast, all the Romantics included in this volume saw Shakespeare as the romantic poet *par excellence* and saw Homer initially as characteristically classical. In this central case the Romantics followed Herder's lead, and then gradually moved in the direction of establishing principles essential to *all* good art, while Schiller on the other hand sought to distinguish two types of good art, and Herder had been content with a historical relativism consistent with either approach. Similarly, in relation to contemporary writers, Schiller's and Schlegel's categories of the sentimental and the romantic did not overlap. Goethe, particularly his *Wilhelm Meister* novel, represented for Schiller the *naiv* type of artist. Friedrich Schlegel, on the other hand, repeatedly (even if inconsistently: see Eichner (1956), 1019, and Lovejoy (1916) for discussion of Schlegel's ambivalent attitude toward Goethe) extolled Goethe's art and particularly *Wilhelm Meister* as preeminent examples of romantic art. Indeed, Schlegel's review of the novel, 'On Goethe's *Meister*', constitutes the major early manifesto of romantic irony (see below, pp. 59–73).

Some of the major distinctions between the predominant tendencies in ancient and modern art emphasized by Schiller and the Romantics can be summarized as, first, the preponderance of the objective in ancient art, second, the subjective in modern art, third the pervasive interest in unifying form in classical as opposed to the interest in multifarious content in modern art – the one displaying a unity, permanence, naturalness, and perfection of form through limitation, the other revealing a variousness and all-encompassing content through its striving for the unattainable infinite. Modern art was extolled for its emphasis upon expressiveness and concern for impressions and ideas, rather than upon nature, external objects, and objectivity of representation generally. The Romantics were obsessed with nature, while rejecting the rational, objective view of nature common to enlightenment thinkers. The goal of modern art was the *interessant* instead of the 'beautiful'; it was didactic and philosophical, and, characteristically, while ancient art was largely based upon mythology, modern art was 'based entirely on a historical' or often real, autobiographical foundation, however fantastic, marvellous, grotesque, or fanciful its elaboration of this real. Furthermore, modern writers were said to portray individual human nature in its peculiar characteristics, only indirectly revealing the universal, thereby giving free play to originality and individual, mannered style.

Friedrich Schlegel was clearly dissatisfied with his own early acceptance of and with Schiller's (and Herder's) apparent acquiescence in a dualistic theory of two types of great art, in Schiller's terms the objective or 'naiv' and the subjective or 'sentimental'. Schlegel set himself to study Shakespeare as the model of the modern tendency in literature in order to be able to articulate the nature of that tendency, and to decide whether or not it might still reveal shared, fundamental aesthetic principles with the ancient, classical mode in spite of extreme differences evident at the surface level. Schlegel found in his study of Shakespeare that he shared the view of his famous brother August Wilhelm, namely, that Shakespeare's judgment and artistry were equal to his instinct and genius. The plays of Shakespeare were not mere instinctual outpourings of an unreflective spirit, as the Storm and Stress encouraged us to believe, but were artistic constructs of an intensely observant and penetrating mind. In this the Schlegel brothers seem to give a hint as to one genuine meaning of Schiller's categorizing of Shakespeare with the 'objective' poets, for Shakespeare showed objective artistic intelligence and not just subjective outpouring of emotion. Yet, confusingly, Schiller further described these poets as 'naiv', implying lack of conscious artistry. 'Objective' and 'naiv' seem to have opposite meanings, but this apparent discrepancy may be a clue to how Schiller meant the term 'naiv' to be understood. A spontaneous detachment from subjective, personal, sentimental involvement in their art is probably a better description of what is meant by naive poets than if we imagine 'naive' to mean the outpourings of the poet, or his naive and primitive descriptions of the natural world – a genius unguided by the rudder of judgment, conscious reflection, or conscious artistry (if such a genius is even possible). Schiller himself was also deeply impressed by Shakespeare's consummate artistry, by his ability to select and abstract from the mass of detail offered by reality the most apt and intense particulars that imbue his language with the compression essential to poetry and his characters with the passion essential to art. It was his consummate artistry and objective, detached passion or imaginative intensity in representing nature and human nature that made Shakespeare a Homeric poet in Schiller's eyes.

Friedrich Schlegel adopted Schiller's insight into Shakespeare's objectivity, universality and detachment from sentimental emotionalism, which the Storm and Stress movement had overlooked in favour of the notion of a 'raw, unfettered genius'. But Schlegel then overcame the dualism of Schiller's aesthetic theory by not only admitting this shared quality with Homer and perhaps with early Greek tragedy. Schlegel also claimed that Schiller's error lay in not recognizing the conclusion that must be drawn from Shakespeare's affinity to the Greeks – namely, that there are not two types of great art, but only one, and that not only Shakespeare and Goethe amongst the moderns were close to the Greeks when the deeper principles of their art were discovered. All truly great modern art is close to Greek literature in its essential aesthetic principles. 'Naiv und sentimental' was rejected as a misleading and inadequate dichotomy, however useful it had been initially in bridging the gap between the ancient and the modern. Schlegel announced Shakespeare's plays as the perfect artistic embodiment of both so-called 'objective' and 'subjective' art. Shakespeare's art was, as was Goethe's *Wilhelm Meister*, at once representative of the universal and of the particular, of objective and subjective, of unified form and multifarious content, of objective nature and subjective consciousness, of detachment and of passion. The difference between disparate literary forms could not be one of fundamental aesthetic principle, as Schiller seemed at least to suggest by his dualism, but merely a matter of emphasis, or of degree rather than kind. Friedrich Schlegel then transformed the original meaning of his term 'romantic' to signify the characteristic synthesis of these pairs of opposites common to all great art, where before 'romantic' had been used merely as a historical term in relation to modern literature.

3. The challenge to unity, authority, and decorum

The effort to articulate the nature of the distinction between ancient and modern literature brought into question the notion of perfection, completeness, unity, and the work of art as a self-contained whole or discrete entity (a question discussed more fully below, where unity is related to the individual's self-cultivation through art). But related assumptions about individual authorship and originality were also questioned, covertly by means of the fragment form, used by several of the Romantics for their first public statements about the new literature and criticism, and which by its nature challenged conventional, technical unity. Romantic collections of fragments of mixed and unidentified authorship also challenged the established notions of authorship, influence and originality as a matter of individuality alone. Fragments represented a self-conscious expression through choice of genre that all genuinely romantic literature must be fragmentary and incomplete, imperfect because it strives for an unattainable infinity. Jean Paul defended the fragment form for the additional reason that 'all life is but a fragment anyway' (*Sämtliche Werke*, 1:2:5). Fragments constituted not only a rejection of the apparent unity and perfection of the closed, consistent system or work of art in favour of a form which could include multiple authorship as a truer expression of the nature of authorship (because authorship involves not merely the individual but previous poets and the literary tradition, as well as contemporary poets as co-authors). Self-contradiction and paradox were also seen as necessary elements of art expressible through the fragment genre, for both were pervasive characteristics of human experience and psychology, and thus necessary to an adequate representation of it.

The fragment form as conceived by the Romantics also represented the nature of language and communication as indirect, imperfect, and dialectical, that is, emphasizing the process of response as an integral, completing part of a necessarily fragmentary formulation. Thus the problem of response and, derivatively, of incomprehensibility became a focus for several of these issues. Friedrich Schlegel, Jean Paul, and Novalis addressed themselves to these aspects of communication, openly rejecting easy, immediate comprehension as unproductive and even delusive. They embraced carefully designed models of incomprehension as a way of stimulating readers, by means of fragmentary and oracular utterances, to grapple with thinking itself and with language as a vehicle of thought. Such a style discouraged reading merely mechanically over linguistic formulations whose significance eludes actual reflection, due to a surface sense that is too readily accessible to provoke active thinking, while it appears to offer determined solutions. Jean Paul explained: 'Ultimately it is best to envelop everything great in dark words so that it cannot be parroted, but only guessed at by those who will not destroy but explore it further . . . Like children, those who are capable will learn through the incomprehensible how to understand' (E. Berend, *Jean Paul's Aesthetik* (Berlin, 1909), 86). Goethe, in a moment of perhaps only apparent agreement, similarly remarked, 'The obscurity of certain maxims is only relative. Not everything which is illuminating to the man who practises it can be made clear to the listener' ('Aphorisms', see below, p. 226). Closely related to this method of stimulating the reader to imaginative labours of thought was the concept of 'preparatives' and 'propadeutics'. In spite of the emphasis by Herder and the Romantics upon the *Roman* as the 'all-encompassing tendency' of modern art, and as the 'poetry in prose' of post-classical literature, the fragment form was important as the 'preparative style' for the development of the genuine *Roman* to come. Indeed, art itself was seen as the essential preparative to raising the mind from unimaginative to creative apprehension of life and reality. Preparatives were necessary to prepare the mind for imaginative response. Jean Paul especially emphasized the importance of 'preparatives', of prefaces and 'delaying techniques'. His *School for Aesthetics* he saw as a prefatory work, just as Novalis saw the fragment form as prefatory to the genuine novel. In his own fiction, as in the *School*, Jean Paul made extensive use of delays – of interruptions, prefaces to prefaces, and extra pages, in order to loosen narrative convention and raise the reader to a pitch of imaginative stimulation, where he could awaken to the realization that the preparative or the delay and the goal, if understood rightly, are identical. This identity of delay and goal and the concept of the preparative are also emphasized by Karl Solger (see below for discussion). The fragment by its very fragmentariness and simultaneous self-contained unity expressed the paradoxical identity of the preparative as also the goal, or the thinking itself as not only the means but the end of thought. A thought posing as a solution and authorized end to thinking about something was seen as a delusory expectation and a false goal. Situations of apparent (surface) incomprehension were designed to reveal the genuine goal to be reflection itself, arrived at through the very situations supposed to be preparatives only.

4. Allegory, symbol, and fragment

The distinction between allegory and symbol made clear by such theorists as Schelling and Karl Solger, and later by Friedrich Schlegel further elaborated the purpose of this calculated and deliberate 'incomprehension' typical of the fragment as a dense and compressed form. Other theorists of the period such as G. H. Schubert and Creuzer followed this work up and explored in detail the distinction and its relation to art and dream-work. The distinction was based largely on Schelling's insistence that the symbol is not merely a sign for something, as allegory is (see *Philosophie der Kunst*, part II, in *Sämtliche Werke*, vol.

v (Stuttgart, 1859), 354f.). Rather, the symbol both signifies and also vitally participates in the idea which it represents. Goethe made a similar distinction between the allegory – which involves the *concept* fully captured and complete in the image that expresses it – and the symbol, which involves not a concept but an idea, which can never be fully captured or expressed completely in the image that seeks to represent it (see 'Aphorisms' below, p. 229, for a brief exposition). Schelling insisted moreover that the value of all mythology is that it is not allegorical, but symbolic (which accounts, for example, for the power of Greek mythology as it occurs in ancient art). The meaning of the symbol verges on the mystical because it cannot be expressed discursively or conclusively and because it eludes any definite linguistic formulation. Its content, incommensurate with its expression taken discursively, stimulates the hearer to active contemplation and energetic participation in the symbolic work. The value of the symbol over allegory then is in its evocative power; in its linguistic expression it is nevertheless a true part or a living fragment of the experience or idea it seeks to represent.

The romantics viewed their collections of fragments as examples of the symbolic mode, on account of the genre itself, but also in many particular cases through the actual content of the fragments, some being more successful examples than others. The fragments were designed not to determine solutions or to give final results, even indirectly, as the allegory does. Nor are they to be conceived as 'signs', which in themselves are not significant but arbitrary. Rather, by portraying the author's mind in an active grappling which remains uncompleted and indecisive, they stir the reader to active thinking. As Jean Paul insisted, the process of the artist's labour to decipher the symbolic language of nature must be repeated as the reader deciphers the 'hieroglyphs' of the aesthetic object. Goethe, in spite of his anti-romantic stance, made a similar point, in the 'Aphorisms', when he insisted that the spectator could derive aesthetic pleasure from even a moderate talent, precisely because the work of art reveals a mind at work in the presence of nature. To the Romantics, a work of art is necessarily incomplete just as nature is, for both communicate through a language of symbols. Novalis and Jean Paul emphasized that poetry was a fragmentary, symbolic, but imperfect representation of the secret, the hidden, and the mystical in human life. Goethe too, in a rare moment of apparent agreement, emphasized the unattainability of symbolic meaning and described beauty as inner necessity concealed from view but nevertheless discoverable in the work of art ('Aphorisms', p. 229). Hegel, that master of such dialectical writing, was impressed by Solger's theoretical contribution to the distinction between allegory and symbol (included in this volume), a distinction that also fascinated Goethe, but other Romantics used the fragment form as a practical contribution to the distinction. Novalis well described this symbolic significance of the fragment form; each fragment, he said, was meant to be for the reader a 'purposeful exercise of the power of thinking', and Jean Paul insisted that the fragment was designed to leave room for the imagination of the reader to act. Novalis called the fragments 'literary seed-houses' and said, 'True, there may be many a barren grain amongst them. But meanwhile if only a few germinate . . .' (*Miscellaneous Writings*, 104) – in the reader's mind, of course. Novalis recognized that many of his fragments might be difficult to comprehend (he described them as like hedgehogs), but, like Jean Paul, he viewed them as deliberately mystical, as, like the symbol, harbouring secrets. The mystical was the romantic expression for the unattainable, ungraspable and 'unendlich' toward which all romantic art strove, but difficulty of comprehension could lead to a deeper understanding, to an ability to accept paradox and the mystical irresolution of profound insight.

5. The reader as a fellow labourer

The fragment form was meant then to represent the incomplete nature of language, communication, and art as parts representing the unattainable perfection toward which they strove, while at the same time the fragment genre instructed the reader in his role as actively participating to create the relations which the artifact could stimulate, rather than in the role of passive recipient or observer of someone else's strivings. Novalis and Jean Paul Richter insisted that the author could not give a reader the truth, but only set him in the direction of truth. For example, wit according to Jean Paul forces the audience to mental exercise, while paradox and even vagueness help to evoke in him the striving for the infinite. Jean Paul also spoke of the necessity for the reader to complete the work of art as if it were an 'outline', sketched by the author, of his perceptions and experiences; Solger might have clarified this idea by calling Jean Paul's 'outline' a symbolic design. Novalis, Jean Paul, and Solger all suggested that the reader, like the author, can never fully grasp, but can only have presentiments and forebodings of truths that must remain forever fragmentary, incomplete and unverifiable by the discursive reason. Thus the author is in no position to offer his readers more than the opportunity to exercise, sharpen, and cultivate their intuition, wit, and imagination; but to the Romantics this was the greatest gift possible. The gift of truth and complete comprehensibility was a delusion, and indicated a major misconception of the nature of truth and communication, and a false expectation of what art or philosophy could offer.

Jean Paul developed his sketch of the relation of the author to his reader in the *School for Aesthetics*, where he was concerned both with explaining the significance of the fragment form, like Novalis and Schlegel, and with articulating the related problem of the nature of language and communication as indirect and symbolic. Jean Paul insisted that the reader and poet are both poets of a sort if the creative activity involved in imaginative reading is properly understood. The failure on the part of the reader to rouse himself to a congenial and imaginative level of response accounts for much of the incomprehensibility of works of art, which cannot be understood at the most basic level if the reader remains in a passive mental posture. In this sense Novalis insisted that 'the true reader must be an expanded author' (*Miscellaneous Writings*, 125), but he insisted on this only in order to indicate the demands of art on the reader, not to glorify the reader's activity as greater than or equal to the poet's. Many of Jean Paul's stylistic devices, his puns and disruptions, his extraordinary imagery and wit, and his surrealistic verbal techniques function to hold the reader attentive and active; his style is not, then, mere mannerism, but an aesthetic device consciously wrought. Jean Paul's theory of indirect communication, of the reader creatively filling in the outline provided by the artist, was based upon his Coleridgean theory of the faculties. He explained that there can be 'no simple reception without production or creation, since every man receives poetic beauty only in parts, like chemical elements which he must compose organically into a whole, in order to contemplate it' (*School for Aesthetics*, 29, and below, p. 163). That is, 'simple', ordinary perception, which Coleridge called primary imagination, involves, originally, active creation, even if ordinary perception degenerates through time into an unimaginative, habitual passivity. For both Coleridge and Jean Paul, imagination is precisely that faculty which has the energy to synthesize parts into wholes, whether at the level of perception or of that of artistic creation (secondary imagination). Thus even the initial perception of the reader, when correctly understood, should involve that 'faculty of faculties', subordinating and unifying parts into a coherent whole. Novalis stressed the nature of the activity involved in aesthetic response in equally Coleridgean terms when he emphasized, 'What I am to understand has to develop organically within me – and what appears to be learning is only nourishment – a stimulus to the organism' (*Miscellaneous Writings*, 19). Friedrich Schlegel had spoken in similar terms in the 'Ideas', 5 (see below, p. 54).

According to Jean Paul, the reader was limited or restricted but also guided by the outline which the text provided for the reader to fill in. Words, according to Jean Paul, cannot express the whole of what the author experiences, but if the reader is congenial and attuned to the author, he can enter into the text and complete it in the fullness of his own activity. Jean Paul explained that art can mediate differences in men's responses to art works by presenting something general which is then interpreted uniquely by each reader. If, however, as Solger claimed, the heart and essence of all art is identical (see below, *Erwin* selections), then the restriction on the reader imposed by the 'outline' or complex of symbols, as Solger might describe it, is not actually a restriction, but only a limitation that is the means of initiating the reader into the aesthetic experience. The poet's individuality draws the reader, through the artistic outline, into a self-activity (*Selbsttätigkeit*), but the particularity and individuality of the outline and of the response to it are joined to a universality as the reader is led to the goal of self-discovery and self-cultivation common to all art. The idea of the 'outline' is not to be understood as some preferred meaning or *authoritative* limitation to interpretative work, but rather as the initiating stimulus to an eventual 'awareness of the inner self and a longing for the infinite'. As the anti-Romantic Goethe also reminded his readers, 'An artist skilled in producing estimable works is not always capable of giving an account of them – neither his own, nor others'' ('Aphorisms', p. 226).

Solger's choice of the dialogue form (and Novalis' brief toying with it, see below) was indicative of his insistence that the reader must engage creatively, doing at least half the labour of the author instead of passively acquiescing in the fruits of others' labours and 'parroting' their insights – for the dialogue form itself provided the reader with a model of response. The dialogue also represented Solger's commitment to the romantic idea of 'Symphilosophie', one of the central goals of Romantic writing, namely to develop a philosophy of life and art in a form communicable and comprehensible rather than esoteric and academic in style, with Plato as the model. Through the dialogue form Solger believed he was expressing his philosophy of art in a form at least coincident with natural, ordinary life, namely conversation and friendly enquiry, thus reuniting philosophy with ordinary linguistic behaviour. Following Plato, he believed that the dialogue form was a type of fragment form necessary to the concept of philosophy as the art of evoking thinking and active response from the listener as the real content to be taught, rather than a static content or dogma parroted by the learner. Thus, like all the Romantics, Solger saw his philosophical method as an art, just as Jean Paul saw his critical-theoretical method, the *School for Aesthetics*, as a work of art. Both fulfilled, in theory at least, Friedrich Schlegel's requirement that both philosophy and criticism must be art if they are to be most valuable. Schleiermacher developed a similar attitude in connection with Solger in terms of the 'Symphilosophie': philosophy should be a matter not of dogma, words, or even abstract thinking, but rather of living and experiencing. Solger summed up the informing principle of 'Symphilosophie': 'Where everything depends on knowledge being not merely spoken, heard, and stored up or preserved in the memory, but rather on becoming our own completely, and the material of our most inner experiences, then the dialogue form must be the best, for it lets our spirit, before our very eyes, come into being within us and develop in our daily lives' (*Nachgelassene Schriften*, II, 195). Like the fragment form, then, the dialogue by its very genre represented the active nature of the genuine response required if philosophy and art were to 'nourish' the reader and stimulate him to the goal common to all art and philosophy, namely, an 'awareness and cultivation of the inner spirit'.

6. The aesthetics of incomprehensibility

Novalis' dialogues, so short and anecdotal as to be only fragments of dialogues, indicate yet another significant aspect of the genre. Novalis argued that the true dialogue should be a pure play with words (see 'Monologue', below): 'It is amazing, the absurd error people make of imagining that they are speaking for the sake of things; no one knows the essential thing about language, that it is only concerned with itself.' He further explained the significance of the dialogue and fragment forms in relation to the symbol and as revealing the fragmentary quality of all art and all experience (as Jean Paul had hinted in saying that all life is itself fragmentary): 'Everything Visible cleaves to the Invisible – the Audible to the Inaudible – the Palpable to the Impalpable. Perhaps the Thinkable to the Unthinkable' (*Studies in the Visual Arts*, paragraph 481). Here Novalis hints at his mystical view of nature as a symbolic language of the infinite, of another life and spirit beyond this life, a view shared in its basic idea with Jean Paul, Schelling, Jacob Boehme, and many other German (and English) writers. This view informed their theory of art as symbolic correspondence and of nature as a hieroglyph to be deciphered, though not into a single definable meaning or even group of meanings. Rather, for these 'symbolists' the activity of decipherment was itself the only solution, as the antidote to literal-mindedness and passivity. In essence, nature and art were incomprehensible to the reason alone, accessible only to the mystical irresolution of profound insight. In his writings on the necessity for incomprehension in art, Friedrich Schlegel expanded this enigma further in relation to the techniques of art for communicating the insoluble mystery of man's relation to reality. In addition to the aesthetic function of incomprehension in relation to reader communication discussed above, Schlegel justified the symbolic import of the fragment form by saying that all texts are only fragmentarily incomprehensible, first because of the cleaving of one thing to its opposite (as explained by Novalis immediately above), and next, because of the nature of language itself as symbolical (that is, having an indeterminate significance beyond the discursively expressible: no words are able to communicate or contain the whole of the author's aesthetic inspiration). Schlegel also maintained that a text must in consequence build into itself space and stimulus for the reader to enliven the words with actual experience and build depth out of the surface, visible text. We must, then, he explained, be interested not only in 'the brilliant outward covering', but also in 'the layering and composition of the strata far within'. We must, as readers, 'delve deeper and deeper, even to the very centre in order to know the construction of the whole' ('On Goethe's *Meister*'). Schlegel concluded that what we should love most as readers is to seek out what the author has hidden from our gaze, a comment related to Goethe's description of aesthetic beauty as the concealing of the inner necessity of a work of art ('Aphorisms', below, p. 229). But Schlegel reminds us not to expect to find any final solution or ultimate meaning, for the goal is rather 'a clear consciousness of eternal agility, of an infinite teeming chaos' ('Ideas', 69). The goal, Schlegel explained, is self-knowledge, or, as Karl Solger insisted, the goal is for the reader to cultivate himself more and more, for art shows the ordinary man the way to raise himself to a higher realization of understanding. Art alone opens the way to this achievement, and acts, according to Solger, as a propaedeutic to philosophy, or to thinking about being.

In discussing incomprehensibility as a necessary element of all art, Friedrich Schlegel had implied that such incomprehensibility was both the expression of the impossibility for man of achieving complete, perfect understanding of the highest truths, and also a reflection of the extent to which the reader as yet had not comprehended or cultivated himself. Goethe as classicist had made a somewhat similar point, when he warned his reader, 'If you would reproach an author with obscurity, look first into yourself, to see if all is lucid there: in twilight, even the clearest writing is unreadable' ('Aphorisms', below, p. 226). On the problem of truth as unattainable, Schlegel wrote: 'All the greatest truths of every sort are completely trivial and hence nothing is more important than to express them forever in a new way, and, whenever possible, forever more paradoxically, so that we won't forget they still exist and that they can never be expressed in their entirety' ('On Incomprehensibility', Firchow, 263 and below, p. 35). Jean Paul illuminated the role of paradox that Schlegel described in saying: 'Only dissimilarity raised to polemic fermentation can grow and sprout. No single element can produce flowers – it can hardly reproduce itself' (*Sämtliche Werke*, 1:1:5). Schlegel amplified Jean Paul's idea in saying that through paradox and incomprehensibility he was determined to try to create before the reader's eyes, 'in spite of him as it were – another reader to my own liking: yes even to deduce him if need be' ('On Incomprehensibility', Firchow, 260 and below, p. 33). In *Critical Fragment* 112 he further insisted that the reader should not be 'calm and dead', but alive and critical; the author must design ways of enticing the reader into a shared experience of philosophizing, so that he can discover for himself and genuinely experience the truth to which the author refers him.

7.   Criticism as poetic play

The fragment and the dialogue forms, along with the distinction between allegorical and symbolical language, point then to the concept that all art is necessarily incomplete, first because man's experience of reality is incomplete, and further because the goal of art is to stimulate men to *strive* to overcome that incompleteness: although the goal of completion is unattainable, a new goal of striving for its own sake is set up. Art provides the 'outline', the symbolic, fragmentary starting point for the reader's striving – his self-cultivation and self-knowledge, which, according to the Romantics, was the essential content of all works of art. Jean Paul, Friedrich Schlegel, Novalis, Solger, and even Goethe in his *Wilhelm Meister* all indicated that this creative self-cultivation of the imaginative reader is essentially akin to the poet's work. They insisted that criticism itself, the product of reading, must also become poetic if it is to fulfil its real task, namely to help readers to see how the work of art is trying to engage them in educating and improving themselves through self-criticism and awareness of their present limitations. Goethe's *Wilhelm Meister* was for the romantics (although they detested its ending), if not for Goethe himself, an example *par excellence* of the romantic work of art, partly because even its overt content is the process of a young man cultivating and educating himself, while the novel itself indirectly reveals a mind 'cultivated to perfection'. This cultivated mind behind the apparent disunity of the novel is its primary unifying energy. The *Roman* as genre challenged the accepted notion that obvious, overt structure or formal unity was a necessary element of good art, and showed that the 'intellectual perspective' of the mind of a genius could provide the focus necessary to hold together an apparently miscellaneous content. For example, Jean Paul distinguished between external and internal unity or form: he called the latter 'symbolic individuality', and explained that the expression of inner unity may violate the conventions of external or technical form. Friedrich Schlegel anticipated this distinction when he spoke of the 'cultivated randomness' of Goethe's genius, and when he maintained that modern art generally reveals a 'cultivated randomness' or surface disunity; the usual expectations of unity and coherence are often disappointed: 'But the reader who possesses a true instinct for system [will find that] the more deeply he probes, the more inner connections and relations and the greater intellectual coherence he will discover in the work ('On Goethe's *Meister*', p. 65). Goethe himself complained of his readers that 'All the richness and concentration which is the sole excellence in a work of art goes unrecognized; everything fruitful and stimulating gets pushed aside; a deep and all-embracing synthesis is readily grasped by no-one' ('Aphorisms', see below, p. 228). The insight into the true unity of a work of art depends then upon the self-cultivation of the reader; modern art dispenses with traditional demands for surface unity precisely in order to force the reader to delve deeper in the search for unity and aesthetic integrity. The probing into the depths and layers is precisely the means by which the reader cultivates, educates, and reveals to himself his areas of knowledge and ignorance. Friedrich Schlegel credited Goethe particularly with stimulating the reader in this way: 'Quite deliberately, it seems, this controlling mind allows itself almost any liberty, with a particular fondness for far-fetched connections' ('On Goethe's *Meister*', p. 72). But it must be remembered that the concept of 'unity' was itself paradoxically expressed by the Romantics. That is, genuine aesthetic unity is not some blatantly revealed objective, formal quality inhering in a work of art; it exists only so far as the energy of the creative activity of a mind of genius is retraceable and recreatable by a reader. 'Unity' as a mechanical, discursive mode of organization is replaced by unity of imaginative perception, so that the reader is expected to recreate and retrace the connections, no matter how far-fetched, in order to grasp the 'sole excellence' and integrity of art, that 'deep, all-embracing synthesis'. The fragment genre was itself designed to break down conventional technical unity in art, and entice the reader to discover the unity of the fragments through relating the ideas they expressed in his own unique way.

Novalis illuminated the importance of this deliberate randomness and disregard for conventional structural unity by crediting Goethe with 'no other intention than to find a poetic way of engaging the imagination in a mysterious kind of play' (*Miscellaneous Writings*, 27), a statement closely related to his view of language in ' Monologue' as a play with itself. Novalis then addressed himself to the matter of artistic unity discovered through self-cultivation, which he identified as 'the highest task of education . . . to seize the mastery of one's transcendental self – to be at the same time the self of one's self . . . without a complete understanding of ourselves we will never truly understand others' (*Miscellaneous Writings*, 28). Later, in the same collection of fragments, he sought to distinguish the genuine reflection which art strives to stimulate in its spectator from the more mechanical, passive attention to the content of this or that thought. He spoke of a 'true disposition of mind toward reflection' as constituting the possibility for progress of the spirit in cultivating itself, as opposed to a mere 'inclination to thinking this or that thought . . . Many scholars do not have the true disposition' (*Miscellaneous Writings*, 45).

8.   Irony as self-criticism

The goal and unity of art as knowledge of the spirit through self-conscious cultivation and self-criticism involves both the spectator and the artist – the latter educates himself and develops his 'transcendental self', his spirit, through creating works of art, the former through recreating these works of art in his 'uniquely personal (but not merely subjective) way'. From both artist and spectator, the ability to disengage the conscious self from a naive and sentimental absorption in the artifact is required in order to achieve a state of detached contemplation of oneself in relation to the work. Novalis hints at this detachment when he writes 'Self-alienation is the source of all abasement, as well as being the ground of all true elevation. The first step will be insight into ourselves – detached contemplation of ourselves' (*Miscellaneous Writings*, 26). Tieck characterized this detachment from the point of view of the artist, who must learn to have 'control over his material' ('Herrschaft über den Stoff'), for 'the poet should not lose himself in his work, but remain above it. Irony protects him from onesidedness and empty idealizing' (Köpke, *Nachgelassene Schriften*, II, 239). Friedrich Schlegel attributes to Goethe this genius, or ironic attitude (as will be further discussed below); he describes Goethe as ironic, 'from the heights of his intellect seeming to smile down upon his masterpiece' though he is at the same time utterly serious about it ('On Goethe's *Meister*', p. 64). Thus the artist must be able to step back from his material and reflect upon it in a detached way, and in a similar way the reader must lift himself (*sich aufheben*) above his emotional involvement in the text in order to gain a perspective of detachment upon his interaction with it. Self-criticism is the goal of this detached reflectiveness, and the means whereby the spirit becomes aware of itself in order to perceive and then overcome its limitations born of incomplete but ever growing cultivation. Jean Paul described this true reflectiveness and detachment as 'that high separation of the self from its whole inner world' (*School for Aesthetics*, 30, and see below, p. 163), while Novalis emphasized repeatedly the need for insight into ourselves and for 'detached contemplation of ourselves'.

The capacity for self-consciousness and self-criticism is connected with the ability to be so detached as to be able to enjoy a parody of oneself because of the limitations which have not yet been overcome. Jean Paul asserts, 'the best reader of the best author would be one who could thoroughly enjoy a humorous lampoon on himself' (*School for Aesthetics*, 94, and see below, p. 179). Schlegel insisted, in a passage that moves us closer to a more specific discussion of romantic irony, that, to a person who has not got it, Socratic irony 'will remain a riddle even after it is openly confessed. It is meant to deceive no one except those who consider it a deception and who either take pleasure in the delightful roguery of making fools of the whole world, or else become angry when they get an inkling they themselves might be included' (*Critical Fragments*, 108). The concept of romantic irony is closely involved with self-criticism and the detached glance in art which makes self-consciousness possible, since art acts as a mirror of the artist's and spectator's spirit (as well as the spirit of his culture), in that it shows him what he knows of himself so far, and how cultivated and 'present' his spirit is, once he realizes that his responses to an artifact tell him more about his stage of cultivation than about the object itself. According to Novalis, 'What [Friedrich] Schlegel characterizes so sharply as irony is to my mind nothing other than the consequence, the character of presence of mind – of the true presence of the spirit. The spirit always appears in *strange and airy form*. To me, Schlegel's irony seems to be genuine humour. One idea can have several names' (*Miscellaneous Writings*, 36, and cf. 43). (This comment is instructive of how we may relate the Romantics to each other in spite of their great terminological differences.) The 'true presence of the spirit' is registered when one has become detached from one's self, when one has in a sense 'alienated one's self', as Novalis and Schlegel explain, and when one has limited that self through reflection or self-awareness, so that the spirit can observe and recognize itself as the object of contemplation in aesthetic experience. But let not this self-watching be decried as egotism. For Solger, we achieve a transcendence out of the world of ego and appearance and subjectivity 'when we find all oppositions . . . suspended in ourselves . . . we know no other genuine existence and activity than that which arises in a steady denial of ourselves in our illusory being' (*Nachgelassene Schriften*, 1, 603). The steady denial involves a parodying, an ironizing of our ego, our illusory being, of the self which seeks to usurp the 'transcendental self'. Novalis elaborates Solger's thought when he remarks that man is most admirable 'when the first impression he gives is the impression of an absolutely witty idea, that is, of being spirit and a certain individual at the same time. Each one of these excellent men must seem to be as it were permeated by an airy spirit, which acts as a kind of ideal parody of the visible phenomenon' (*Miscellaneous Writings*, 58). Thus the connection between romantic irony and wit or humour, as Jean Paul called it, begins to emerge. Like irony, Jean Paul's 'humour' is based upon self-criticism and self-annihilation, but like irony, that annihilation also involves a positive, earnest recreation.

The self-criticism that involves a humorous parody of ironizing of the self and leads to transcendence of the self as ego is represented in the work of art when it, too, ironizes itself, and when the author ironizes himself or his audience. As Ludwig Tieck aptly put it, 'the theatre can make fun of itself' (*Kritische Schriften*, I, viii); it jokes with itself, 'as we see already in Aristophanes; he can hardly leave off ironizing himself' (*Kritische Schriften*, v, 81). Tieck likened Aristophanes' effects to those of Shakespeare's, the master of 'Herrschaft über den Stoff', and explained: 'Irony is the power that constitutes a poet's control over his material' (Köpke, *Nachgelassene Schriften*, II, 239). Jean Paul called his concept of humour the 'romantic comic', which, he said, 'annihilates the finite' (*School for Aesthetics*, 88, and see below, p. 174), and described humour as the high, self-conscious, self-parodying spirit of criticism. He gave as an example Tieck's *Zerbino*, in which the *dramatis personae* 'finally believe themselves to be merely fictive non-entities, thus drawing the audience themselves onto the stage . . .' (*School for Aesthetics*, 93, and see below, p. 178). Jean Paul's comment refers to *Illusionstörung*, the disturbance or destruction of illusion characteristic of much romantic writing, as for example in Tieck's 'theatre playing with itself' in *Puss-in-Boots* (*Der gestiefelte Kater*). But Jean Paul himself regularly played a role in his own fiction, and made a distinction between the author and the implied author. In 'Course VII on the Novel' (in *School for Aesthetics*, see below) he praised this destruction of illusion, especially as found in Tieck and Sterne. Both Tieck and Karl Solger cautioned, however, against the error of thinking that *Illusionstörung* constituted romantic irony. Tieck seems to have named it 'direct irony' as opposed to a deeper irony (Köpke, *Nachgelassene Schriften*, I, 173). Furthermore, Tieck often distinguished between crude or common and high irony; the former he attributed to such writers as Swift, while to Plato and Shakespeare he attributed higher, romantic irony:

In most definitions irony is taken too one-sidedly, too prosaically and too materially. Hegel misunderstood Solger on this point. He imagined, that Solger was thinking about common irony, that crude irony of Swift. But already in Plato, it is clear that there is another completely different higher irony. The irony of which I speak is not derision, mockery, persiflage or what in a similar vein is usually understood by the term. Rather irony is the most profound seriousness, yet bound up with play and genuine joviality. Irony is not merely negative, it is rather through and through positive.

(Köpke, *Nachgelassene Schriften*, II, 238–9).

Tieck thus stressed the close relation in irony between the oppositions of play and seriousness, just as did Jean Paul and Friedrich Schlegel. Similarly Goethe emphasized that art should include both 'gravity' and 'fun' ('Aphorisms', below, p. 228), though he probably had nothing like romantic irony in mind when he wrote this. Self-criticism and artistic production were a form of play that was of the most profound seriousness for the realization of the spirit in man, a point emphasized repeatedly by Schiller, and which explains in part the close relation of tragedy and comedy and tragedy and irony. Tieck explained that 'in humour, play and seriousness are paired with each other, as in Sterne'. He then added, 'One may wonder if Jean Paul is actually a humorist, since there play and sentimentality are united' (Köpke, *Nachgelassene Schriften*, ii, 236).

9.   'Destructive' creativity, or the reconciliation of opposites

Karl Solger along with these other writers also emphasized the unity of play and earnestness. The play involved in *Illusionstörung* is not, however, all that there is to irony, however excellent an example of romantic irony when fully appreciated. Certainly irony could be said to be a 'permanent parabasis', a continual self-consciousness of the work itself, which *Illusionstörung* perfectly represents and exemplifies. Understood symbolically, *Illusionstörung* can represent one of the deepest meanings of irony, namely a recognition of the necessity for the artifact not only to criticize itself, the author, or the reader, but also to 'destroy' itself in a certain sense. Friedrich Schlegel hinted at this idea: 'Life at its highest vitality creates as it destroys, and if it cannot destroy anything outside itself, it must turn upon itself and upon its own creation' (*Prosaische Jugendschriften*, ed. Minor, i, 18). Such a concept of self-destruction and of self-nullification is discussed below as a central formulation of the concept of irony. The close involvement of tragedy with irony and humour may be traced in part to this destructive creativity. But the destruction of illusion was only one possible, even if exemplary, technique for embodying irony. Like Tieck and Solger, Friedrich Schlegel insisted that romantic irony was not just satire, persiflage, parody, wit, or *Illusionstörung*. He pointed out that Socratic irony was the precondition for the concept of romantic irony. Novalis, in equating Jean Paul's humour with Friedrich Schlegel's irony, went some way towards indicating the scope of the concepts of irony and humour: 'Humour is a capriciously assumed style . . . Humour is the result of a free combination of the Absolute and the conditioned. Humour gives a general interest and an objective value to what is peculiar and conditioned' (*Miscellaneous Writings*, 30). Jean Paul used almost exactly the same words in his discussion of humour in the *Aesthetics*, and added that the truly humorous author helps the reader to extrapolate from individual instances a general pattern, whereas classical art had given preeminence to general human nature. These comments hint at a complementary formulation of irony as the synthesis of the universal and the particular, which could equally well serve as a general definition of the symbol, to which irony is of course closely related (see the foregoing discussion on symbol and fragment).

Solger had certainly pushed towards this relation between irony, symbol, and humour when he described romantic irony as the constant irresolvable tension between the conditioned and the unconditioned, or as Tieck called it, the 'divine-human in poetry'. For Solger, appearances did not suffice to reach the unconditioned, even in its highest form as art. Art symbolizes the unconditioned, but it is limited by not actually being the unconditioned. Solger explained that irony was partly the attitude of the artist who is aware of the close relation of art to the divine, and who realizes that art is not mere appearance. But this artist also knows that while his art is an expression of the essence of things, the expression itself presents only a limited, finite embodiment of what is essentially unlimited and infinite; hence if taken literally the representation is false, and the literal, concrete expression must be cancelled as invalid. On the other hand, if taken symbolically, the artistic representation has no adequate discursive, strictly conceptual meaning; its meaning is in its ability to stimulate its community of readers to an imaginative insight into the profound, mystical nature of things. As Goethe said, through the symbol the idea 'remains infinitely powerful and unattainable in the image' ('Aphorisms', below, p. 229). But any idea that emerges of the nature of things can emerge only in the garb of concepts or images, which are, by definition, conditioned. Hence, according to Solger, not only the meaning as object but also the meaning as idea must be marred and invalid. Goethe, in his characteristically lucid if nevertheless Classical way, partly captured this more abstract formulation when he commented, 'we know of no world but with relation to man; we desire no art but the art which is the imprint of this relation' ('Aphorisms', see below, p. 227). The tendency of the mind to mistake its relation for a super-human reality partly explains the necessity for an ironic detachment and a procedure of self-watching and cancellation or restriction. But the inexpressibility even of the relation of man to world adds to the need for an awareness of the latent contradiction or irony in all efforts to express it.

Solger described irony from the artist's point of view as the act of stepping back from his work of art, from his creative involvement, in order to observe himself and his creativity as an object of attention and as part of the work of art. Likewise, Solger demanded that the reader should distance himself from *his* creative involvement, for reasons discussed earlier, and constantly glance back over his response. Irony for the romantics is that single, all-encompassing 'Blick' or 'Schau' – a glance back over the artifact which hovers over the entire work, 'work' including not just the notionally independent artifact, but the all-inclusive 'work', namely the object and the response to the object. The word 'artifact' represents then not just some allegedly independent object, but a subject-object. The backward glance, which in a single sweep takes in the unity of the whole, is the glance of the self-conscious mind detached from its apparently independent object of attention and attending to the experience of interaction in order to uncover the limitations of its response and to overcome them. At the same time, the self-conscious glance recognizes both the representation in the artifact of a striving for the infinite, and the ultimate failure to reach that infinite, the ultimate failure to decipher the 'hieroglyph' of nature and of mind. In this paradoxical recognition of the success in striving through the creation of beauty and the creation of imaginative design, with the simultaneous failure to reach the goal of the striving, irony reveals the creative tension of life and of thought in activity rather than in the stasis of a delusive finality. The glance of irony sees the intense seriousness of the quest, and at the same time cancels out the representation of it, annihilating its claim to truth in play and jest, in self-parody and self-criticism. Solger explains that the true arena of art is the moment when the idea itself, embodied in the artifact, is necessarily affirmed and revoked simultaneously by the only faculty that can apprehend meaning in such contradiction, the imagination. But all the Romantics insisted that irony is not primarily negative; in Tieck's words, it is 'through and through positive', for while it invalidates any formulation or representation as adequate to express the infinity of nature or totality, it affirms with the most profound seriousness and in a genuinely Socratic spirit the necessity for this perpetual play of expression and cancellation as the essence of life. According to Solger only by way of the invalidation of the conditioned representation as it claims to represent truth could the realization gradually be won that the conditioned is actually one with the unconditioned. Ultimately, for Solger, the conditioned is itself illusion, for it is certainly not reality, by definition. But the illusory quality of conditionality is not in the world as object; rather, it is in the subject's way of perceiving the world. To the Romantic theorist, duality and opposition arise in consciousness – indeed they are the preconditions of human consciousness – while irony describes the ability to see unity in that duality and opposition, and to *reconcile* contradictions *without*, however, resolving or dissolving them. Reconciliation is not the removal of the tension, but the insight into the common ground or unity which makes possible and sustains the oppositions and tension. Opposites are reconciled in ironic awareness, then, but the tension is not resolved, for reconciliation demands that the paradox be sustained for the faculty of reasoning; but resolution wholly dissipates the paradox into a 'clear' falsifying choice. For Solger and for Hegel, tragedy reaches its apex in the moment when the conditioned and the unconditioned interpenetrate in reconciliation, but not resolution, for the fundamental tension is not released or resolved however completely the surface conflict may be terminated.

Solger explained in terms very similar to Friedrich Schlegel's that this spirit of paradox or contradiction, of the conditioned and unconditioned, reconciled but not resolved since still in opposition, is the true spirit of irony. Moreover, irony, he says, 'is the essential centre of art'; it is 'the most perfect fruit of the artist's understanding' (*Erwin*, 394, and below, p. 150). It is not composed merely of discrete and identifiable techniques or gestures scattered throughout the work of art; rather 'it hovers over the whole of the work', as both Tieck (above) and Schlegel explained (see 'On Goethe's *Meister*', p. 67). Jean Paul pointed out that it was precisely this creation and perception of poetic unity that distinguishes talent from genius (*School for Aesthetics*, 31, and see below, p. 165); this perception is achieved by the unifying backward glance of irony, reconciling oppositions and relating apparently unrelated parts. Novalis, too, reaffirmed the importance of the unity or whole in art in saying that 'the idea of a whole must dominate and modify a work of art throughout' (*Novalis Schriften*, II, 277). Goethe insisted that 'not even the finest artist always succeeds in turning a number of sketches into a whole', but that 'to grasp the whole' was crucial to the appreciation of art. Friedrich Schlegel elaborated the point when he described the unity of a work of art as residing in the single intellectual perspective which it adopted, not in some surface organization or superficially orderly arrangement of parts accessible to the understanding alone (see discussion above).

This 'intellectual perspective' which best constituted the unity of the work, we can now see to be identical with the artist's glance back over his material, with Tieck's idea of control over the artistic material, with the posture of irony (in the high Socratic sense in which the Germans revived the concept of irony). In this constant glancing back over his work as he creates it (for it is not a final glance back over a finished product but a continuous distancing during the process of creation), the artist, positively affirming his idea by embodying it in a work of art, also nullifies its claim to true representation of the infinite and unconditional and cancels its validity by recognizing it as a limited, conditioned work: it is only a representation of essence, and not essence itself. This continuous gesture of 'nullification' ('vernichten') is built into the structure and unity of the artifact (indeed, at a certain level of generalization it constitutes the unity), and is a constant revealing of the artist's awareness, as Novalis maintained in 'Monologue', that his art and language are ultimately about nothing so much as about art and language; overt 'content' is the medium for revealing the relation of language and art to experience and reality. According to Solger, 'the spirit of the artist must unite in one single glance all tendencies in his work, and this glance, hovering over the whole and yet also cancelling out everything, this glance we call irony. The entire being and essence of art is resolved in irony' (*Erwin*, 387, and below, p. 146). Solger adds, 'that man who has not the courage to grasp the idea itself in its transience and nullity is, at least for art, completely lost' (*Erwin*, 388, and below, p. 146). This affirmation and simultaneous cancellation is the essence of Solger's dialectical idealism, as opposed to the dogmatic idealism of later *expounders* of Solger, Plato, Hegel, and others. This dynamic and dialectical emphasis upon methods of thinking and response, which constitutes the heart of traditional (Platonic) methodology, is no doubt what appealed to Hegel in Solger's aesthetics. Each statement, each concept, each claim, each idea must be cancelled out and transcended ('aufgehoben') both in order to keep the movement essential to thinking alive, and because of the paradoxical nature of the concept's or idea's existence – that is, its striving to represent the absolute or unconditioned at the same time that it remains relative and conditioned in its formulation or representation. Only in the striving itself, in the 'Aufhebung', the raising of itself above stasis, can the thought discover itself and participate in the

unconditioned as one with it, rather than merely parroting formulations or
clinging to transitional expressions, as if they were final truths. As Goethe
pithily remarked, perhaps however referring to the (quasi-Platonic) ideas he
believed were immanent throughout nature, 'nature and idea are not to be
separated without destroying both art and life' ('Aphorisms', below, p. 226).
The idea cannot then be entirely torn from the finiteness of nature even in its
striving to represent infinity. The corollary of this view is that the sensible and
the intelligible are also indissolubly united, even if their relation is an enigma to
the reason.

10.   The unity of poetry and philosophy

Thus for the romantic ironists, art and poetry were not absolutely distinct and
separable from philosophy; rather they strove through beauty and the sensible
toward precisely the same goal, namely self-cultivation, as philosophy, often
even using the same methods. Jean Paul affirms the closeness of the two modes
in the *School*: 'This is equally true of the philosophical genius, whom I (unlike
Kant) cannot specifically distinguish from the poetic genius . . . The *inventive*
philosophers were all poetic, that is, the truly systematic ones. Something
different are the *sifting* philosophers, who never create an organic system, but at
best clothe, nourish, amputate, etc.' (*School for Aesthetics*, 35, and below, p. 242).
Novalis made a very similar point in criticizing the pseudo-scholars and
philosophers and their mechanical systems: 'They have learned how to draw
inferences and conclusions in the same way as a shoemaker has learned to make
shoes, without ever coming upon the underlying design or troubling to discover
the first principles behind the thought . . . they have only sought [a System] in
order to be relieved of the labour of any further reflection' (*Miscellaneous
Writings*, 45). For the Romantics, the unity of genuinely organic, open systems
of philosophy and reflection arises from the same intellectual genius which
creates the unity of art, and the creativity of art and philosophy (as well as of
science and mathematics) derives from the same imaginative source of energy.
Jean Paul concludes, 'The reflectiveness of the poet, which we are inclined to
presuppose also among philosophers, confirms the kinship of the two' (*School for
Aesthetics*, 37, and below, p. 168). Friedrich Schlegel concurred: 'The whole
history of modern poetry is a running commentary on the following brief
philosophical text: all art should become science and all science art; poetry and
philosophy should be made one' (*Critical Fragments*, 115). Elsewhere he
amplifies: 'All philosophy is idealism, and there exists no true realism except
that of poetry. But poetry and philosophy are only extremes' (*Ideas*, 96, and cf.
48, 67, 90).
   This view, which sought on the one hand to expand the conception of
philosophy so that its artistic method should be recognized as crucial to its
content, and on the other to reveal the intense reflectiveness and 'the spirit of

contemplation and withdrawal into the self' ('On Goethe's *Meister*', p. 69) of all great art, also led further to the close relation of art and criticism from two perspectives. First, romantic poetry (in the fullest sense of the phrase) included self-criticism, that is, criticism of the work itself within the structure of the artifact. Friedrich Schlegel gave his favourite example from contemporary literature as *Wilhelm Meister*: 'Perhaps we should judge the book and at the same time refrain from judging it; which does not seem to be at all an easy task. Fortunately, it turns out to be one of those books which carries its own judgment within itself, and spares the critic his labours. Indeed, not only does it judge itself; it also describes itself' ('On Goethe's *Meister*', p. 65). One might make this claim for Schlegel's own novel, *Lucinde*, an example of a self-conscious novel whose confusion and disorder are carefully planned as a 'cultivated random-ness' and parody of mechanical, technical unity. From the second perspective, on the other hand, criticism must become poetry, in the widest sense of the term: 'Poetry can be criticized only by way of poetry' (*Critical Fragments*, 117). According to the Romantics, the critical work must, either in its substance or in its form and 'open tone', be a work of art. Novalis credited Friedrich Schlegel with having achieved this goal: 'Schlegel's writings are philosophy as lyric. His essays on Forster and Lessing are first rate minor poetry' (*Miscellaneous Writings*, 105). Similarly, Schlegel described Goethe's criticism of *Hamlet* in *Wilhelm Meisters Lehrjahre* as 'not so much criticism as high poetry', adding: 'All criticism must go beyond the visible work, because every great work, of whatever kind, knows more than it says, and aspires to more than it knows' ('On Goethe's *Meister*', p. 69). Jean Paul described good criticism as first uniting taste and sense, and then gradually becoming a higher criticism, indeed an aesthetics, in that it should transfer its interest from its initial and proper concern for the text toward the principles of aesthetic experience which inform the individual work and which it embodies. Schlegel named this higher criticism 'poetic criticism', which 'does not act as a mere inscription, and merely say what the thing is' ('On Goethe's *Meister*', p. 69), as does ordinary criticism. Rather, poetic criticism must form again what the work of art created; it must 'add to the work, restore it, and shape it afresh', so that it 'represents the representation' ('On Goethe's *Meister*', p. 69).

The unification of poetry and criticism is then two-fold: modern literature should be critical – more particularly self-critical in describing and judging itself. But criticism must become poetry, either in substance or in form. Schlegel postulated that the best of higher criticism should in a sense 'transcend' poetry, but only in the sense that it is the 'understanding of understanding', and only in so far as it reconstitutes the aesthetic object in the light of the multiplicity of perspectives that the critic's distance allows. But art must continue to be the genuine creation and embodiment of understanding; criticism can certainly not be said to 'transcend' poetry in a value sense, but only in a logical sense, as a deliberate move toward thinking about thinking. The critic and reader, if they are to gain what art has to offer, must then become a kind of artist too, according to the romantic ironists. They must seek not to render discursively hidden yet nevertheless discoverable or favoured meanings of a text, but to grasp meaningfulness in its dynamic or symbolic form. The text, says Novalis, is more like an onion than a fruit with a pit of meaning at its centre. The unfolding and discovery of the layers and their inexhaustible and complex interrelationships *is* the meaning, and the 'poetic critic' seeks rather to elucidate some of these possibilities and these symbolic interconnections in order not to bring into view determinate meanings, but to help the reader to cultivate his response and elucidate his aesthetic experience. The poetic critic 'restores' the work of art by redrawing 'outlines' of the text obliterated by the accretion of custom, of expectation, and of the received opinion which passes itself off for the text. It then reveals these lines as the text 'in play with itself', in play with its medium, language, and with the expectations and responses of its community of readers. But the concept of irony adds the proviso that these outlines restored by the poetic critic must be viewed as provisional; they must erase themselves when their function of clearing the mists of earlier received opinion has exhausted itself and they have similarly become mistaken for the text. Poetic criticism should be rich enough that new lines can be drawn out of its content, lines which illustrate the dynamic but elusive nature of artistic meaning. Irony reveals discursive meaning to be radically unstable, and it seeks to express meaning as residing in the interplay between experience and art. Higher criticism as conceived by the Romantics transcends subjectivity, even if it must begin in subjectivity, by identifying the goal of criticism to be the process of cultivation of the human spirit through the awareness of the imaginative complexity of the work of art, as it reflects the cultivated mind of human genius in its infinite variety. 'Symphilosophie' and 'Sympoesie' expressed the transcendence of subjectivity and solipsism through a 'Gesellschaft', a socially shared community of experience and background which makes it possible to relate the unique, personal responses of each reader to an intersubjective context.

Not only did the romantics seek to reunite poetry and philosophy, taking Shakespeare as their model on the one hand, and Plato on the other; they also sought to reunite art and religion, inspired by Greek tragedy. Novalis and Solger insisted upon the vital importance of this process and sought to achieve it in their writings, emphasizing the role of art in religion through mythologizing and symbol-making, and through the concept of nature as a hieroglyph. Tieck and Friedrich Schlegel also called for the close relation of the two, Schlegel uniting them in his novel, *Lucinde*, in his fragments, and in his researches into world mythology. Art was seen as the most adequate representation possible for man of the divine; indeed Tieck had defined the essence of irony as the 'divine-human in poetry' (Köpke, *Nachgelassene Schriften*, II, 238–9). Goethe once observed that 'Art rests upon a kind of religious sense, upon a profound, unshakeable seriousness, that is why it unites so readily with religion' ('Aphorisms', below, p. 228), though what he understood by 'religious' was probably quite different from what the romantics meant. Jean Paul called poetry a higher, vaster love akin to spiritual devotion, but Novalis most succinctly expressed the interrelationship between art, philosophy and religion in one of his fragments, his 'seeds', as he called them, on Goethe; he concluded on a high note with the declaration: 'Poetry is the true and absolute reality. This is the heart of my philosophy. The more poetic, the more true' ('On Goethe', in *Novalis Schriften*, 473, and below, p. 108).

Part 1

Friedrich Schlegel

Friedrich Schlegel

(1772–1829)

Friedrich Schlegel, major theorist of the romantic school, brought to the forefront of literary criticism Herder's earlier attempts to relate modern and ancient literature through an analysis of the 'essentially modern', with Shakespeare as the model and standard of the modern tendency in art. 'Über das Studium der griechischen Poesie' (1795, published 1797) was one of Schlegel's first published attempts to articulate the disparities between ancient and modern, 'interessante' literature. Schiller's article, 'Über Naiv und Sentimentalische Dichtung' (Dec. 1795), opened the way, through its admiration of modern techniques, for Schlegel's re-evaluation of his own critical position, a re-evaluation influenced by Kant's aesthetic relativism. By 1797, Schlegel had published his first fragments in the journal, *Lyceum der Schöne Künste*, in which he developed his idea of 'romantische Poesie' out of the earlier concept of 'interessante' literature, leaving behind his purist tendencies and embracing a non-objective, relativist aesthetic. In 1798, he published his critical masterpiece, 'Über Goethes *Meister*', in which he realized aesthetically many of his critical principles; by 1800 he had written his manifesto of Romanticism, *Gespräch über Poesie*. Many of his publications appeared first in the *Athenäum*, a journal founded in 1798 by himself and his brother, August Wilhelm, as an organ of criticism, and, as Friedrich described it, 'an experiment, or series of experiments' on the possibility of communication, especially by means of irony. In the journal, several collections of fragments of mixed and unidentified authorship were published, including contributions from the Schlegels, Novalis, and Schleiermacher, the aphoristic genre having been inspired by the French writer, S.R.N. Chamfort (1741–94).

For Friedrich Schlegel, criticism should be concerned primarily with the literary text itself, and only secondarily with broad historical or literary generalizations. Schlegel distinguished between analytical and poetic criticism, the former producing only discursive 'Charakteristiks', the latter emphasizing the activity of interpretation as an endless play with the relations in the text and the infinite variety of meaningful responses possible. Poetic criticism sought to discover the 'central intellectual perspective' which unified the imaginative complexity of relations that constituted the text. Only once the initial enthusiasm of the critic (or poet) for his material had subsided could the detachment and ironic self-consciousness necessary for understanding the artifact emerge (the relation between enthusiasm and irony is one of the major topics of the Solger–Tieck letters; see below). Schlegel rejected as improper and misguided any search by the critic for an objective (even if hidden) truth in the text, any privileged interpretation, and insisted upon the analysis of response as itself a crucial part of critical procedure, crucial because it was the means of 'self-cultivation', the ultimate aim of all art for Schlegel, and the other Romantics. The novel was seen by Schlegel as an absolutely new form of composition best expressing the modern sensibility, due in part to its all-inclusive content, its poetic-prose style, its mixed genre, and its emphasis on the particular and concrete. However, in order for modern literature to reach its highest possible achievement, Schlegel saw the need for a new mythology which would revitalize the language of poetry.

Schlegel's other major publications include a highly controversial novel, *Lucinde* (translated into English), attacked in its own time and later by Kierkegaard as 'lewd sensuality', but also criticized for its apparent disunity; 'Über Lessing' (1797), a critical study; and numerous essays on ancient literature as well as essays and lectures on contemporary literature and on philosophy.

Of the following selections, 'Critical Fragments' appeared in the journal, *Lyceum der Schöne Künste*, in 1797; the 'Athenäum Fragments' in *Athenäum*, 1798, as did 'On Goethe's *Meister*'. The 'Dialogue on Poetry' from which the 'Letter about the Novel' is taken, and 'On Incomprehensibility' appeared in *Athenäum*, 1800. The 'Ideas', inspired by Schleiermacher's *Reden Über die Religion* (1799), were also published in 1800, and all of these writings can be found in Jacob Minor, *Friedrich Schlegel, 1794–1802. Seine prosaischen Jugendschriften* (Vienna, 1882). The sources of the selections are as follows: (1) 'On Incomprehensibility': English text from *Lucinde and the Fragments*, translated P. Firchow (Minneapolis, Minn., 1971), 257–71, based on *Kritische Friedrich–Schlegel–Ausgabe* (hereafter *KFSA*). (2) From 'Critical Fragments': English text from Firchow, 143–159, based on *KFSA*. (3) From 'Athenäum Fragments': English text from Firchow, 161–240, based on *KFSA*. (4) From 'Ideas': English text from Firchow, 241–56, based on *KFSA*. (5) 'On Goethe's *Meister*', English text follows the German *KFSA*, II, 126–46. (6) 'Letter about the Novel': English text from *Dialogue on Poetry and Literary Aphorisms*, ed. and translated Ernst Behler and R. Struc (Pennsylvania and London, 1968), pp. 94–105.

'On Incomprehensibility'
'Über die Unverständlichkeit' (1800)

Because of something either in them or in us, some subjects of human thought stimulate us to ever deeper thought, and the more we are stimulated and lose ourselves in these subjects, the more do they become a Single Subject, which, depending on whether we seek and find it in ourselves or outside of ourselves, we designate the Nature of Things or the Destiny of Man. Other subjects perhaps would never be able to attract our attention if we were to withdraw into holy seclusion and focus our minds exclusively on this subject of subjects, and if we did not have to be together with people and hence busy our minds with real and hypothetical human relationships which, when considered more carefully, always become more numerous and complex and thereby make us diverge into directions contrary to this single subject.

Of all things that have to do with communicating ideas, what could be more fascinating than the question of whether such communication is actually possible? And where could one find a better opportunity for carrying out a variety of experiments to test this possibility or impossibility than in either writing a journal like the *Athenaeum* oneself or else taking part in it as a reader?

Common sense which is so fond of navigating by the compass of etymologies – so long as they are very close by – probably did not have a difficult time in arriving at the conclusion that the basis of the incomprehensible is to be found in incomprehension. Now, it is a peculiarity of mine that I absolutely detest incomprehension, not only the incomprehension of the uncomprehending but even more the incomprehension of the comprehending. For this reason, I made a resolution quite some time ago to have a talk about this matter with my reader, and then create before his eyes – in spite of him as it were – another new reader to my own liking: yes, even to deduce him if need be. I meant it quite seriously and not without some of my old bent for mysticism. I wanted for once to be really thorough and go through the whole series of my essays, admit their frequent lack of success with complete frankness, and so gradually lead the reader to being similarly frank and straightforward with himself. I wanted to prove that all incomprehension is relative, and show how incomprehensible Garve,[1] for example, is to me. I wanted to demonstrate that words often understand themselves better than do those who use them, wanted to point out that there must be a connection of some secret brotherhood among philosophical words that, like a host of spirits too soon aroused, bring everything into confusion in their writings and exert the invisible power of the World Spirit on even those who try to deny it. I wanted to show that the purest and most genuine incomprehension emanates precisely from science and the arts – which by their very nature aim at comprehension and at making comprehensible – and from philosophy and philology; and so that the whole business shouldn't turn around in too palpable a circle I had made a firm resolve really to be comprehensible, at least this time. I wanted to focus attention on what the greatest thinkers of every age have divined (only very darkly, to be sure) until Kant discovered the table of categories[2] and there was light in the spirit of man: I mean by this a real language, so that we can stop rummaging about for words and pay attention to the power and source of all activity. The great frenzy of such a Cabala where one would be taught the way the human spirit can transform itself and thereby perhaps at last bind its transforming and ever transformed opponent in chains – I simply could not portray a mystery like this as naively and nakedly as, when with the thoughtlessness of youth, I made *Lucinde* reveal the nature of love in an eternal hieroglyph. Consequently I had to think of some popular medium to bond chemically the holy, delicate, fleeting, airy, fragrant, and, as it were, imponderable thought. Otherwise, how badly might it have been misunderstood, since only through its well-considered employment was an end finally to be made of all understandable misunderstandings? At the same time, I noted with sincere pleasure the progress of our country – not to speak of our age! The same age in which we too have the honour to live; the age that, to wrap it all up in a word, deserves the humble but highly suggestive name of the Critical Age,[3] so that soon now everything is going to be criticized, except the age itself, and everything is going to become more and more critical, and artists can already begin to cherish the just hope that humanity will at last rise up in a mass and learn to read.

Only a very short while ago this thought of a real language occurred to me again and a glorious prospect opened up before my mind's eye. In the

nineteenth century, so Girtanner[4] assures us, in the nineteenth century man will
be able to make gold; and isn't it now more than mere conjecture that the
nineteenth century is shortly going to begin? With laudable confidence and
some huffing and puffing, the worthy man says: 'Every chemist, every artist will
make gold; the kitchen utensils are going to be made of silver, of gold.' How
gladly all artists will now resolve to go on being hungry for the slight,
insignificant remainder of the eighteenth century, and in future no longer fulfill
this sacred duty with an aggrieved heart; for they know that in part they
themselves, and in part also (and all the more certainly) their descendants will
shortly be able to make gold. That he should specify precisely kitchen utensils is
due to the fact that what this ingenious prophet finds really beautiful and great
in this catastrophe is that we won't be swallowing so much vile vinegary wine
out of ordinary, ignoble, base metals like lead, copper, iron, and suchlike.

I saw the whole thing from another point of view. I had often secretly
admired the objectivity of gold, I might say even worshipped it. Among the
Chinese, I thought, among the English, the Russians, in the island of Japan,
among the natives of Fez and Morocco, even among the Cossacks, Cheremis,
Bashkirs, and Mulattoes, in short, wherever there is even a little enlightenment
and education, silver and gold are comprehensible and through them
everything else. When it comes to pass that every artist possesses these materials
in sufficient quantity, then he will be allowed only to write his works in bas-
relief, with gold letters on silver tablets. Who would want to reject so beautifully
printed a book with the vulgar remark that it doesn't make any sense?

But all these things are merely chimeras or ideals: for Girtanner is dead and
consequently for the moment so far removed from being able to make gold that
one might extract with all possible artistry only so much iron out of him as
might be necessary to immortalize his memory by way of a little medallion.

Furthermore, the complaints of incomprehensibility have been directed so
exclusively and so frequently and variously at the *Athenaeum* that my deduction
might start off most appropriately right at the spot where the shoe actually
hurts.

A penetrating critic in the *Berliner Archiv der Zeit* has already been good
enough to defend the *Athenaeum* against these attacks and in so doing has used as
an example the notorious fragment about the three tendencies. What a
marvellous idea! This is just the way one should attack the problem. I am going
to follow the same procedure, and so as to let the reader perceive all the more
readily that I really think the fragment good, I shall print it once more in these
pages:

The French Revolution, Fichte's philosophy, and Goethe's *Meister* are the greatest
tendencies of the age. Whoever is offended by this juxtaposition, whoever cannot take
any revolution seriously that isn't noisy and materialistic, hasn't yet achieved a lofty,
broad perspective on the history of mankind. Even in our shabby histories of civilization,
which usually resemble a collection of variants accompanied by a running commentary
for which the original classical text has been lost; even there many a little book, almost
unnoticed by the noisy rabble at the time, plays a greater role than anything they did.[5]

I wrote this fragment with the most honourable intentions and almost without any irony at all. The way that it has been misunderstood has caused me unspeakable surprise because I expected the misunderstanding to come from quite another quarter. That I consider art to be the heart of humanity and the French Revolution a marvellous allegory about the system of transcendental idealism is, to be sure, only one of my most extremely subjective opinions. But I have let this opinion be known so often and in so many different ways that I really might have hoped the reader would have gotten used to it by now. All the rest is mere cryptology. Whoever can't find Goethe's whole spirit in *Wilhelm Meister* won't be able to find it anywhere else. Poetry and idealism are the focal points of German art and culture; everybody knows that. All the greatest truths of every sort are completely trivial and hence nothing is more important than to express them forever in a new way and, wherever possible, forever more paradoxically, so that we won't forget they still exist and that they can never be expressed in their entirety.

Up to this point I have not been ironical and by all rights I ought not to be misunderstood; and yet it has happened, to the extent in fact of having the well-known Jacobin, Magister Dyk of Leipzig,[6] even find democratic leanings in it.

To be sure, there is something else in the fragment that might in fact be misunderstood. This lies in the word *tendencies* and this is where the irony begins. For this word can be understood to mean that I consider the *Theory of Knowledge*, for example, to be merely a tendency, a temporary venture like Kant's *Critique of Pure Reason* which I myself might perhaps have a mind to continue (only rather better) and then bring to completion; or else that I wish to use the jargon that is most usual and appropriate to this kind of conception, to place myself on Fichte's shoulders, just as he placed himself on Reinhold's[7] shoulders, Reinhold on Kant's shoulders, Kant on Leibniz's, and so on infinitely back to the prime shoulder. I was perfectly aware of this, but I thought I would like to try and see if anyone would accuse me of having had so bad an intention. No one seems to have noticed it. Why should I provide misunderstandings when no one wants to take them up? And so I now let irony go to the winds and declare point-blank that in the dialect of the *Fragments* the word means that everything now is only a tendency, that the age is the Age of Tendencies. As to whether or not I am of the opinion that all these tendencies are going to be corrected and resolved by me, or maybe by my brother or by Tieck, or by someone else from our group, or only some son of ours, or grandson, great-grandson, grandson twenty-seven times removed, or only at the last judgment, or never: that I leave to the wisdom of the reader, to whom this question really belongs.

Goethe and Fichte: that is still the easiest and fittest phrase for all the offence the *Athenaeum* has given, and for all the incomprehension it has provoked. Here too probably the best thing would be to aggravate it even more: when this vexation reaches its highest point, then it will burst and disappear, and then the process of understanding can set to work immediately. We haven't gotten far enough in giving offence; but what is not yet may still come to be. Yes, even those names are going to have to be named again – more than once. Just today my brother wrote a sonnet which I can't resist passing along to the reader because of the charming puns which he (the reader) loves almost more than he loves irony:

> Go, admire idols[8] that are finely made
> And leave us Goethe to be master, guide and friend:
> When his spirit's rosy dawns do fade
> Apollo's golden day no joy will send.
>
> He lures no new spring green from barren trunks,
> But cuts them down to give us warmth and fire.
> And so the time will come when all the Muse's clunks
> Will curse themselves to stone and stiffened mire.
>
> Not to know Goethe means to be a Goth.
> Fools are first blinded by every new, bright flame,
> Then too much light kills them, like the moth.
>
> Goethe, you who by the mercy of the gods came
> To us, an angel from the stars: we are not loth
> To call you godly in form, look, heart, and name.

A great part of the incomprehensibility of the *Athenaeum* is unquestionably due to the *irony* that to a greater or lesser extent is to be found everywhere in it. Here too I will begin with a text from the *Lyceum* [*Critical*] *Fragments*:

Socratic irony is the only involuntary and yet completely deliberate dissimulation. It is equally impossible to feign it or divulge it. To a person who hasn't got it, it will remain a riddle even after it is openly confessed. It is meant to deceive no one except those who consider it a deception and who either take pleasure in the delightful roguery of making fools of the whole world or else become angry when they get an inkling they themselves might be included. In this sort of irony, everything should be playful and serious, guilelessly open and deeply hidden. It originates in the union of *savoir vivre* and scientific spirit, in the conjunction of a perfectly instinctive and a perfectly conscious philosophy. It contains and arouses a feeling of indissoluble antagonism between the absolute and the relative, between the impossibility and the necessity of complete communication. It is the freest of all licenses, for by its means one transcends oneself; and yet it is also the most lawful, for it is absolutely necessary. It is a very good sign when the harmonious bores are at a loss about how they should react to this continuous self-parody, when they fluctuate endlessly between belief and disbelief until they get dizzy and take what is meant as a joke seriously and what is meant seriously as a joke. For Lessing irony is instinct; for Hemsterhuis it is classical study; for Hülsen it arises out of the philosophy of philosophy and surpasses these others by far.[9]

Another one of these fragments recommends itself even more by its brevity:

Irony is the form of paradox. Paradox is everything which is simultaneously good and great.[10]

Won't every reader who is used to the *Athenaeum* fragments find all this simply trifling – yes, even trivial? And yet at the time it seemed incomprehensible to many people because of its relative novelty. For only since then has irony become daily fare, only since the dawn of the new century has such a quantity of great and small ironies of different sorts sprung up, so that I will soon be able to say, like Boufflers,[11] of the various species of the human heart:

> J'ai vu des coeurs de toutes formes,
> Grands, petits, minces, gros, médiocres, énormes.

In order to facilitate a survey of the whole system of irony, we would like to mention here a few of the choicest kinds. The first and most distinguished of all is coarse irony. It is to be found in the real nature of things and is one of the most widespread of substances; it is properly at home in the history of mankind. Next there is fine or delicate irony; then extra-fine. Scaramouche employs the last type when he seems to be talking amicably and earnestly with someone when really he is only waiting for the chance to give him – while preserving the social amenities – a kick in the behind. This kind of irony is also to be found in poets, as well as straightforward irony, a type that flourishes most purely and originally in old gardens where wonderfully lovely grottoes lure the sensitive friend of nature into their cool wombs only to be-splash him plentifully from all sides with water and thereby wipe him clean of delicacy. Further, dramatic irony; that is, when an author has written three acts, then unexpectedly turns into another man and now has to write the last two acts. Double irony, when two lines of irony run parallel side-by-side without disturbing each other: one for the gallery, the other for the boxes, though a few little sparks may also manage to get behind the scenes. Finally, there is the irony of irony. Generally speaking, the most fundamental irony of irony probably is that even it becomes tiresome if we are always being confronted with it. But what we want this irony to mean in the first place is something that happens in more ways than one. For example, if one speaks of irony without using it, as I have just done; if one speaks of irony ironically without in the process being aware of having fallen into a far more noticeable irony; if one can't disentangle oneself from irony anymore, as seems to be happening in this essay on incomprehensibility; if irony turns into a mannerism and becomes, as it were, ironical about the author; if one has promised to be ironical for some useless book without first having checked one's supply and then having to produce it against one's will, like an actor full of aches and pains; and if irony runs wild and can't be controlled any longer.

What gods will rescue us from all these ironies? The only solution is to find an irony that might be able to swallow up all these big and little ironies and leave no trace of them at all. I must confess that at precisely this moment I feel that mine has a real urge to do just that. But even this would only be a short-term solution. I fear that if I understand correctly what destiny seems to be hinting at, then soon there will arise a new generation of little ironies: for truly the stars augur the fantastic. And even if it should happen that everything were to be peaceful for a long period of time, one still would not be able to put any faith in this seeming calm. Irony is something one simply cannot play games with. It can have incredibly long-lasting after effects. I have a suspicion that some of the most conscious artists of earlier times are still carrying on ironically, hundreds of years after their deaths, with their most faithful followers and admirers. Shakespeare has so infinitely many depths, subterfuges, and intentions. Shouldn't he also, then, have had the intention of concealing insidious traps in his works to catch the cleverest artists of posterity, to deceive them and make them believe before they realize what they're doing that they are somewhat like Shakespeare themselves? Surely, he must be in this respect as in so many others much more full of intentions than people usually think.

I've already been forced to admit indirectly that the *Athenaeum* is incomprehensible, and because it happened in the heat of irony, I can hardly take it back without in the process doing violence to that irony.

But is incomprehensibility really something so unmitigatedly contemptible and evil? Methinks the salvation of families and nations rests upon it. If I am not wholly deceived, then states and systems, the most artificial products of man, are often so artificial that one simply can't admire the wisdom of their creator enough. Only an incredibly minute quantity of it suffices: as long as its truth and purity remain inviolate and no blasphemous rationality dares approach its sacred confines. Yes, even man's most precious possession, his own inner happiness, depends in the last analysis, as anybody can easily verify, on some such point of strength that must be left in the dark, but that nonetheless shores up and supports the whole burden and would crumble the moment one subjected it to rational analysis. Verily, it would fare badly with you if, as you demand, the whole world were ever to become wholly comprehensible in earnest. And isn't this entire, unending world constructed by the understanding out of incomprehensibility or chaos?

Another consolation for the acknowledged incomprehensibility of the *Athenaeum* lies in the very fact of this acknowledgment, because precisely this has taught us that the evil was a passing one. The new age reveals itself as a nimble and quick-footed one. The dawn has donned seven-league boots. For a long time now there has been lightning on the horizon of poetry; the whole thunderous power of the heavens had gathered together in a mighty cloud; at one moment, it thundered loudly, at another the cloud seemed to move away and discharge its lightning bolts in the distance, only to return again in an even more terrible aspect. But soon it won't be simply a matter of one thunderstorm, the whole sky will burn with a single flame, and then all your little lightning rods won't help you. Then the nineteenth century will indeed make a beginning of it and then the little riddle of the incomprehensibility of the *Athenaeum* will also be solved. What a catastrophe! Then there will be readers who will know how to read. In the nineteenth century everyone will be able to savour the fragments with much gratification and pleasure in the after-dinner hours and not need a nutcracker for even the hardest and most indigestible ones. In the nineteenth century every human being, every reader will find *Lucinde* innocent, *Genoveva*[12] Protestant, and A. W. Schlegel's didactic *Elegies*[13] almost too simple and transparent. And then too what I prophetically set forth as a maxim in the first fragments will hold true:

A classical text must never be entirely comprehensible. But those who are cultivated and who cultivate themselves must always want to learn more from it.[14]

The great schism between understanding and not understanding will grow more and more widespread, intense, and distinct. Much hidden incomprehension will still erupt. But understanding too will reveal its omnipotence: understanding that ennobles disposition into character, elevates talent into genius, purifies one's feelings and artistic perceptions. Understanding itself will be understood, and people will at last see and admit that everyone can achieve the highest degree and that up to now humanity has been neither malicious nor stupid but simply clumsy and new.

I break off at this point so as not to profane prematurely the worship of the highest divinity. But the great principles, the convictions on which this worship depends may be revealed without profanation; and I have attempted to express the essentials by adding on something myself, by way of what the Spanish call a gloss, to one of the profound and admirable verses of the poet. And now all I have left to wish for is that one of our excellent composers will find my lines worthy of being set to music. There is nothing more beautiful on earth than poetry and music mingled in sweet compliance for the greater ennoblement of mankind.[15]

> The rights of Jove are not for all.
> Don't go too far,
> Stay where you are,
> Look how you stand, or else you'll fall.

> One man is very humble,
> Another's cheeks swell up with pride;
> This one's brains are all a jumble,
> Another's still less well supplied.
> I love a fool, his hair and hide,
> I love it when he roars and rants,
> And love his languid, flowery dance.
> Forever will I now recall
> What in the master's heart I spied:
> The rights of Jove are not for all.

> To keep the mighty pyre burning
> A host of tender souls must be
> Who fresh to every labour turning
> Will make the heathen light to see.
> Now let the din grow loud and louder:
> Watch where you bite,
> Watch what you write,
> For when the fools with gun and powder
> Crawl from their lairs, think who they are:
> Don't go too far.

> Some few have caught and kept the spark
> That we have lighted.
> The masses still are in the dark:
> The dolts remain united.
> Lack of understanding understood
> Confers a lasting gloom
> On all that issues from the womb.
> The latest word brings lust for blood,
> The wasps fly in from near and far:
> Stay where you are.

Let them talk from now till doomsday
They never will understand.
Some are born to go astray,
Artists buried in the sand. –
There are sparrows every season
Exulting in their song:
Does this seem wrong?
Let them live by their own reason,
Just make sure you're big and tall:
Look how you stand, or else you'll fall.

From 'Critical Fragments'
'Kritische Fragmente' (1797)

4. There is so much poetry and yet there is nothing more rare than a poem! This is due to the vast quantity of poetical sketches, studies, fragments, tendencies, ruins, and raw materials.

8. A good preface must be at once the square root and the square of its book.

9. Wit is absolute social feeling, or fragmentary genius.

14. In poetry too every whole can be a part and every part really a whole.

16. Though genius isn't something that can be produced arbitrarily, it is freely willed – like wit, love, and faith, which one day will have to become arts and sciences. You should demand genius from everyone, but not expect it. A Kantian would call this the categorical imperative of genius.

20. A classical text must never be entirely comprehensible. But those who are cultivated and who cultivate themselves must always want to learn more from it.

21. Just as a child is only a thing which wants to become a human being, so a poem is only a product of nature which wants to become a work of art.

22. The flame of the most brilliantly witty idea should radiate warmth only after it has given off light; it can be quenched suddenly by a single analytic word, even when it is meant as praise.

23. Every good poem must be wholly intentional and wholly instinctive. That is how it becomes ideal.

25. The two main principles of the so-called historical criticism are the Postulate of Vulgarity and the Axiom of the Average. The Postulate of Vulgarity: everything great, good, and beautiful is improbable because it is extraordinary and, at the very least, suspicious. The Axiom of the Average: as we and our surroundings are, so must it have been always and everywhere, because that, after all, is so very natural.

26. Novels are the Socratic dialogues of our time. And this free form has become the refuge of common sense in its flight from pedantry.

27. The critic is a reader who ruminates. Therefore he ought to have more than one stomach.

28. Feeling (for a particular art, science, person, etc.) is divided spirit, is self-restriction: hence a result of self-creation and self-destruction.

29. Gracefulness is life lived correctly, is sensuality contemplating and shaping itself.

33. The overriding disposition of every writer is almost always to lean in one of two directions: either not to say a number of things that absolutely need saying, or else to say a great many things that absolutely ought to be left unsaid. The former is the original sin of synthetic, the latter of analytic minds.

37. In order to write well about something, one shouldn't be interested in it any longer. To express an idea with due circumspection, one must have relegated it wholly to one's past; one must no longer be preoccupied with it. As long as the artist is in the process of discovery and inspiration, he is in a state which, as far as communication is concerned, is at the very least intolerant. He wants to blurt out everything, which is a fault of young geniuses or a legitimate prejudice of old bunglers. And so he fails to recognize the value and the dignity of self-restriction, which is after all, for the artist as well as the man, the first and the last, the most necessary and the highest duty. Most necessary because wherever one does not restrict oneself, one is restricted by the world; and that makes one a slave. The highest because one can only restrict oneself at those points and places where one possesses infinite power, self-creation, and self-destruction. Even a friendly conversation which cannot be broken off at any moment, completely arbitrarily, has something intolerant about it. But a writer who can and does talk himself out, who keeps nothing back for himself, and likes to tell everything he knows, is to be pitied. There are only three mistakes to guard against. First: What appears to be unlimited free will, and consequently seems and should seem to be irrational or supra-rational, nonetheless must still at bottom be simply necessary and rational; otherwise the whim becomes wilful, becomes intolerant, and self-restriction turns into self-destruction. Second: Don't be in too much of a hurry for self-restriction, but first give rein to self-creation, invention, and inspiration, until you're ready. Third: Don't exaggerate self-restriction.

42. Philosophy is the real homeland of irony, which one would like to define as logical beauty: for wherever philosophy appears in oral or written dialogues – and is not simply confined into rigid systems – there irony should be asked for and provided. And even the Stoics considered urbanity a virtue. Of course, there is also a rhetorical species of irony which, sparingly used, has an excellent effect, especially in polemics; but compared to the sublime urbanity of the Socratic muse, it is like the pomp of the most splendid oration set over against the noble style of an ancient tragedy. Only poetry can also reach the heights of philosophy in this way, and only poetry does not restrict itself to isolated ironical passages, as rhetoric does. There are ancient and modern poems that are pervaded by the divine breath of irony throughout and informed by a truly transcendental buffoonery. Internally: the mood that surveys everything and rises infinitely above all limitations, even above its own art, virtue, or genius;

externally, in its execution: the mimic style of an averagely gifted Italian *buffo*.

44. You should never appeal to the spirit of the ancients as if to an authority. It's a peculiar thing with spirits: they don't let themselves be grabbed by the hand and shown to others. Spirits reveal themselves only to spirits. Probably here too the best and shortest way would be to prove one's possession of the only true belief by doing good works.

48. Irony is the form of paradox. Paradox is everything simultaneously good and great.

51. To use wit as an instrument for revenge is as shameful as using art as a means for titillating the senses.

55. A really free and cultivated person ought to be able to attune himself at will to being philosophical or philological, critical or poetical, historical or rhetorical, ancient or modern: quite arbitrarily, just as one tunes an instrument, at any time and to any degree.

56. Wit is logical sociability.

57. If some mystical art lovers who think of every criticism as a dissection and every dissection as a destruction of pleasure were to think logically, then 'wow' would be the best criticism of the greatest work of art. To be sure, there are critiques which say nothing more, but only take much longer to say it.

62. We already have so many theories about poetic genres. Why have we no concept of poetic genre? Perhaps then we would have to make do with a single theory of poetical genres.

65. Poetry is republican speech: a speech which is its own law and end unto itself, and in which all the parts are free citizens and have the right to vote.

70. People who write books and imagine that their readers are the public and that they must educate it soon arrive at the point not only of despising their so-called public but of hating it. Which leads absolutely nowhere.

73. What is lost in average, good, or even first-rate translations is precisely the best part.

78. Many of the very best novels are compendia, encyclopedias of the whole spiritual life of a brilliant individual. Works which have this quality, even if they are cast in a completely different mould – like *Nathan*[16] – thereby take on a novelistic hue. And every human being who is cultivated and who cultivates himself contains a novel within himself. But it isn't necessary for him to express it and write it out.

84. From what the moderns aim at, we learn what poetry should become; from what the ancients have done, what it has to be.

85. Every honest author writes for nobody or everybody. Whoever writes for some particular group does not deserve to be read.

86. The function of criticism, people say, is to educate one's readers! Whoever wants to be educated, let him educate himself. This is rude: but it can't be helped.

88. Nothing is more piquant than a brilliant man who has manners or mannerisms. That is, if he has them: but not at all, if they have him. That leads to spiritual petrification.

89. Isn't it unnecessary to write more than one novel, unless the artist has become a new man? It's obvious that frequently all the novels of a particular author belong together and in a sense make up only one novel.

96. A good riddle should be witty; otherwise nothing remains once the answer has been found. And there's a charm in having a witty idea which is enigmatic to the point of needing to be solved: only its meaning should be immediately and completely clear as soon as it's been hit upon.

100. The poetry of one writer is termed philosophical, of another philological, of a third, rhetorical, etc. But what then is poetical poetry?

101. Affectation doesn't arise so much out of a striving to be new as out of a fear of being old.

102. To want to judge everything is a great fallacy, or a venial sin.

104. What's commonly called reason is only a subspecies of it: namely, the thin and watery sort. There's also a thick, fiery kind that actually makes wit witty, and gives an elasticity and electricity to a solid style.

108. Socratic irony is the only involuntary and yet completely deliberate dissimulation. It is equally impossible to feign it or divulge it. To a person who hasn't got it, it will remain a riddle even after it is openly confessed. It is meant to deceive no one except those who consider it a deception and who either take pleasure in the delightful roguery of making fools of the whole world or else become angry when they get an inkling they themselves might be included. In this sort of irony, everything should be playful and serious, guilelessly open and deeply hidden. It originates in the union of *savoir vivre* and scientific spirit, in the conjunction of a perfectly instinctive and a perfectly conscious philosophy. It contains and arouses a feeling of indissoluble antagonism between the absolute and the relative, between the impossibility and the necessity of complete communication. It is the freest of all licenses, for by its means one transcends oneself; and yet it is also the most lawful, for it is absolutely necessary. It is a very good sign when the harmonious bores are at a loss about how they should react to this continuous self-parody, when they fluctuate endlessly between belief and disbelief until they get dizzy and take what is meant as a joke seriously and what is meant seriously as a joke. For Lessing irony is instinct; for Hemsterhuis[17] it is classical study; for Hülsen[18] it arises out of the philosophy of philosophy and surpasses these others by far.

109. Gentle wit, or wit without a barb, is a privilege of poetry which prose can't encroach upon: for only by means of the sharpest focus on a single point can the individual idea gain a kind of wholeness.

112. The analytic writer observes the reader as he is; and accordingly he makes his calculations and sets up his machines in order to make the proper impression on him. The synthetic writer constructs and creates a reader as he should be; he doesn't imagine him calm and dead, but alive and critical. He allows whatever he has created to take shape gradually before the reader's eyes, or else he tempts him to discover it himself. He doesn't try to make any particular impression on him, but enters with him into the sacred relationship of deepest symphilosophy or sympoetry.

114. There are so many critical journals of varying sorts and differing intentions! If only a society might be formed sometime with the sole purpose of gradually making criticism – since criticism is, after all, necessary – a real thing.

115. The whole history of modern poetry is a running commentary on the following brief philosophical text: all art should become science and all science art; poetry and philosophy should be made one.

117. Poetry can be criticized only by way of poetry. A critical judgment of an artistic production has no civil rights in the realm of art if it isn't itself a work of art, either in its substance, as a representation of a necessary impression in the state of becoming, or in the beauty of its form and open tone, like that of the old Roman satires.

120. Whoever could manage to interpret Goethe's *Meister* properly would have expressed what is now happening in literature. He could, so far as literary criticism is concerned, retire forever.

121. The simplest and most immediate questions, like Should we criticize Shakespeare's works as art or as nature? and Are epic and tragedy essentially different or not? and Should art deceive or merely seem to do so? are all questions that can't be answered without the deepest consideration and the most erudite history of art.

123. It is thoughtless and immodest presumption to want to learn something about art from philosophy. There are many who start out that way as if they hope to find something new there, since philosophy, after all, can't and shouldn't be able to do more than order the given artistic experiences and existing artistic principles into a science, and raise the appreciation of art, and create here as well that logical mood which unites absolute tolerance with absolute rigour.

126. The Romans knew that wit is a prophetic faculty; they called it nose.

From 'Athenäum Fragments'
'Athenäums Fragmente' (1798)

1. Nothing is more rarely the subject of philosophy than philosophy itself.

24. Many of the works of the ancients have become fragments. Many modern works are fragments as soon as they are written.

27. Most people are, like Leibniz's possible worlds, only equally rightful pretenders to existence. Few exist.

32. One should have wit, but not want to have it. Otherwise, you get persiflage, the Alexandrian style of wit.

35. A *cynic* should really have no possessions whatever: for a man's possessions, in a certain sense, actually possess him. The solution to this problem is to own possessions as if one didn't own them. But it's even more artistic and cynical not to own possessions as if one owned them.[19]

37. Many witty ideas are like the sudden meeting of two friendly thoughts after a long separation.

39. Most thoughts are only the profiles of thoughts. They have to be turned around and synthesized with their antipodes. This is how many philosophical works acquire a considerable interest they would otherwise have lacked.

41. Those people who have made a profession of explaining Kant to us were either of the sort that lacked the capacity to gain an understanding for themselves of the subjects about which Kant has written; or else such people as had only the slight misfortune of understanding no one except themselves; or such as expressed themselves even more confusedly than he did.

43. Philosophy is still moving too much in a straight line; it's not yet cyclical enough.

44. Every philosophical review should simultaneously be a philosophy of reviews.

46. According to the way many philosophers think, a regiment of soldiers on parade is a system.

51. Naive is what is or seems to be natural, individual, or classical to the point of irony, or else to the point of continuously fluctuating between self-creation and self-destruction. If it's simply instinctive, then it's childlike, childish, or silly; if it's merely intentional, then it gives rise to affectation. The beautiful, poetical, ideal naive must combine intention and instinct. The essence of intention in this sense is freedom, though intention isn't consciousness by a long shot. There is a certain kind of self-infatuated contemplation of one's own naturalness or silliness that is itself unspeakably silly. Intention doesn't exactly require any deep calculation or plan. Even Homeric naiveté isn't simply instinctive; there is at least as much intention in it as there is in the grace of lovely children or innocent girls. And even if Homer himself had no intentions, his poetry and the real author of that poetry, Nature, certainly did.

53. It's equally fatal for the mind to have a system and to have none. It will simply have to decide to combine the two.

54. One can only become a philosopher, not be one. As soon as one thinks one is a philosopher, one stops becoming one.

63. Every uncultivated person is a caricature of himself.

64. The demand for moderation is the spirit of castrated intolerance.

66. When an author doesn't know anymore what sort of answer to make to a critic, then he usually says: But you can't do it any better. That's like a dogmatic philosopher accusing the sceptic of not being able to create a system.

71. People always talk about how an analysis of the beauty of a work of art supposedly disturbs the pleasure of the art lover. Well, the real lover just won't let himself be disturbed!

76. An intellectual point of view is the categorical imperative of any theory.[20]

77. A dialogue is a chain or garland of fragments. An exchange of letters is a dialogue on a larger scale, and memoirs constitute a system of fragments. But as yet no genre exists that is fragmentary both in form and in content, simultaneously completely subjective and individual, and completely objective and like a necessary part in a system of all the sciences.

78. Usually incomprehension doesn't derive from a lack of intelligence, but from a lack of sense.

96. Whoever doesn't pursue philosophy for its own sake, but uses it as a means to an end, is a sophist.

99. At the words 'his philosophy, my philosophy', one is always reminded of that line in *Nathan*:[21] 'Who owns God? What kind of God is that who belongs to a man?'

104. The world considers anyone a Kantian who is interested in the latest German philosophical writings. According to the school definition, a Kantian is only someone who believes that Kant is the truth, and who, if the mail coach from Königsberg[22] were ever to have an accident, might very well have to go without the truth for some weeks. According to the outmoded Socratic concept of disciples being those who have independently made the spirit of the great master their own spirit, have adapted themselves to it, and, as his spiritual sons, have been named after him, there are probably only a very few Kantians.

111. The teachings that a novel hopes to instil must be of the sort that can be communicated only as wholes, not demonstrated singly, and not subject to exhaustive analysis. Otherwise the rhetorical form would be infinitely preferable.

114. A definition of poetry can only determine what poetry should be, not what it really was and is; otherwise the shortest definition would be that poetry is whatever has at any time and at any place been called poetry.

116. Romantic poetry[23] is a progressive, universal poetry. Its aim isn't merely to reunite all the separate species of poetry and put poetry in touch with philosophy and rhetoric. It tries to and should mix and fuse poetry and prose, inspiration and criticism, the poetry of art and the poetry of nature; and make poetry lively and sociable, and life and society poetical; poeticize wit and fill and saturate the forms of art with every kind of good, solid matter for instruction, and animate them with the pulsations of humour. It embraces everything that is purely poetic, from the greatest systems of art, containing within themselves still further systems, to the sigh, the kiss that the poetizing child breathes forth in artless song. It can so lose itself in what it describes that one might believe it exists only to characterize poetical individuals of all sorts; and yet there still is no form so fit for expressing the entire spirit of an author: so that many artists who started out to write only a novel ended up by providing us with a portrait of themselves. It alone can become, like the epic, a mirror of the whole circumambient world, an image of the age. And it can also – more than any other form – hover at the midpoint between the portrayed and the portrayer, free of all real and ideal self-interest, on the wings of poetic reflection, and can raise that reflection again and again to a higher power, can multiply it in an endless succession of mirrors. It is capable of the highest and most variegated refinement, not only from within outwards, but also from without inwards; capable in that it organizes – for everything that seeks a wholeness in its effects – the parts along similar lines, so that it opens up a perspective upon an

infinitely increasing classicism. Romantic poetry is in the arts what wit is in philosophy, and what society and sociability, friendship and love are in life. Other kinds of poetry are finished and are now capable of being fully analysed. The romantic kind of poetry is still in the state of becoming; that, in fact, is its real essence: that it should forever be becoming and never be perfected. It can be exhausted by no theory and only a divinatory criticism would dare try to characterize its ideal. It alone is infinite, just as it alone is free; and it recognizes as its first commandment that the will of the poet can tolerate no law above itself. The romantic kind of poetry is the only one that is more than a kind, that is, as it were, poetry itself: for in a certain sense all poetry is or should be romantic.

120. They have so little regard for wit because its expressions aren't long and wide enough, since their sensitivity is only a darkly imagined mathematics; and because wit makes them laugh, which would be disrespectful if wit had real dignity. Wit is like someone who is supposed to behave in a manner representative of his station, but instead simply *does* something.

149. The systematic Winckelmann[24] who read all the ancients as if they were a single author, who saw everything as a whole and concentrated all his powers on the Greeks, provided the first basis for a material knowledge of the ancients through his perception of the absolute difference between ancient and modern. Only when the perspective and the conditions of the absolute identity of ancient and modern in the past, present, and future have been discovered will one be able to say that at least the contours of classical study have been laid bare and one can now proceed to methodical investigation.

162. In investigating ancient Greek mythology, hasn't too little attention been paid to the human instinct for making analogies and antitheses? The Homeric world of gods is a simple variation of the Homeric world of men, while the Hesiodic world, lacking the principle of heroic contrast, splits up into several opposing races of gods. In that old remark of Aristotle that one gets to know people through their gods, one finds not only the self-illuminating subjectivity of all theology, but also the more incomprehensible innate spiritual dualism of man.

164. The mistakes of the Greek sophists were errors more of excess than omission. Even the confidence and arrogance with which they presumed and pretended to know everything has something quite philosophical about it: not intentionally but instinctively. For surely the philosopher has only the choice of knowing either everything or nothing. And certainly no philosophy worthy of the name tries to teach only some particular thing or some melange of things.

165. In Plato we find unmixed all the pure types of Greek prose in their classic individuality, and often incongruously juxtaposed: the logical, the physical, the mimical, the panegyrical, and the mythical. The mimical style is the foundation and general component of all the rest; the others often occur only episodically. And then he has a further type of prose that is particularly characteristic of him and makes him most Platonic: the dithyrambical. It might

be called a mixture of the mythical and panegyrical if it didn't also have
something of the conciseness and simple dignity of the physical.

167. Almost all criticisms of art are too general or too specific. The critics
should look for the golden mean here, in their own productions, and not in the
works of the poets.

168. Cicero ranks philosophies according to their usefulness to the orator;
similarly, one might ask what philosophy is fittest for the poet. Certainly no
system at variance with one's feelings or common sense; or one that transforms
the real into the illusory; or abstains from all decisions; or inhibits a leap into the
suprasensory regions; or achieves humanity only by adding up all the externals.
This excludes eudaemonism, fatalism, idealism, scepticism, materialism, or
empiricism. Then what philosophy is left for the poet? The creative philosophy
that originates in freedom and belief in freedom, and shows how the human
spirit impresses its law on all things and how the world is its work of art.

206. A fragment, like a miniature work of art, has to be entirely isolated from
the surrounding world and be complete in itself like a porcupine.

216. The French Revolution, Fichte's philosophy, and Goethe's *Meister* are
the greatest tendencies of the age. Whoever is offended by this juxtaposition,
whoever cannot take any revolution seriously that isn't noisy and materialistic,
hasn't yet achieved a lofty, broad perspective on the history of mankind. Even
in our shabby histories of civilization, which usually resemble a collection of
variants accompanied by a running commentary for which the original
classical text has been lost; even there many a little book, almost unnoticed by
the noisy rabble at the time, plays a greater role than anything they did.[25]

220. If wit in all its manifestations is the principle and the organ of universal
philosophy, and if all philosophy is nothing but the spirit of universality, the
science of all the eternally uniting and dividing sciences, a logical chemistry:
then the value and importance of that absolute, enthusiastic, thoroughly
material wit is infinite, that wit wherein Bacon and Leibniz, the chief
representatives of scholastic prose, were masters, the former among the first,
chronologically speaking, the latter among the greatest. The most important
scientific discoveries are bons mots of this sort – are so because of the surprising
contingency of their origin, the unifying force of their thought, and the
baroqueness of their casual expression. But they are, of course, in respect to
content, much more than the unsatisfied and evanescent expectation of purely
poetical wit. The best ones are *echappées de vue* into the infinite. Leibniz's whole
philosophy consists of a few fragments and projects that are witty in this sense. It
may be that Kant – the Copernicus of philosophy – has even more natural
syncretistic spirit and critical wit than Leibniz, but his situation and his
education aren't as witty; and furthermore the same thing has happened to his
ideas that happens to popular songs: the Kantians have sung them to death.
Therefore it's quite easy to be unfair to him and think him less witty than he
really is. Of course, philosophy will only be healthy when it no longer expects
and counts on getting brilliant ideas, when it's able to make continuous

progress, relying, naturally, on enthusiastic energy and brilliant art, but also on a sure method. But are we to despise the few still extant products of synthesizing genius because no unifying art and science exists as yet? And how could they exist as long as we still simply spell out most sciences like schoolchildren and imagine that we've achieved our object when we can decline and conjugate one of the many dialects of philosophy but have no notion of syntax and can't construct even the shortest periodic sentence?

234. It's only prejudice and presumption that maintain there is only a single mediator between God and man. For the perfect Christian – whom in this respect Spinoza probably resembles most – everything would really have to be a mediator.[26]

238. There is a kind of poetry whose essence lies in the relation between ideal and real, and which therefore, by analogy to philosophical jargon, should be called transcendental poetry. It begins as satire in the absolute difference of ideal and real, hovers in between as elegy, and ends as idyll with the absolute identity of the two. But just as we wouldn't think much of an uncritical transcendental philosophy that doesn't represent the producer along with the product and contain at the same time within the system of transcendental thoughts a description of transcendental thinking: so too this sort of poetry should unite the transcendental raw materials and preliminaries of a theory of poetic creativity – often met with in modern poets – with the artistic reflection and beautiful self-mirroring that is present in Pindar, in the lyric fragments of the Greeks, in the classical elegy, and, among the moderns, in Goethe. In all its descriptions, this poetry should describe itself, and always be simultaneously poetry and the poetry of poetry.

247. Dante's prophetic poem is the only system of transcendental poetry, and is still the greatest of its kind. Shakespeare's universality is like the centre of romantic art. Goethe's purely poetical poetry is the most complete poetry of poetry. This is the great triple chord of modern poetry, the inmost and holiest circle among all the broad and narrow spheres of a critical anthology of the classics of modern poetry.

249. The poetizing philosopher, the philosophizing poet, is a prophet. A didactic poem should be and tends to become prophetic.

250. Whoever has imagination, or pathos, or a gift for mimicry ought to be able to learn poetry like any other mechanical art. Imagination consists of both enthusiasm and invention; pathos, of soul and passion; and mimicry, of penetration and expression.

252. A real aesthetic theory of poetry would begin with the absolute antithesis of the eternally unbridgeable gulf between art and raw beauty. It would describe their struggle and conclude with the perfect harmony of artistic and natural poetry. This is to be found only among the ancients and would in itself constitute nothing but a more elevated history of the spirit of classical poetry. But a philosophy of poetry as such would begin with the independence of beauty, with the proposition that beauty is and should be distinct from truth

and morality, and that it has the same rights as these: something that – for those who are able to understand it at all – follows from the proposition I = I. It would waver between the union and the division of philosophy and poetry, between poetry and practice, poetry as such and the genres and kinds of poetry; and it would conclude with their complete union. Its beginning would provide the principles of pure poetics; its middle the theory of the particular, characteristically modern types of poetry: the didactic, the musical, the rhetorical in a higher sense, etc. The keystone would be a philosophy of the novel, the rough outlines of which are contained in Plato's political theory. Of course, to the ephemeral, unenthusiastic dilettantes, who are ignorant of the best poets of all types, this kind of poetics would seem very much like a book of trigonometry to a child who just wants to draw pictures. Only a man who knows or possesses a subject can make use of the philosophy of that subject; only he will be able to understand what that philosophy means and what it's attempting to do. But philosophy can't inoculate someone with experience and sense, or pull them out of a hat – and it shouldn't want to do so. To those who knew it already, philosophy of course brings nothing new; but only through it does it become knowledge and thereby assume a new form.

253. In the nobler and more original sense of the word correct – meaning a conscious main and subordinate development of the inmost and most minute aspects of a work in line with the spirit of the whole – there probably is no modern poet more correct than Shakespeare. Similarly, he is also systematic as no other poet is: sometimes because of those antitheses that bring into picturesque contrast individuals, masses, even worlds; sometimes through musical symmetry on the same great scale, through gigantic repetitions and refrains; often by a parody of the letter and an irony on the spirit of romantic drama; and always through the most sublime and complete individuality and the most variegated portrayal of that individuality, uniting all the degrees of poetry, from the most carnal imitation to the most spiritual characterization.

255. The more poetry becomes science, the more it also becomes art. If poetry is to become art, if the artist is to have a thorough understanding and knowledge of his ends and means, his difficulties and his subjects, then the poet will have to philosophize about his art. If he is to be more than a mere contriver and artisan, if he is to be an expert in his field and understand his fellow citizens in the kingdom of art, then he will have to become a philologist as well.

256. The basic error of sophistic aesthetics is to consider beauty merely as something given, as a psychological phenomenon. Of course, beauty isn't simply the empty thought of something that should be created, but at the same time the thing itself, one of the human spirit's original ways of acting: not simply a necessary fiction, but also a fact, that is, an eternally transcendental one.

258. All poetry that wants to produce an effect, and all music that tries to imitate the comic or tragic excesses and exaggerations of eccentric poetry for the sake of exhibiting itself or of making an impression, is rhetorical.

262. Every good human being is always progressively becoming God. To

become God, to be human, to cultivate oneself are all expressions that mean the same thing.

263. True mysticism is morality at its most exalted.

267. The more one knows, the more one still has to learn. Ignorance increases in the same proportion as knowledge – or rather, not ignorance, but the knowledge of ignorance.

270. As is well known, Leibniz went to Spinoza to have his glasses made; and that's the only contact he had with him or his philosophy. If only he had also ordered his eyes there, so that he might have gazed at least from a distance into that continent of philosophy that was unknown to him and where Spinoza has his home.

274. Every philosophy of philosophy that excludes Spinoza must be spurious.

275. People are always complaining that German authors write for such a small circle, and even sometimes just for themselves. That's how it should be. This is how German literature will gain more and more spirit and character. And perhaps in the meantime an audience will spring into being.

278. Much seeming stupidity is really folly, which is more common than one might think. Folly is an absolute wrongness of tendency, a complete lack of historical spirit.

281. Fichte's theory of knowledge is a philosophy about the subject matter of Kant's philosophy. He doesn't say much about form because he is a master of it, but if the essence of the critical method is that the theory of the determining ability and the system of determined affective impressions should be intimately united in it, like object and idea, in a pre-stabilized harmony, then it might very well be that even formally he is a Kant raised to the second power, and the theory of knowledge much more critical than it seems to be. Especially the new version of the theory of knowledge is always simultaneously philosophy and philosophy of philosophy. There may be valid meanings of the word critical that don't apply to every work of Fichte's, but in Fichte one has to look as he does – without paying attention to anything else – only at the whole and at the one thing that really matters. Only in this way can one see and understand the identity of his philosophy with Kant's. And besides, one can never be too critical.

298. In vain do the orthodox Kantians seek the principle of their philosophy in Kant. It's to be found in Bürger's[27] poems, and reads: 'The words of the Emperor shouldn't be twisted and turned.'

301. Philosophers still admire only Spinoza's consistency, just as the English praise only Shakespeare's truth.

302. Jumbled ideas should be the rough drafts of philosophy. It's no secret how highly these are valued by connoisseurs of painting. For a man who can't draw philosophical worlds with a crayon and characterize every thought that has a physiognomy with a few strokes of the pen, philosophy will never be an art and consequently never a science. For in philosophy the way to science lies only

through art, just as the poet, on the other hand, finds his art only through
science.

304. Philosophy too is the result of two conflicting forces – of poetry and
practice. Where these interpenetrate completely and fuse into one, there
philosophy comes into being; and when philosophy disintegrates, it becomes
mythology or else returns to life. The wisdom of the Greeks was created out of
poetry and law. The most sublime philosophy, some few surmise, may once
again turn to poetry; and it is in fact a common occurrence that ordinary people
only begin to philosophize according to their own lights after they've stopped
living. It seems to me that Schelling's real vocation is to describe better this
chemical process of philosophizing, to isolate, wherever possible, its dynamic
laws and to separate philosophy – which always must organize and disorganize
itself anew – into its living, fundamental forces, and trace these back to their
origins. On the other hand, his polemics, particularly his literary critique of
philosophy, seem to me to represent a false tendency; and his gift for
universality is probably still not sufficiently developed to be able to discover in
the philosophy of physics what it seeks.

305. Intention taken to the point of irony and accompanied by the arbitrary
illusion of its self-destruction is quite as naive as instinct taken to the point of
irony. Just as the naive plays with the contradictions between theory and
practice, so the grotesque plays with the wonderful permutations of form and
matter, loves the illusion of the random and the strange and, as it were,
coquettes with infinite arbitrariness. Humour deals with being and nonbeing,
and its true essence is reflection. Hence its closeness to the elegy and to
everything transcendental; and hence its arrogance and its bent for the
mysticism of wit. Just as genius is necessary to naïveté, so too an earnest, pure
beauty is a requisite of humour. Most of all humour likes to hover about the
gently and clearly flowing rhapsodies of philosophy or poetry, and abhors
cumbersome masses and disconnected parts.

393. In order to translate perfectly from the classics into a modern language,
the translator would have to be so expert in his language that, if need be, he
could make everything modern; but at the same time he would have to
understand antiquity so well that he would be able not just to imitate it but, if
necessary, recreate it.

395. In true prose, everything has to be underlined.

402. In trying to see if it's possible to translate the classical poets, the
important thing is to decide whether or not even the most faithful German
translation isn't still Greek. To judge by the reaction of the most sensitive and
intelligent laymen, there are valid grounds for such a suspicion.

418. Even by the most ordinary standards, a novel deserves to become
famous when it portrays and develops a thoroughly new character interest-
ingly. *William Lovell*[28] undeniably does this, and the fact that all the rest of its
staging and scenery is either commonplace or a failure, just like the great stage
manager behind it all, and the further fact that what's extraordinary about it is

only the ordinary turned inside out would probably not have done the book a great deal of damage, except that unfortunately the character was poetical. Lovell, like his insufficiently differentiated alter ego, Balder, is a complete phantast in every good and every bad, every beautiful and every ugly sense of the word. The whole book is a struggle between prose and poetry, in which prose is trodden underfoot and poetry stumbles and breaks its neck. Besides, it suffers from the fault of many first productions: it wavers between instinct and intention because it doesn't have enough of either. Hence the repetitions whereby the description of sublime boredom at times shifts into a communication of the thing itself. This is the reason why the absolute imaginativeness of this novel could have been misunderstood even by the initiates of poetry and disdained as mere sentimentalism. And this is the reason too why the reasonable reader, who likes to be moderately moved in return for his money, didn't like at all – in fact thought quite mad – the sentimentality of the novel. Tieck has perhaps never again portrayed a character so profoundly and thoroughly. But *Sternbald* combines the seriousness and vitality of *Lovell* with the artificial religiosity of the *Klosterbruder* and with everything that, taken as a whole, is most beautiful in those poetical arabesques he fabricated out of old fairy tales: namely their fantastic richness and facility, their sense of irony, and particularly their intentional variety and uniformity of coloration. Here too everything is clear and transparent, and the romantic spirit seems to be daydreaming pleasantly about itself.

421. Perhaps the great mass likes Friedrich Richter's novels only because of their apparent adventurousness. All in all he is probably interesting in the greatest variety of ways and for the most contradictory reasons. Although the educated businessman sheds quantities of noble tears while reading him, and the exacting artist hates him as the bloody symbol of the triumphant unpoetry of his nation and his age, the man of universal tendency can idolize his arbitrariness or else find great pleasure in those grotesque porcelain figures that his pictorial wit drums together like imperial soldiers. Richter is a unique phenomenon: an author who hasn't mastered the first principles of his art, who can't express a bon mot properly and can't tell a story in a better than average way, and yet someone who – if only because of a humorous dithyramb like the mulish, pithy, tense, and magnificent Leibgeber's letter to Adam[29] – cannot justly be denied the name of a great poet. Even if his works don't have a great deal of cultivation, they are nonetheless cultivated. The whole is like the part, and vice versa; in short, he is accomplished. It is a great advantage of *Siebenkäs* that its execution and descriptions are even better than those of his other works; and it has the far greater advantage of having so few Englishmen in it. To be sure, his Englishmen are ultimately Germans too, but in idyllic surroundings and with sentimental names; still, they always have a strong resemblance to Louvet's Poles and so belong with those false tendencies he is so given to. In the same category is also where his women, philosophy, the Virgin Mary, delicacy, ideal visions, and self-criticism belong. His women have red eyes and are

paragons, puppets who serve as occasions for psycho-moralistic reflections on womanhood or infatuation. In fact, he almost never comes down to the level of portraying his characters; it is enough for him to have thought of them, and now and then to say something striking about them. And so he sides with the passive humorists, the people who are actually nothing more than humorous objects; the active ones seem more self-sufficient, but they share too much of a family likeness amongst themselves and with the author to make us think of their self-sufficiency as a merit. His decor consists of leaden arabesques in the Nuremberg style. It is here that the monotony of his imagination and intelligence – bordering almost on destitution – becomes most noticeable; but here too do we find that charming dullness of his, and that piquant tastelessness which we can censure only on the grounds that he doesn't seem to be aware of it. His madonna is a sentimental sexton's wife, and his Christ is cast in the role of an enlightened student of divinity. The more moral his poetical Rembrandts are, the more common and ordinary they become; the funnier, the closer to the good; the more dithyrambical and provincial, the more divine: for he conceives of the village primarily as the City of God. His humorous poetry is separating itself more and more from his sentimental prose; often it appears, like interpolated songs, as an episode, or else it destroys the book in the shape of an appendix. But at times large masses of it still escape from him into the universal chaos.

431. To sacrifice to the Graces means, when said to a philosopher, as much as: create irony and aspire to urbanity.

438. Urbanity is wit of harmonious universality, and that is the beginning and the end of historical philosophy and Plato's most sublime music. The humanities are the gymnastics of this art and science.

446. Consistent empiricism ends in contributions toward settling mis-understandings, or in a subscription to truth.

450. Rousseau's polemic against poetry is really only a bad imitation of Plato. Plato is more against poets than he is against poetry; he thought of philosophy as the most daring dithyramb and the monodic music. Epicurus is the real enemy of art, for he wants to root out imagination and retain sense only. Spinoza might be viewed as the enemy of poetry in quite a different way: because he demonstrates how far one can get with philosophy and morality unaided by poetry, and because it is very much in the spirit of his system not to isolate poetry.

From 'Ideas'
'Ideen' (1800)

5. The mind understands something only in so far as it absorbs it like a seed into itself, nurtures it, and lets it grow into blossom and fruit. Therefore scatter holy seed into the soil of the spirit, without any affectation and any added superfluities.

8. The mind, says the author of the *Talks on Religion*,[30] can understand only the universe. Let imagination take over and you will have a God. Quite right: for the imagination is man's faculty for perceiving divinity.

11. Only through religion does logic become philosophy; only from it comes everything that makes philosophy greater than science. And instead of an eternally rich, infinite poetry, the lack of religion gives us only novels or the triviality that now is called art.

13. Only someone who has his own religion, his own original way of looking at infinity, can be an artist.

15. Every particular conception of God is mere gossip. But the idea of God is the Idea of ideas.

16. The priest as such exists only in the invisible world. In what guise is it possible for him to appear among men? His only purpose on earth will be to transform the finite into the infinite; hence he must be and continue to be, no matter what the name of his profession, an artist.

19. To have genius is the natural state of humanity. Nature endowed even humanity with health, and since love is for women what genius is for men, we must conceive of the golden age as a time when love and genius were universal.

20. Everyone is an artist whose central purpose in life is to educate his intellect.

21. The need to raise itself above humanity is humanity's prime characteristic.

24. The symmetry and organization of history teach us that mankind, for as long as it existed and developed, has really always been and has always become an individual, a person. In the great person of mankind, God became a man.

26. Wit is the appearance, the outward lightning bolt of the imagination. Hence the divinity and witty appearance of mysticism.

27. Plato's philosophy is a worthy preface to the religion of the future.

28. Man is Nature creatively looking back at itself.

33. The morality of a work is to be found not in its subject or in the relation of the speaker to his audience, but in the spirit of its execution. If this is infused with the whole wealth of humanity, then the work is moral. If it is only the product of a particular ability or art, then it is not.

34. Whoever has religion will speak in poetry. But to seek and find religion, you need the instrument of philosophy.

36. Every complete human being has some sort of genius. True virtue is genius.

37. Culture is the greatest good and it alone is useful.

39. The Kantians' conception of duty relates to the commandment of honour, the voice of God and of one's calling in us, as the dried plant to the fresh flower on the living stem.

40. A definite relationship to God must seem as intolerable to the mystic as a particular conception or notion of God.

42. If one is to believe the philosophers, then what we call religion is simply

intentionally popular or instinctively artless philosophy. The poets, however, seem to prefer to think of it as a variety of poetry which, unsure of its own lovely playfulness, takes itself too seriously and too one-sidedly. Still, philosophy already admits and begins to recognize that it must start with religion and achieve perfection in religion, and poetry strives only for the infinite and despises wordly practicality and culture as the real opposites of religion. Hence eternal peace among artists is no longer a distant prospect.

43. What men are among the other creatures of the earth, artists are among men.

45. An artist is someone who carries his centre within himself. Whoever lacks such a centre has to choose some particular leader and mediator outside of himself, not, to be sure, forever, but only to begin with. For a man cannot live without a vital centre, and if he does not yet have one within himself, then he can only seek it in another man, and only a man and a man's centre can stimulate and awaken his own.

46. Poetry and philosophy are, depending on one's point of view, different spheres, different forms, or simply the component parts of religion. For only try really to combine the two and you will find yourself with nothing but religion.

47. God is everything that is purely original and sublime, consequently the individual himself taken to the highest power. But aren't nature and the world also individuals?

48. Where philosophy stops, poetry has to begin. An ordinary point of view, a way of thinking, natural only in opposition to art and culture, a mere existing: all these are wrong; that is, there should be no kingdom of barbarity beyond the boundaries of culture. Every thinking part of an organization should not feel its limits without at the same time feeling its unity in relation to the whole.

54. The artist should have as little desire to rule as to serve. He can only create, do nothing but create, and so help the state only by making rulers and servants, and by exalting politicians and economists into artists.

55. Versatility consists not just in a comprehensive system but also in a feeling for the chaos outside that system, like man's feeling for something beyond man.

60. Individuality is precisely what is original and eternal in man; personality doesn't matter so much. To pursue the cultivation and development of this individuality as one's highest calling would be a godlike egoism.

63. The really central insight of Christianity is sin.

64. Artists make mankind an individual by connecting the past with the future in the present. Artists are the higher organ of the soul where the vital spirits of all external humanity join together, and where inner humanity has its primary sphere of action.

65. Only by being cultivated does a human being, who is wholly that, become altogether human and permeated by humanity.

69. Irony is the clear consciousness of eternal agility, of an infinitely teeming chaos.

73. There is no dualism without primacy; and therefore morality is not equal to religion, but subordinate to it.

74. Join the extremes and you will find the true middle.

79. There is only a single sense incorporating all the others. The most spiritual sense is the most original; all others derive from it.

83. Only through love and the consciousness of love does man become man.

85. The kernel, the centre of poetry, is to be found in mythology and the mysteries of antiquity. Satiate the feeling of life with the idea of infinity, and you will understand both the ancients and poetry.

86. Beautiful is what reminds us of nature and thereby stimulates a sense of the infinite fullness of life. Nature is organic, and whatever is most sublimely beautiful is therefore always vegetal, and the same is true of morality and love.

87. A true human being is one who has penetrated to the centre of humanity.

92. The only significant opposition to the religion of man and artist now springing up everywhere is to be expected from the few remaining real Christians. But they too, when the sun really begins to dawn, will fall down and worship.

95. The new, eternal gospel that Lessing prophesied will appear as a bible: but not as a single book in the usual sense. Even what we now call the Bible is actually a system of books. And that is, I might add, no mere arbitrary turn of phrase! Or is there some other word to differentiate the idea of an infinite book from an ordinary one, than Bible, the book per se, the absolute book? And surely there is an eternally essential and even practical difference if a book is merely a means to an end, or an independent work, an individual, a personified idea. It cannot be this without divine inspiration, and here the esoteric concept is itself in agreement with the exoteric one; and, moreover, no idea is isolated, but is what it is only in combination with all other ideas. An example will explain this. All the classical poems of the ancients are coherent, inseparable; they form an organic whole, they constitute, properly viewed, only a single poem, the only one in which poetry itself appears in perfection. In a similar way, in a perfect literature all books should be only a single book, and in such an eternally developing book, the gospel of humanity and culture will be revealed.

96. All philosophy is idealism, and there exists no true realism except that of poetry. But poetry and philosophy are only extremes. If one were to say that some people are pure idealists and others very definitely realists, then that remark would be quite true. Stated differently, it means that there as yet exist no wholly cultivated human beings, that there still is no religion.

105. So Fichte is supposed to have attacked religion? If an interest in the world beyond the senses is the essence of religion, then his whole doctrine is religion in the form of philosophy.

108. Whatever can be done while poetry and philosophy are separated has been done and accomplished. So the time has come to unite the two.

109. Imagination and wit are everything to you! Explain a beautiful illusion and take playfulness seriously, and you will apprehend what is at the centre and

rediscover your revered art in a more sublime light.

110. The difference between religion and morality is to be found quite simply in the old classification of all things into divine and human, if only it were understood properly.

115. If you want to achieve great things, then inspire and educate women and young men. Here, if anywhere, fresh strength and health are still to be found, and this is the way that the most important reformations have been accomplished.

118. What blindness to talk of atheism! Are there any theists? Did any human mind ever encompass the idea of divinity?

127. Women have less need for the poetry of poets because their very essence is poetry.

129a. You're not really supposed to understand me, but I want very much for you to listen to me.[31]

131. The hidden meaning of sacrifice is the annihilation of the finite because it is finite. In order to demonstrate that this is its only justification, one must choose to sacrifice whatever is most noble and most beautiful: but particularly man, the flower of the earth. Human sacrifices are the most natural sacrifices. But man is more than the flower of the earth; he is reasonable, and reason is free and in itself nothing but an eternal self-destination into the infinite. Hence man can only sacrifice himself, and he does so in an omnipresent sanctity the mob knows nothing of. All artists are Decians,[32] and to become an artist means nothing but consecrating oneself to the gods of the underworld. In the enthusiasm of annihilation, the meaning of the divine creation is revealed for the first time. Only in the midst of death does the lightning bolt of eternal life explode.

133. To begin with, I speak only to those who are already facing the Orient.

134. You suspect something greater even in me and ask why I keep silent precisely at the threshold? It's because it's still so early in the day.

137. The piety of philosophers is theory, pure contemplation of the divinity, calm and gay in silent solitude. Spinoza is the ideal of the species. The religious state of the poet is more passionate and more communicative. At the root of things lies enthusiasm, and at the end there remains mythology. Whatever stays at the midpoint possesses the character of life to the point of sexual differentiation. Mysteries are, as I said before, female; and orgies seek, in the happy exuberance of their male strength, to overcome everything around them or fertilize it.

139. There is no self-knowledge except historical self-knowledge. No one knows what he is if he doesn't know what his contemporaries are, particularly the greatest contemporary of the brotherhood, the master of masters, the genius of the age.

141. Oh, how wretched are your conceptions of genius (I mean the best among you). Where you see genius, I often see a wealth of false tendencies, the very centre of incompetence. A little talent and a lot of humbug are things

everyone praises, and which even lead everyone to proclaim that genius is incorrect, must be incorrect. So, this idea is gone too? Isn't the thoughtful man the one who is fittest to perceive the language of the spirit? Only the spiritual man has a spirit, a genius, and every genius is universal. Whoever is merely representative, merely has talent.

146. Even in their outward behaviour, the lives of artists should differ completely from the lives of other men. They are Brahmins, a higher caste: ennobled not by birth, but by free self-consecration.

148. Who unlocks the magic book of art and frees the imprisoned holy spirit? Only a kindred spirit.

149. Without poetry, religion becomes murky, false, and evil; without philosophy, extravagant in its lewdness and lustful to the point of self-emasculation.

150. You can neither explain nor understand the universe, but only contemplate and reveal it. Only stop calling the system of empiricism the universe, and if you haven't yet understood Spinoza, discover for the present the true religious conception of the universe in the *Talks on Religion*.[33]

153. All self-sufficiency is radical, is original, and all originality is moral, is originality of the whole man. Without originality, there is no energy of reason and no beauty of disposition.

155. I have expressed a few ideas pointing toward the heart of things, and have greeted the dawn in my own way, from my own point of view. Let anyone who knows the road do likewise in his own way, from his own point of view.

156. *To Novalis*: You don't stay at the threshold of things. On the contrary, your spirit is deeply suffused with poetry and philosophy. It was closest to me in these images of uncomprehended truth. What you've thought I think; what I've thought you will think or have already thought. There are misunderstandings that serve only to confirm the greatest shared understanding. Every doctrine of the eternal Orient belongs to all artists. I name you instead of all the others.

'On Goethe's *Meister*'
'Über Goethes *Meister*' (1798)

With no presumption, no sound and fury, like the quiet unfolding of an aspiring spirit, like the new-created world rising gently from within, the lucid tale begins. There is nothing extraordinary about what happens or what is said in it; the figures who appear first of all are neither great nor marvellous: a shrewd old woman who always has an eye to her own advantage and supports the wealthier suitor; a girl who escapes the snare of this dangerous schemer in order to give herself passionately to her lover; a pure youth who devotes the sweet ardour of his first love to an actress. Moreover, it is all there right before our eyes, appealing and alluring. The outlines are light and general, but they are sharp, precise and sure. The smallest trait is meaningful, every touch a gentle hint; and everything is enhanced by clear and lively contrasts. There is nothing here to enflame the passions, nothing at the outset to make violent claims upon our sympathies. But of their own accord the sprightly tableaux remain fixed in a mind cheerfully disposed to quiet enjoyment, just as we might retain the strangely clear and ineradicable memory of a landscape of simple and modest charm, which for a moment appears new and unique, suffused in a rare and beautiful illumination, or tempered by a marvellous mood of our feelings. The feelings are gently touched by the cheerful story, sweetly stirred in many ways. Without being entirely familiar with them, the reader already feels as if he has met these people, before he ever knows or even asks how it was he made their acquaintance. The reader feels the same about them as the company of actors did towards the Stranger on their gay excursion on the river. He thinks he must have met them already, because they look like real human beings, not like any mere Tom, Dick or Harry. They do not owe this appearance to their nature or their education: for only in one or two cases do these approach the general level, and even then in different ways and to a different extent. It is rather the manner of the representation, which endows even the most circumscribed character with the appearance of a unique, autonomous individual, while yet possessing another aspect, another variation of that general human nature which is constant in all its transformations, so that each variation is a small part of the infinite world. That is the great thing about this novel: every cultured reader believes he recognizes only himself in it, whereas he is raised far beyond himself; which is only as it should be, and yet far more than one might expect.

Benevolently, the delighted reader follows Wilhelm's tender memories of the puppet plays that filled the inquisitive boy with greater happiness than any other delicacy, at a time when he still drank in at random every spectacle and pictures of all kinds, with the same pure thirst with which the new-born child takes the sweet nourishment from his fond mother's breast. Wilhelm's credulity makes the good-natured children's stories of that time important, indeed sacred to him, for then he would yearn passionately to see everything that was new and unfamiliar to him, and promptly try to imitate what he had just seen. Now his affection paints them in the most charming colours, and his hope lends them the most flattering significance. It is these attractive characteristics that make up the fabric of his dearest ambition: to use the theatre to elevate, enlighten and ennoble mankind and to become the creator of a new and greater age in the history of his country's stage. His childish inclination burns ardently for this idea, intensified by his virtue and redoubled by his love. Though our response to such feelings and desires cannot be wholly without misgivings, still it is absorbing and delightful to read how for the first time Wilhelm is sent by the two fathers on a short journey, how he encounters an adventure that begins seriously and develops amusingly, and in which he glimpses the image of his own enterprise – not, it is true, reflected very flatteringly, but that cannot make him untrue to his enthusiasm. Meanwhile, all unnoticed, the tale has become more vivid and passionate. In the balmy night when Wilhelm, believing he is close to an eternal union with his Mariane, lingers lovingly and ecstatically about her house, the ardent yearning that seems to lose itself in itself, soothed and revived in the enjoyment of its own sounds, rises to a climax until Wilhelm's passion is suddenly extinguished by sad certainty and Norberg's base letter: the entire dream-world of the young man in love is destroyed at a blow.

The first book closes with this harsh dissonance. The end resembles a music of the spirit, in which the most various voices change rapidly and vehemently, like so many inviting sounds from a new world whose wonders are to unfold before us. And the sharp contrast can season and salve with a dash of impatience that tension roused first a little and then more than we expected, without ever disturbing the most even-tempered enjoyment of what is going on, or removing the most delicate features from the secondary development nor the slightest hints from our perception of the work, desiring as we do to understand every glance and changing expression of the poetic spirit made visible in the work.

But in order that our feelings should not strive merely in an empty infinity, but rather that the eye might estimate the distance according to some higher point of view and set some bounds to the vast prospect, the Stranger is there – so rightly called the Stranger. Alone and incomprehensible, like a manifestation from another, nobler world, as different from the real world surrounding Wilhelm as *it* is from the possible world of his dreams, the Stranger acts as a measure of the heights to which the work has yet to rise, where art will become a science, and life an art.

The mature intelligence of this cultivated man is separated by an abyss from the flourishing imagination of the young man in love. But the transition from Wilhelm's serenade to Norberg's letter is not a gentle one, and the contrast between his poetry and Mariane's prosaic, nay, low surroundings, is stark. Introductory to the whole work, the first book is a series of varied situations and picturesque contrasts, each casting a new and brighter light on Wilhelm's character from a different, noteworthy perspective; and each of the smaller, clearly distinct chapters and blocks of narrative forms in itself more or less a picturesque whole. Wilhelm has already won the reader's complete good-will, to whom he utters (as much as to himself) the noblest sentiments in the most splendid words. His entire nature consists of feeling, willing, aspiring; and although we can foresee that he will come to act as a mature man only very late (or perhaps never), his easy adaptability is a sure promise that men and women will make his education their business and their pleasure. Perhaps without knowing or even wishing it, they will thereby stimulate in numerous ways that gentle, many-sided receptivity which gives his mind such great appeal; and they will develop his dim, early awareness of the whole world into a beautiful form. He will have to be able to learn wherever he goes, and he will not be without his trials and temptations. But if a kindly destiny or a friend with a wide scope of experience supports him with good will, guiding him with warnings and promises, then his years of apprenticeship cannot but end happily.

The second book begins with a musical recapitulation of what has happened up to the end of the first book, concentrating the issues into a few focal points, and pushing them to the farthest possible extent. At first, the gradual but complete destruction of the poetry of Wilhelm's childish dreams and his first love is examined with a sparing generality of representation. The reader's mind, having sunk to these depths in sympathy with Wilhelm and become as inactive as he, is reenlivened and roused into pulling itself out of this vacancy by the most passionate recollections of Mariane and by the young man's inspired praise of poetry, transposing us into the ominous past of ancient heroes and the still innocent world of poetry.

Then follows his entry into the world, made neither formally, nor tumultuously, but as sweetly and gently as the wanderings of someone caught between melancholy and expectation, or wavering between bitter-sweet memories and desires heavy with presentiments. A new scene opens, a new world stretches out beckoning to us. Here everything is strange, significant, marvellous, enveloped by a mysterious enchantment. Events and characters move more rapidly, and each character is like a new act. Even events not in themselves unusual appear surprising. But these events are only the natural element of the characters, in whom the spirit of this entire massive system is most clearly revealed. They too express a fresh sense of the present, a magic hovering between forwards and backwards. Philine is the seductive symbol of easy sensuality; likewise, the volatile Laertes lives only for the moment, and to complete the merry company, the fair-haired Friedrich represents a hale and hearty loutishness. The old Harper breathes and laments all that is touching of memory and melancholy and remorse, out of fathomless depths of grief, seizing our hearts with a sudden sadness. The holy child Mignon excites an even sweeter spasm, a delicious shudder, and with her appearance the innermost spring of this strange work is released. Now and again Mariane's image appears like a dream of great import; suddenly the mysterious Stranger enters the scene and then vanishes like lightning. The Melinas too reappear, but changed, in their true colours. The clumsy vanity of Madame Melina's excessive sensibility makes a pretty contrast with the lightness of the dainty sinner Philine. The reading of the drama of chivalry offers overall a profound glance behind the scenes of theatrical enchantment, as if into a comic world in the background. Humour, feeling, mystery, allure are all marvellously interwoven in the Finale, and the conflicting voices clash harshly with one another. This harmony of dissonance is even more beautiful than the music with which the First Book ended. It is more delightful, and yet it cuts deeper; it is more overwhelming, and yet it leaves us more composed.

It is a beautiful and indeed necessary experience when reading a poetic work to give ourselves up entirely to its influence, to let the writer do with us what he will; perhaps only in matters of detail is it necessary to pause and confirm our emotional response with a moment's reflection, raise it into a thought, and where there is room for doubt or dispute, decide and amplify the matter. This is the prime, the most essential response. But it is no less necessary to be able to abstract from all the details, to have a loose general concept of the work, survey it en bloc, and grasp it as a whole, perceive even its most hidden parts, and make connections between the most remote corners. We must rise above our own affection for the work, and in our thoughts be able to destroy what we adore; otherwise, whatever our talents, we would lack a sense of the whole. Why should we not both breathe in the perfume of a flower and at the same time, entirely absorbed in the observation, contemplate in its infinite ramifications the vein-system of a single leaf? The whole man who feels and thinks in universal terms is interested not only in the brilliant outward covering, the bright garment of this beautiful earth; he also likes to investigate the layering and the composition of the strata far within; he would wish to delve deeper and deeper, even to the very centre, if possible, and would want to know the construction of the whole. So we gladly tear ourselves away from the poet's spell, after we have willingly let him cast his enchantment upon us; what we love most is to seek out what he has hidden from our gaze or was reluctant to reveal at first, what it is that most makes him an artist: the hidden intentions he pursues in secret. In a genius whose instinct has become will, there are many more intentions than we can take for granted.

Both the larger and the smaller masses reveal the innate impulse of this work, so organized and organizing down to its finest detail to form a whole. No break is accidental or insignificant; and in this novel, where everything is at the same time both means and end, it would not be wrong to regard the first part, irrespective of its relationship to the whole, as a novel in itself. If we look at the preferred topics of conversation, at all the incidental developments, at the preferred relationships between all the incidents, characters, and their surroundings, we are struck by the fact that everything is concerned with spectacle, drama, representation, art, and poetry. It was so much the poet's intention to set up a comprehensive theory of art, or rather to represent one in living examples and aspects, that this purpose can divert him into introducing events which are really only episodes, such as the comedy presented by the factory-workers, or the play put on by the miners. It is possible, indeed, to find a system in the author's presentation of this physics of poetry – not by any means the dead framework of a didactic structure, but stage after stage of every natural history and educational theory in living progression. For example, in this period of his apprenticeship, Wilhelm is concerned with the first, most elementary beginnings of the art of living. Hence this is where the simplest ideas about art are also presented, the most basic facts and the crudest efforts – in short, the rudiments of poetry: the puppet plays, the early childhood years of poetic instinct common to all people of sensibility, even those without any particular talent. Then there are the observations about how the learner should practise his art and make his judgments, and about the impressions made by the miners and by the tight-rope walkers; there are the poetic passages on the

Golden Age of early poetry, and on the acrobat's art, and there is the improvised comedy during the excursion on the river. But this natural history of the fine arts is not restricted only to the actors' skills and related arts. The romantic songs of Mignon and the Harper also reveal poetry as the natural language and natural music of beautiful souls.

With this intention, the actor's world was bound to become both the setting and the foundation of the whole work, because his art is not only the most versatile, but also the most sociable of all the arts, and because it makes the perfect meeting-place for poetry and life, for the world and the times; whereas the solitary studio of the painter or sculptor does not offer so much material, and poets only live as poets within themselves, no longer forming a separate social guild of artists.

This might suggest that the novel is as much an historical philosophy of art as a true work of art, and that everything which the poet so lovingly presents as his true aim and end is ultimately only means. But that is not so: it is all poetry – high, pure poetry. Everything has been thought and uttered as though by one who is both a divine poet and a perfect artist; and even the most delicate secondary features seem to exist in their own right and to rejoice in their own independent life, even against the laws of petty, inauthentic probability. What is lacking in the paeans of praise that Werner and Wilhelm raise to Trade and to Poetry but the metre, for everyone to acknowledge them as high poetry? Every page offers us golden fruits upon silver platters. This marvellous prose is prose, and yet it is poetry. Its richness is graceful, its simplicity significant and profound, and its noble and delicate development is without stubborn rigour. Though the main threads of this style are on the whole drawn from the cultivated speech of social life, it also takes pleasure in rare and strange metaphors which aim at establishing a resemblance between the highest and the purest on the one hand, and some aspect peculiar to this or that everyday trade or skill on the other, or such similar spheres which, according to public commonplace, are utterly remote from poetry.

But we should not be deceived into thinking that the poet is not utterly serious about his masterpiece, even though he himself seems to take the characters and incidents so lightly and playfully, never mentioning his hero except with some irony and seeming to smile down from the heights of his intellect upon his work. We should think of this work in connection with the very highest ideas, and not read it as it is usually taken on the social level: as a novel in which the persons and incidents are the ultimate end and aim. For this book is absolutely new and unique. We can learn to understand it only on its own terms. To judge it according to an idea of genre drawn from custom and belief, accidental experiences and arbitrary demands, is as if a child tried to clutch the stars and the moon in his hand and pack them in his satchel.

Our feelings too protest against an orthodox academic judgment of this divine organism. Who would review a feast of the finest and choicest wit with all the usual fuss and formalities? An academic review of *Wilhelm Meister* would look like the young man who went walking in the woods with a book under his arm and drove away Philine as well as the cuckoo.

Perhaps then we should judge it, and at the same time refrain from judging it; which does not seem to be at all an easy task. Fortunately it turns out to be one of those books which carries its own judgment within it, and spares the critic his labour. Indeed, not only does it judge itself; it also describes itself. A mere description of the impression it makes, quite apart from being superfluous, would be bound to come off badly, even if it were not the worst of its kind. It would lose out not only to the poet, but also to the thoughts of the kind of reader who knows the highest when he sees it and has the capacity to worship, a reader who can tell at once without art or science what he should worship, and who responds to the real, right thing as though struck by lightning.

Our usual expectations of unity and coherence are disappointed by this novel as often as they are fulfilled. But the reader who possesses a true instinct for system, who has a sense of totality or that anticipation of the world in its entirety which makes Wilhelm so interesting, will be aware throughout the work of what we might call its personality and living individuality. And the more deeply he probes, the more inner connections and relations and the greater intellectual coherence he will discover in it. If there is any book with an indwelling genius, it is this. And if this genius could characterize itself in detail and as a whole, then there would be no need for anyone else to say what it is all about, or how it should be taken. A little elaboration is possible here, and some explanation need not seem unnecessary or superfluous, for despite this feeling of its wholeness, the beginning and the end of the work, as well as one or two parts in the middle, are generally felt to be superfluous and unrelated. Even the reader who is able to recognize the divine nature of its cultivated randomness, and do it honour, has a sense of something isolated at the beginning and the end as if despite the most beautiful coherence and innermost unity of the work, it lacked the ultimate interdependence of thoughts and feelings. Many readers, to whom one cannot deny this sense, are uneasy about several parts of the work, for in such developing natures, idea and feeling are mutually extended, sharpened and formed by one another.

The differing nature of the individual sections should be able to throw a great deal of light on the organization of the whole. But in progressing appropriately from the parts to the whole, observation and analysis must not get lost in over-minute detail. Rather analysis must pause, as if the detail were merely a matter of simple parts, at those major sections whose independence is also maintained by their free treatment, and by their shaping and transformation of what they have taken over from the previous section; and whose inner, unintentional homogeneity and original unity the poet himself has acknowledged in using the most various, though always poetic, means, in a deliberate effort to shape them into a rounded whole. The development within the individual sections ensures the overall coherence, and in pulling them together, the poet confirms their variety. And in this way each essential part of the single and indivisible novel becomes a system in itself. The means of connection and progression are more or less the same in all sections. In the second volume, Jarno and the appearance of the Amazons raise our expectations in the same way as the Stranger and Mignon had done in the first; and they likewise rouse our interest in the far distance and point forward to heights of education not yet visible. Here too, every book opens with a new scene and a new world; here too the old figures reappear with youth renewed; here too every book contains the germ of the next, and with vital energy absorbs into its own being what the previous book has yielded. And the third book, distinguished by the freshest and happiest colouring, is beautifully framed, as if by the blossoms of youth still burgeoning but already mature, first by Mignon's song 'Kennst du das Land . . .' and at the end by Wilhelm's and the Countess's first kiss. Where there is so much to be noticed, there would be little point in drawing attention to something that has been there already, or recurs again and again with a few changes. Only what is quite new and individual requires commentary – but of the sort which should by no means make everything clear for everybody. It deserves the name of excellence only when the reader who understands *Wilhelm Meister* completely finds it utterly familiar and when the reader who does not understand it at all finds it as stupid and empty as the work it is supposed to elucidate. On the other hand, the reader who only half-understands the work would find such a commentary only half-comprehensible; it would enlighten him in some respects, but perhaps only confuse him the more in others – so that out of this disturbance and doubt, knowledge might emerge, or the reader might at least become aware of his incompleteness. The second volume in particular has least need of explanations. It is the fullest, but also the most charming. It is full of keen understanding, but still very understandable.

In the sequence of grades of these apprentice years in the art of living, this volume represents for Wilhelm the higher degree in temptations, and the time of errors and instructive but dearly purchased experiences. It is true that his principles and his actions run, as ever, side by side like parallel lines, without ever crossing or touching. But in the meantime he does finally reach the stage whereby he has gradually raised himself out of that baseness which originally adheres even to the noblest natures or accidentally forms their environment – or at least he has seriously endeavoured to rise above it. At first, Wilhelm's infinite impulse towards education only lived and moved within him, even to the point of bringing about the self-destruction of his first love, and of his aspirations as an artist. Then, after it had led him to venture out into the world, it was natural that his aspirations should carry him to the very heights, even though it were only the heights of an ordinary theatre stage; it was natural that his highest aim should become all that was noble and distinguished, even if that were only the representative mode of existence of a not very cultivated nobility. This is probably the only way such an aspiration, in its origins so worthy of our respect, could have worked out successfully, for Wilhelm was still so innocent and so young. That is why the Third Book was bound to come so close to comedy, all the more so as its intention was to shed the fullest light on Wilhelm's unworldliness, and on the contrast between the magic of the play, and the common, ordinary life of the players. In the earlier sections, only individual traits were distinctly comic – perhaps a few figures in the foreground, or an indefinite one in the distance. But here the entire Book, the setting and the action are themselves comic. Indeed, we might call it a comic world, for in fact it contains infinite cause for amusement. The nobility and the actors form two quite separate bodies, neither of whom yield the prize for absurdity to the other, and who manoeuvre against each other in the most amusing way. The elements in this comedy are not at all dainty or delicate or noble. Rather, much of it is the kind of thing we are all accustomed to laughing at heartily, such as the contrast between high expectations and bad management. The contrasts between hope and success, and between imagination and reality, play a great part throughout: the claims of reality are asserted with cruel severity, and the pedant even gets knocked about because he is also an idealist. In sheer infatuation, his fellow, the Count, is pleased to acknowledge him across the enormous gulf of their different social positions. For sheer intellectual silliness, the Baron yields pride of place to no one, nor the Baroness for moral turpitude. The Countess herself is at best a charming excuse for a beautiful justification of adornment. And apart from their social class, the only superiority these nobles show over the actors is that they are more thoroughly common. But these people, whom we should call figures rather than people, are sketched with the light touch and delicate brush we might imagine in the daintiest caricatures of the finest painting. It is foolishness shaped into transparency. This freshness of colour, this child-like variety, this love of trimmings and trappings, the wit, the lightness of heart, the fleeting high spirits are characterized by something we might call an ethereal merriment, whose impression is too fine and delicate for the mere letter of commentary to be able to reflect and reproduce. Only reading it aloud with total understanding can convey to those with a feeling for it the irony which hovers over the entire work, but becomes beautifully clear here. This illusion of dignity and importance, mocking itself gently, in the periodic style, this apparent negligence, these seeming tautologies, determine the work so perfectly, that they themselves become subject to its conditions, together with everything else in the world of the novel. This style enables the narrator to say or to seem to want to say everything or nothing; this highly prosaic tone in the midst of the poetic mood of the subject presented or turned into comedy, this delicate breath of poetic pedantry on the most prosaic occasions – often it all depends upon a single word, or indeed on the merest matter of emphasis.

Perhaps there is no section of the work as free and independent of the whole as this third book. But not everything in it is playful, or intended for the pleasure of the moment. Jarno makes to Wilhelm and the reader a powerful affirmation of his faith in a grand and dignified reality and in serious endeavour in the world and his works. His dry and simple common sense is the perfect antithesis to Aurelia's sophistical sensibility, which is half natural and half affected. She is

actress through and through, even in her own character; all she can do, all she
wants to do, is represent and perform, best of all herself; she puts everything on
display, even her femininity and her love. Both figures are distinguished only by
common sense. For the poet gives Aurelia a good measure of shrewdness. But
she lacks judgment and a sense of propriety, as much as Jarno lacks
imagination. They are excellent persons, but thoroughly limited, and certainly
not great, and the book's distinct pointers towards this limitation are proof that
it is far less of a eulogy of common sense than might first appear. Each acts as a
foil to the other, as the deeply feeling Mariane does to the light and promiscuous
Philine; and like them, they both stand out more strongly than would be
necessary merely to furnish the theories of art under discussion with examples,
or provide the complications of the plot as a whole with characters. They are
major figures, and each of them in its substantiality sets the tone. They earn
their places because they too want to shape Wilhelm's mind; they too have his
education at heart. Despite the honest concern of so many pedagogues in his
personal and moral education, their pupil, it is true, seems to have acquired
little more than the external graces, which he imagines he has learned from the
great variety of his social acquaintance, and from his practice in dancing and
fencing. However, it seems he does make great advances in art, at least, more as
a natural development of his own mind than because others have urged him
towards it. And he now makes the acquaintance of real experts, and their
conversations about art – quite apart from the fact that they lack the heavy
splendour of what is known as concentrated brevity – are real conversations,
with many voices engaging with one another, not mere one-sided sham
conversations. Serlo is in a certain sense a generally representative human
being, and even the story of his youth is appropriate to one with such a distinct
talent and an equally distinct absence of any sense of higher things. In this
respect he resembles Jarno: in the last resort, both are masters only of the
mechanical aspects of their craft. There is an immeasureably wide gulf between
the first apprehensions and elements of poetry with which the first volume
concerned Wilhelm and the reader, and the point where man becomes capable
of grasping both the highest and the most profound. And if the passage from the
one to the other, which always has to be a leap, were brought about by the
mediation of a great model, as is only fitting, what poet could perform this
function more appropriately than the one who deserves so eminently to be
called unlimited? This is the view of Shakespeare which Wilhelm seizes upon
first of all, and since the greatness of his nature is less important to this theory
than his profound artistry and purposefulness, the choice was bound to fall on
Hamlet, for there is probably no other play that offers the occasion for such
varied and interesting debate on what the secret intention of the artist might be,
or what the accidental flaws in the work are.[34] This drama also plays its part
beautifully in the theatrical plot and setting of the novel, and almost of its own
accord it raises the question of how far it is possible to alter a finished
masterpiece or perform it unchanged on the stage. With its retarding action,

which is also the very essence of the novel, *Hamlet* can seem so closely related to *Wilhelm Meister* as to be mistaken for it. Also, the spirit of contemplation and withdrawal into the self, of which the novel is so full, is a characteristic common to all intellectual poetry, so much so that even this terrible tragedy which represents the visible earth as a rank garden of luxurious sin, and its hollow depths as the seat of punishment and pain, and which is founded on the harshest ideas of honour and duty, even this drama can in one characteristic at least tend towards the happy prentice years of a young artist.

The view of *Hamlet* to be found scattered partly here and partly in the next volume is not so much criticism as high poetry. What else but a poem can come into being when a poet in full possession of his powers contemplates a work of art and represents it in his own? This is not because his view makes suppositions and assertions which go beyond the visible work. All criticism has to do that, because every great work, of whatever kind, knows more than it says, and aspires to more than it knows. It is because the aims and approach of poetic criticism are something completely different. Poetic criticism does not act as a mere inscription, and merely say what the thing is, and where it stands and should stand in the world. For that, all that is required is a whole and undivided human being who has made the work the centre of his attention for as long as necessary. If he takes pleasure in communication, by word of mouth or in writing, he will enjoy developing and elaborating an insight which is fundamentally single and indivisible. That is how a critical characterization of a work actually comes into being. The poet and artist on the other hand will want to represent the representation anew, and form once more what has already been formed; he will add to the work, restore it, shape it afresh. He will only divide the whole into articulated parts and masses, not break it down into its original constituents, which in respect of the work are dead things, because their elements are no longer of the same nature as the whole; however, in respect of the universe they are certainly living, and could be articulated parts or masses there. The ordinary critic relates the object of his art to these, and so he is inevitably bound to destroy his living unity, sometimes breaking it down into its elements, sometimes regarding it as an atom itself within a greater mass.

The fifth book moves from theory to practice, considered and proceeding according to certain principles. And the crudeness and selfishness of Serlo and the others, Philine's frivolity, Aurelia's extravagance, the old man's melancholy and Mignon's longing also pass over into action. Hence the not infrequent approach to madness, which seems to be a preferred tone and relationship in this Book. Mignon as Fury is a brilliant blaze of light – but there are many. On the whole, however, the work seems to lapse somewhat from the heights of the second volume. It seems to be already preparing itself to plunge into the furthermost depths within man, from thence to climb to even greater heights – indeed the greatest, where it is able to remain. In general, the work appears to be at a crossroads, and caught up in an important crisis. The complication and confusion reaches a climax, as does the tense expectation, about the outcome of so many interesting riddles and enjoyable marvels. Also, the false direction Wilhelm has taken assumes the form of maxims. But the strange warning admonishes the reader too not to believe too credulously that Wilhelm has reached his goal, or is even on the right way to it. None of the parts seems so dependent on the whole, or to serve merely as a means, as this one. It even indulges in merely theoretical afterthoughts and interpolations, such as the ideal of the prompter, the sketch of the connoisseur of acting, or the theoretical basis for the distinction between novel and drama.

By contrast, the 'Confessions of a Beautiful Soul' come as a surprise in their unaffected singularity, their apparent isolation from the whole, and the arbitrariness of their involvement in it, or rather their absorption into it, which has no precedent in the earlier parts of the novel. But on closer reflection, Wilhelm probably ought not to be without any relationship to his aunt before his marriage, just as her Confessions should have some connection with the novel as a whole. After all, these are also years of apprenticeship when nothing else than how to exist is learnt, to live according to his particular principles or his unalterable nature. And if Wilhelm continues to interest us only by virtue of his own capacity to be interested in everything, the way in which his aunt is interested in herself gives her the right to communicate her feelings. Fundamentally she too lives a theatrical life, only with this difference: that she combines all the roles which in the Count's residence had been distributed among many figures who all acted and performed to one another; moreover her heart is the stage on which she is at the same time actor and spectator and mistress of the intrigues behind the scenes. She constantly stands before the mirror of her conscience, prinking and preening her feelings. In this figure the highest degree of inwardness is reached – which was bound to happen, for the work has from the start displayed a decided inclination towards distinguishing sharply between the inner and the outer life, and to contrasting them. In this section, the inner life has as it were undermined itself. It is the very peak of consciously articulated one-sidedness, to which is contrasted the image of the mature generality of a great purpose. For the uncle is present in the background of this picture, like a mighty building in the grand old style devoted to the art of living, with proportions of noble simplicity, in the purest, finest marble. His appearance comes as something quite new in this sequence of educative examples. Writing confessions would surely not have been his favourite pastime; and since he was self-taught, he cannot have had any years of apprenticeship, like Wilhelm. But with the energy of maturity he shaped the natural world around him into a classical world which circled about his independent spirit as if he were its centre.

It is wholly in accord with the artistic spirit of the whole work that religion too should be presented here as an inborn pastime which creates its own room to develop and grows stage by stage into perfect art. And this is only the most striking example to show how the spirit of the work would like to treat everything thus, and see it treated so. The uncle's forebearance towards the aunt is the strongest symbolization of how incredibly tolerant those great men were, in whom the universal spirit of the work is most immediately manifest. The presentation of a nature constantly gazing upon itself as though into infinity was the finest proof an artist could give of the unfathomable depths of his range. He painted even external objects with the light and shade and colour with which this spirit, seeing everything in its own reflected light, must inevitably have mirrored and represented itself. But it could not be his intention to present this with any greater depth and fullness than would be right and necessary for the intention of the whole; still less his duty to resemble a definite reality. In general the characters in this novel resemble the portrait in the way they are presented, but they are more or less general and allegorical by nature. For that reason they provide an excellent collection of examples and inexhaustible material for moral and social enquiry. For this purpose, the conversations in *Wilhelm Meister* about the characters can be most interesting, although for the understanding of the work itself they can only have an episodic effect. But conversations they had to be, for this form removes any one-sidedness. For if one single figure were to discuss each of these persons solely from his individual point of view, and give his own moral testimonial to them, it would be the most fruitless way possible of regarding *Wilhelm Meister*. And in the end it would tell us no more than that the speaker's opinions on these matters were as stated.

With the fourth volume, the work comes of mature and marriageable age, as you might say. It has now become clear that the work is intended to embrace not only what we call theatre or poetry, but the great spectacle of humanity itself, and the art of all arts, the art of living. We also perceive that Wilhelm is the last person these years of apprenticeship would and could turn into a fit and able artist and man. The intention is not to educate this or that human being, but to represent Nature, Education itself in all the variety of these examples, and concentrated into single principles. The 'Confessions of a Beautiful Soul' made us believe that we were suddenly translated from the world of poetry into the world of morality; similarly we are presented with the sound results of a philosophy founded on the higher spirit and feeling, which aspires with equal ardour towards both the strict separation and the noble universality of all human arts and faculties. Wilhelm himself will probably be taken care of at the end, but he has become the butt of the novel, perhaps more than is either fair or mannerly. He is even educated by little Felix, who shames him into an awareness of how little he knows. After a few less than tragic attacks of fear, defiance and remorse, his independence vanishes from the society of the living. He resigns all claim to a will of his own. And now his years of apprenticeship are really completed, and Nathalie becomes the 'Supplement', as she puts it (Book 8, Chapter 7), to the novel. She is the most beautiful embodiment of kindness and womanliness, and this makes her an agreeable contrast to the rather practical Therese. Nathalie makes her benevolent influence felt by her mere presence in society; Therese creates a similar world about herself, as the uncle did. They furnish examples and instances for a theory of womanly virtue which has an essential place in the grand theory of the art of life. The sociability of good manners and morals, and domestic activity, each embodied in a romantically beautiful figure, are the two archetypes, or the two halves of one archetype, which are put forward for this part of humankind.

How disappointed the reader of this novel might be by the end, for nothing comes of all these educational arrangements but an unassuming charm; and behind all those amazing chance occurrences, prophetic hints and mysterious appearances, there is nothing but the most lucid poetry; the final threads of the entire action are guided merely by the whim of a mind cultivated to perfection. And indeed, quite deliberately it seems, this controlling mind allows itself almost any liberty, with a particular fondness for the most far-fetched connections. Barbara's speeches possess the tremendous power, the dignity and the grandeur of ancient tragedy; of one of the most interesting figures in the entire book we learn nothing more circumstantial than his affair with a smallholder's daughter; immediately after the fall of Mariane, who interests us not as Mariane, but as the epitome of deserted, distracted womanhood, we are promptly entertained by the sight of Laertes counting out the ducats; and even the most important minor figures, such as the surgeon, are deliberately presented as odd and eccentric. The true centre of this waywardness is the secret society of pure intellect, which makes a mock of both Wilhelm and itself, and finally turns out to be right and just and useful and economical. But on the other hand, Chance itself is here a cultivated man, and since the presentation gives and takes everything else on a large scale, why should it not make use of traditional poetic licence on a large scale too? It goes without saying that treatment of this kind and in this spirit will not spin out all the threads slowly and long. Nevertheless, the end of the fourth volume, coming as it does so swiftly and then unexpectedly so long drawn out like Wilhelm's allegorical dream at the beginning, does remind us of many of the most interesting figures and themes in the novel as a whole. Among others, there are the Count and his blessing, a pregnant Philine in front of the mirror as a warning and an example of comic nemesis; and the boy thought to be dying who demands a piece of bread and butter, the burlesque height of comic absurdity.

The first volume of this novel is distinguished by its modest charm; the second by its brilliance and beauty; the third by the depth of its artistry and purposefulness. And the true character of the fourth volume – and of the entire work – lies in its grandeur. Even the articulation of the parts is nobler, the light and colouring brighter and more intense; everything is as well-made as it is captivating, and the surprises come thick and fast. But not only are the dimensions enlarged; the characters too appear on a grander scale. Lothario, the Abbé, and the Uncle each in his own way to a certain extent represent the genius of the book itself; the others are only its creatures. This is why they withdraw modestly into the background, like an old master by his painting, although from this point of view they are really the main characters. The Uncle has a great heart, the Abbé a great intellect, and he moves over the whole work like the spirit of God. Since he enjoys playing the role of fate, that is the part he has to take over in this book. Lothario is a great man. There is something heavy and sprawling about the Uncle, something meagre about the Abbé, but Lothario is entire. His appearance is simple, his mind constantly moving forward; he has no flaws, except the original flaw of all great men: he is also capable of destruction. He is the dome rising to heaven, they are the mighty pillars on which it rests. These architectonic natures encompass, bear and support the whole. The others, presented so amply that we could take them to be the most important, are only the minor pictures and decorations in the temple. They are infinitely interesting to the mind and a constant stimulus to discussion about whether we should or could respect them or love them, but to our hearts they are still only marionettes, allegorical playthings. This does not apply to Mignon, Sperata and Augustino, the holy family of natural poetry, who fill the whole work with music and romantic enchantment. It is as if their sorrow would tear our hearts in two, but this sorrow has the form, the tone of some lamenting dignity, and its voice swells upon waves of melody like the devotions of great choirs.

It is as if everything that had gone before were only a witty, interesting game, and now the novel were to become serious. The fourth volume is really the work itself; the previous parts are only preparation. This is where the curtain of the holy of holies is drawn back, and we suddenly find ourselves upon a height where everything is god-like and serene and pure, and in which Mignon's exequies appear as important and significant as the necessary coming of her end.

'Letter about the Novel'
'Brief über den Roman' (1799)

[In this extract, Antonio, one of the main interlocutors of the *Dialogue*, speaks to Amalia. The context becomes clear below.]

I must retract, my dear lady, what I seemed to say yesterday in your defence, and say that you are almost completely wrong. You yourself admitted as much at the end of the argument, having become involved so deeply, because it is against female dignity to come down in tone, as you so aptly put it, from the innate element of gay jest and eternal poetry to the thorough or heavy-handed earnestness of the men. I agree with you against yourself that you are wrong. Indeed, I maintain that it is not enough to recognize the wrong; one must make amends for it and, as it seems to me, proper amends for having degraded yourself with your criticism would now be that you force yourself to the necessary patience and read this critical epistle about the subject of yesterday's conversation.

What I want to say I could have said yesterday; or rather I could not have because of my mood and the circumstances. What kind of opponent are you dealing with, Amalia? Certainly he understands quite well what it is all about, as it could not otherwise be with a clever virtuoso. He could have talked about it as well as anyone else, provided he could talk at all. This the gods have denied him; he is, as I have already said, a virtuoso and that's it; the Graces, unfortunately, stayed away. Since he was not quite certain what you meant in the deepest sense, and externally the right was so completely on your side, I made it my business to argue for you with all my might, to prevent the convival balance from being destroyed. And besides, it is more natural for men, if it really has to be done, to give written instructions rather than oral which I feel violate the dignity of conversation.

Our conversation began when you asserted that Friedrich Richter's[35] novels are not novels but a colourful hodgepodge of sickly wit; that the meagre story is too badly presented to be considered a story; one simply had to guess it. If, however, one wanted to put it all together and just tell it, it would at best amount to a confession. The individuality of the man is much too visible, and such a personality at that.

I disregard this last point because it is only a question of individuality. I admit the colourful hodgepodge of sickly wit; but I shall defend it and emphatically maintain that such grotesques and confessions are the only romantic productions of our unromantic age.

On this occasion let me get something off my mind that I have been thinking about for a long time.

With astonishment and inner anger, I have often seen your servant carry piles of volumes in to you. How can you touch with your hands those dirty volumes? And how can you allow the confused and crude phrases to enter through your eye to the sanctuary of your soul? To yield your imagination for hours to people with whom, face to face, you would be ashamed to exchange even a few words? It serves no purpose but to kill time and to spoil your imagination. You have read almost all the bad books from Fielding to La Fontaine.[36] Ask yourself what you profited by it. Your memory scorns this vulgar stuff which has become a necessity through an unfortunate habit of your youth; what has to be acquired so laboriously, is entirely forgotten.

But then perhaps you remember that there was a time when you loved Sterne and enjoyed assuming his manner, partially to imitate, partially to ridicule him. I still have a few jocular letters of this kind from you which I will carefully save. Sterne's humour did make a definite impression on you. Even though it was no ideally perfect form, yet it was a form and a witty one which captivated your imagination. And an impression that is so definite that we make use of it and cultivate it in seriousness and jest is not lost. And what can have a more fundamental value than those things which in some way stimulate or nourish the play of our inner makeup.

You feel yourself that your delight in Sterne's humour was pure and of an entirely different nature than the suspense which can be often forced upon us by a thoroughly bad book, at the very time that we find it bad. Now ask yourself if your enjoyment was not related to what we often experience while viewing the witty paintings called arabesques. In case you cannot deny some sympathy with Sterne's sensibility, I am sending you a book, but I have to warn you about it so that you will be careful with regard to strangers, for it has the fortune or misfortune to be somewhat notorious. It is Diderot's[37] *The Fatalist*. I think you will like it and will find in it an abundance of wit, quite free of sentimental admixtures. It is designed with understanding and executed with a firm hand. Without exaggerating, I can call it a work of art. To be sure, it is not a work of high rank, but only an arabesque. But for that reason it has in my eyes no small merit; for I consider the arabesque a very definite and essential form or mode of expression of poetry.

This is how I think of the matter. Poetry is so deeply rooted in man that at times, even under the most unfavourable circumstances, it grows without cultivation. Just as we find in almost every nation songs and stories in circulation and, even though crude, some kind of plays in use, so in our unfantastic age, in the actual estate of prose, and I mean the so-called educated and cultured people, we will find a few individuals who, sensing in themselves a certain originality of the imagination, express it, even though they are still far removed from true art. The humour of a Swift, a Sterne is, I believe, natural poetry of the higher classes of our age.

I am far from putting them next to the great ones; but you will admit that whoever has a sense for these, for Diderot, has a better start on the way to learning to appreciate the divine wit, the imagination of an Ariosto, Cervantes, Shakespeare, than one who did not even rise to that point. We simply must not make exaggerated demands on the people of our times; what has grown in such a sickly environment naturally cannot be anything else but sickly. I consider this circumstance, however, rather an advantage, as long as the arabesque is not a work of art but a natural product, and therefore place Richter over Sterne because his imagination is far more sickly, therefore far more eccentric and fantastic. Just go ahead and read Sterne again. It has been a long time since you read him and I think you will find him different. Then compare our German with him. He really does have more wit, at least for one who takes him wittily, for he could easily put himself in the wrong. And this excellence raises his sentimentality in appearance over the sphere of English sensibility.

There is another external reason why we should cultivate in ourselves this sense for the grotesque and remain in this mood. It is impossible in this age of books not to have to leaf through very many bad books, indeed, read them. Some of them always – one can depend on it – are fortunately of a silly kind, and thus it is really up to us to find them entertaining by looking at them as witty products of nature. Laputa is everywhere or nowhere, my dear friend; without an act of our freedom and imagination we are in the midst of it. When stupidity reaches a certain height, which we often see now when everything is more severely differentiated, stupidity equals foolishness even in the external appearance. And foolishness, you will admit, is the loveliest thing that man can imagine, and the actual and ultimate principle of all amusement. In such a mood I can often break out in almost incessant laughter over books which seem in no way meant to provoke it. And it is only fair that nature gave me this substitute, since I cannot laugh at all at many a thing nowadays called anecdote and satire. For me, on the other hand, learned journals, for example, become a farce, and the one called *Die Allgemeine Zeitung* I subscribe to very obstinately, as the Viennese keep their Jack Pudding.[38] Seen from my point of view, it is not only the most versatile of them all but in every way the most incomparable: having sunk from nullity to a certain triviality and from there to a kind of stupidity, now by way of stupidity it has finally fallen into that foolish silliness.

This in general is too learned a pleasure for you. If, however, you were to carry on what unfortunately you cannot stop doing, then I will no longer scorn your servant when he brings you the stacks of books from the loan library. Indeed, I offer myself as your porter for this purpose and promise to send you any number of the most beautiful comedies from all areas of literature.

I now take up the thread again: for I am determined to spare you nothing but to follow up your statements step by step.

You also criticized Jean Paul, in an almost cavalier manner, for being sentimental.

May the gods grant it was in the sense in which I understand the word and as I feel I must understand it according to its origin and nature. For according to my point of view and my usage, that is romantic which presents a sentimental theme in a fantastic form.

Forget for a moment the usual notorious meaning of the sentimental, by which one understands almost everything which, in a shallow way, is maudlin and lachrymose and full of those familiar noble feelings whose awareness makes people without character feel so unspeakably happy and great.

Think rather of Petrarch or Tasso, whose poetry in comparison to the more fantastic Romanzo of Ariosto can well be called sentimental; I cannot recall offhand an example where the contrast is so clear and the superiority so decisive as here.

Tasso is more musical, and the picturesque in Ariosto is certainly not the worst. Painting is no longer as fantastic, if I can trust my feeling, as it was prior to its best period: in numerous masters of the Venetian school, also in Correggio, and perhaps not only in the arabesque of Raphael. Modern music, on the other hand, as far as the ruling power of man in it is concerned, has remained true on the whole to its character, so that I would dare to call it without reservation a sentimental art.

What then is this sentimental? It is that which appeals to us, where feeling prevails, and to be sure not a sensual but a spiritual feeling. The source and soul of all these emotions is love, and the spirit of love must hover everywhere invisibly visible in romantic poetry. This is what is meant by this definition. As Diderot so comically explains in *The Fatalist*, the gallant passions which one cannot escape in the works of the moderns from the epigram to tragedy are the least essential, or more, they are not even the external letter of that spirit; on occasion they are simply nothing or something very unlovely and loveless. No, it is the sacred breath which, in the tones of music, moves us. It cannot be grasped forcibly and comprehended mechanically, but it can be amiably lured by mortal beauty and veiled in it. The magic words of poetry can be infused with and inspired by its power. But in the poem in which it is not everywhere present nor could be everywhere, it certainly does not exist at all. It is an infinite being and by no means does it cling and attach its interest only to persons, events, situations, and individual inclinations; for the true poet all this – no matter how intensely it embraces his soul – is only a hint at something higher, the infinite, a hieroglyph of the one eternal love and the sacred fullness of life of creative nature.

Only the imagination can grasp the mystery of this love and present it as a mystery; and this mysterious quality is the source of the fantastic in the form of all poetic representation. The imagination strives with all its might to express itself, but the divine can communicate and express itself only indirectly in the sphere of nature. Therefore, of that which originally was imagination there remains in the world of appearances only what we call wit.

One more thing resides in the meaning of the sentimental which concerns precisely the peculiar tendency of romantic poetry in contrast with ancient. No consideration is taken in it of the difference between appearance and truth, play and seriousness. Therein resides the great difference. Ancient poetry adheres throughout to mythology and avoids the specifically historical themes. Even ancient tragedy is play, and the poet who presented a true event of serious concern for the entire nation was punished. Romantic poetry, on the other hand, is based entirely on a historical foundation, far more than we know and believe. Any play you might see, any story you read – if it has a witty plot – you can be almost sure has a true story at its source, even if variously reshaped. Boccaccio is almost entirely true history, just as all the other sources are from which all Romantic ideas originate.

I have set up a definite characteristic of the contrast between the antique and the Romantic. Meanwhile, please do not immediately assume that the Romantic and the Modern are entirely identical for me. I consider them approximately as different as the paintings of Raphael and Correggio are from the etchings which are fashionable now. If you wish to realize the difference clearly, read just *Emilia Galotti*,[39] which is so extremely modern and yet not in the least Romantic, and then think of Shakespeare, in whom I would like to fix the actual centre, the core of the Romantic imagination. This is where I look for and find the Romantic – in the older moderns, in Shakespeare, Cervantes, in Italian poetry, in that age of knights, love, and fairytales in which the thing itself and the word for it originated. This, up to now, is the only thing which can be considered as a worthy contrast to the classical productions of antiquity; only these eternally fresh flowers of the imagination are worthy of adorning the images of the ancient gods. Certainly all that is best in modern poetry tends toward antiquity in spirit and even in kind, as if there were to be a return to it. Just as our literature began with the novel, so the Greek began with the epic and dissolved in it.

The difference is, however, that the Romantic is not so much a literary genre as an element of poetry which may be more or less dominant or recessive, but never entirely absent. It must be clear to you why, according to my views, I postulate that all poetry should be Romantic and why I detest the novel as far as it wants to be a separate genre.

Yesterday when the argument became most heated, you demanded a definition of the novel; you said it as if you already knew that you would not receive a satisfactory answer. I do not consider this problem insolvable. A novel is a romantic book. You will pass that off as a meaningless tautology. But I want to draw your attention to the fact that when one thinks of a book, one thinks of a work, an existing whole. There is then a very important contrast to drama, which is meant to be viewed; the novel, on the other hand, was from the oldest times for reading, and from this fact we can deduce almost all the differences in the manner of presentation of both forms. The drama should also be romantic, like all literature; but a novel is that only under certain limitations, an applied novel. On the contrary, the dramatic context of the story does not make the novel a whole, a work, if the whole composition is not related to a higher unity than that of the letter which it often does and should disregard; but it becomes a work through the bond of ideas, through a spiritual central point.

Having made this allowance, there is otherwise so little contrast between the drama and the novel that it is rather the drama, treated thoroughly and historically, as for instance by Shakespeare, which is the true foundation of the novel. You claimed, to be sure, that the novel is most closely related to the narrative, the epic genre. On the other hand, I want to admonish you that a song can as well be romantic as a story. Indeed, I can scarcely visualize a novel but as a mixture of storytelling, song, and other forms. Cervantes always composed in this manner and even the otherwise so prosaic Boccaccio adorns his collections of stories by framing them with songs. If there is a novel in which this does not or cannot occur, it is only due to the individuality of the work and not the character of the genre; on the contrary, it is already an exception. But this is only by the way. My actual objection is as follows. Nothing is more contrary to the epic style than when the influence of the subjective mood becomes in the least visible; not to speak of one's ability to give himself up to his humour and play with it, as it often happens in the most excellent novels.

Afterwards you forgot your thesis or gave it up, and decided to claim that all those divisions lead to nothing; that there is *one* poetry, and what counts is whether something is beautiful, and only a pedant would bother with titles and headings. You know what I think of the classifications in current use. And yet I realize that it is quite necessary for each virtuoso to limit himself to a well-defined goal. In my historical research I came upon several fundamental forms which are not further reducible. Thus, in the sphere of Romantic poetry, for instance, novellas and fairy tales seem to me, if I may say so, infinitely contrasted. I only wish that an artist would rejuvenate each of these genres by restoring them to their original character.

If such examples became known, then I would have the courage for a *theory of the novel* which would be a theory in the original sense of the word; a spiritual viewing of the subject with calm and serene feeling, as it is proper to view in solemn joy the meaningful play of divine images. Such a theory of the novel would have to be itself a novel which would reflect imaginatively every eternal tone of the imagination and would again confound the chaos of the world of the knights. The things of the past would live in it in new forms; Dante's sacred shadow would arise from the lower world, Laura would hover heavenly before us, Shakespeare would converse intimately with Cervantes, and there Sancho would jest with Don Quixote again.

These would be true arabesques which, together with confessions, as I claimed at the outset of my letter, are the only romantic products of nature in our age.

It will no longer appear strange to you that I include confessions here, when you have admitted that true story is the foundation of all romantic poetry; and you will – if you wish to reflect on it – easily remember and be convinced that what is best in the best of novels is nothing but a more or less veiled confession of the author, the profit of his experience, the quintessence of his originality.

Yet I appreciate all the so-called novels to which my idea of romantic form is altogether inapplicable, according to the amount of self-reflection and represented life they contain. And in this respect even the followers of Richardson, however much they are on the wrong track, are welcome. From a novel like *Cecilia Beverley*,[40] we at least learn how they lived there in London in boredom, since it was the fashion, and also how a British lady for all her daintiness finally tumbles to the ground and knocks herself bloody. The cursing, the squires, and the like in Fielding are as if stolen from life, and *Wakefield*[41] grants us a deep insight into the world view of a country preacher; yes, this novel would perhaps – if Olivia regained her lost innocence at the end – be the best among all the English novels.

But how sparingly and only drop by drop even the small amount of the real in all those books is handed out. Which travelogue, which collection of letters, which autobiography would not be a better novel for one who reads them in the romantic sense than the best of these?

Confessions, especially, mainly by way of the naive, develop of themselves into arabesques. But at best those novels rise to the arabesque only at the end, when the bankrupt merchants regain their money and credit, all the poor devils get to eat, the likeable scoundrels become honest, and the fallen women become virtuous again.

The *Confessions* of Rousseau is in my opinion a most excellent novel, *Héloïse* only a very mediocre one.

I will send you the autobiography of a famous man which, as far as I know, you are not acquainted with: Gibbon's *Memoirs*. It is an infinitely civilized and infinitely funny book. It will meet you half way, and really the comic novel contained in it is almost complete. You will see before your eyes, as clearly as you could wish, the Englishman, the gentleman, the virtuoso, the scholar, the bachelor, the well-bred dandy in all his affected absurdity, through the dignity of the historic periods. One can go through many bad books and many insignificant men before finding so much to laugh about gathered in one place.

After Antonio had read this epistle, Camilla began to praise the goodness and forebearance of women: that Amalia did not object to receiving such an amount of instruction and, that in general, women were a model of modesty since they remained patient in the face of men's seriousness and, what is more, remained serious and even expressed a certain belief in the art of men. If by modesty you mean this belief, added Lothario, this premise of an excellence which we do not yet possess, but whose existence and dignity we begin to realize; then it would be the firmest basis of a noble education for excellent women. Camilla asked if pride and self-complacency had this function for men, since every one of them considered himself the more unique the more incapable he was of understanding what the other wanted. Antonio interrupted her by remarking that he hoped for the sake of mankind that that belief was not as necessary as Lothario thought, for it was a rare quality. Women, he said, as far as he could observe, think of art, antiquity, philosophy, and such as of unfathomed traditions, prejudices with which men impress each other in order to pass the time.

Part 2

Novalis

Novalis (Friedrich von Hardenberg)

(1772–1801)

Novalis, mystical philosopher-poet of the Romantic period and writer of fragments and novels, was a central figure of the Romantic School. He met Friedrich Schlegel in 1792 in Leipzig, and remained close friends with him for a decade; he met Tieck, with whom he shared a deep interest in Jakob Boehme and mysticism, in 1799, and he knew Herder, Goethe, Schelling, Schleiermacher, A. W. Schlegel, Henrik Steffens, and other prominent literati and scientists of the day. Most of the selections here stem from the period 1797–8, when Novalis worked closely with Friedrich Schlegel to develop a 'symphilosophy'. Their ideas arose in the midst of studies of Shakespeare, Kant, and Hemsterhuis, and from talks with Schelling and Hülsen, and at first took the form of fragments for publication. Novalis referred to his fragments as mystical, 'mystical' meaning something secret, hidden, and intuitively grasped. Novalis sought in his researches into chemistry, physics, and physiology to discover connections between sensible and intelligible experience. He developed mystical expressions and a 'special language' of tropes and enigmas in order to represent and communicate these connections. Nature Novalis saw as a hieroglyph for a hidden and other world of intelligence. Mysticism for Novalis and for the other Romantics was a symbol for the infinite, incomprehensible, and unknowable, that 'Urwelt' which must remain secret and mystical, but which forever enthralled the artist-thinker. Novalis valued his 'mystical fragment' as itself a formal symbol of the method necessary for communicating his own discoveries of that 'Urwelt' to others; he insisted that all communication was only a beginning, a push for the reader toward self-activity and self-discovery. He considered his fragments to be seeds that might become mature if nourished by his audience.

The first selection, *Vermischte Bemerkungen*, or *Miscellaneous Writings*, is the name given to the only manuscript known to survive of *Blütenstaub*, the collection of fragments published in the first number of the *Athenäum* in 1798. It differs considerably from *Blütenstaub*, but whether due to Novalis' own changes or to editing by Friedrich Schlegel is not always determinable. These fragments were published as a unity in testimony to their beauty, according to Friedrich Schlegel, except for thirteen that were published in the next number of the *Athenäum* in the middle of fragments by the Schlegels and Schleiermacher. Apart from a single poem published in 1791, the *Blütenstaub* collection is Novalis' first publication.

The selection 'Monologue' (composition date uncertain) is a concentrated and impressive example of romantic irony, fusing content and method, subject matter and style, and of the positive negation and self-criticism at the heart of irony. The 'Dialogues' (1798) continue a strong vein of irony and are often fragment-like in form, illustrating Novalis' comment in 'Monologue' that 'the genuine dialogue is sheer word-play'. Dialogue 1 is about the catalogue provided for every Leipzig book fair; it and the second dialogue are closely connected with the fragments at the end of the *Miscellaneous*

Writings. The references to mining and mechanics reflect Novalis' years of study in Freiberg. Dialogues 3, 4, and 5 can be seen to connect with the so-called 'Teplitzer Fragmente' (in *Schriften*, II, 596–622). In Dialogue 6, Novalis argues against Schelling's mode of philosophizing, or his 'Naturphilosophie'. All of the dialogues are thoroughly ironic, though this does not of course exclude the serious play characteristic of parts of them.

The selection 'On Goethe' (summer 1798) is related to the fragments on the natural sciences, for Novalis, in keeping with his idea of connections between the sensible and intelligible world, is interested in examining Goethe as both scientist and artist. In the 'Studies in the Visual Arts' (1798), Novalis continues this theme of the mystical connection between the physical world and art.

Novalis' major publications include *Die Lehrlinge zu Sais* (1798), *Die Christenheit oder Europa* (1799), *Geistliche Lieder* (1799), *Heinrich von Ofterdingen* (1799–1800), and *Hymnen an die Nacht* (1800). The reader is referred to the critical edition of *Novalis Schriften*, edited by Paul Kluckhorn and Richard Samuel, 4 vols. (Stuttgart, 1960–75).

The sources of the selections are in every case *Novalis Schriften*, ed. Kluckhorn and Samuel (Stuttgart, 1960–75), II, pp. 413–70, 672–3, 661–71, 640–7, 648–51.

From *Miscellaneous Writings*[1]
Vermischte Bemerkungen (1797)

1. We *look* everywhere for the Unconditional Absolute, and all we *find* are the conditions.[2]

6. We will never understand ourselves entirely, but we are capable of perceptions of ourselves which far surpass understanding.

8. The distinction between illusion and truth lies in the difference in their vital functions.
Illusion lives off truth – truth has its life within itself. We destroy illusion as we destroy diseases – and accordingly illusion is but an inflammation or an expiration of the intellect – the affliction of the fanatic or of the Philistine. The after-effect of the former is usually an *apparent failure of the power to think*, which can be remedied only by a diminishing series of incentives (coercive means). The latter often changes into a *deceptive animation*, the dangerous revolutionary symptoms of which can be dispelled only by an increasing sequence of violent measures.

Both conditions can be changed only by means of a thorough regimen strictly pursued.

9. Our entire perceptive faculty resembles the eye. The objects must pass through contrary media in order to appear correctly on the pupil.

10. Experience is the test of the rational – and the other way round.

The inadequacy of *mere* theory when it comes to application, so often remarked on by the practical man, has its counterpart in the rational application of *mere* experience. This is remarked distinctly enough by your true philosopher, but with the self-knowledge that this consequence is necessary. This is why the practical man rejects mere theory in its entirety, without any inkling of how fraught with problems the answer might be to the question: whether theory exists for the sake of practice, or practice for the sake of theory.

11. Death is an overcoming of the self, and like all self-conquest creates a new, and lighter, existence.

12. Perhaps we need to expend so much energy and effort on the common and ordinary because for the true human self there is nothing more uncommon, nothing more out of the ordinary, than the commonplace everyday?

The highest is the most comprehensible – the nearest, the most indispensable. Only if we have no acquaintance with ourselves, if we have lost the custom and habit of ourselves, something beyond comprehension will emerge which is itself incomprehensible.

14. Nature is the enemy of eternal possessions. According to strict laws she destroys all signs of property and obliterates all distinctive marks of its formation. The earth belongs to all the generations – each one has a rightful claim to everything. The earlier ones may not owe any advantage to this accident of primogeniture. The right of ownership lapses at certain times. The process of improvement and deterioration is determined by certain unchangeable conditions. But if my body is a possession by which I acquire only the rights of an active citizen of this earth, to lose this possession will not make me lose myself. I shall lose nothing but a place in this school for princes[3] – and I shall enter into a higher corporate state whither my dear fellow scholars will follow me.

15. Life is the beginning of death. Life exists for the sake of death. Death is at once end and beginning. At once separation and an even closer amalgam of the self. Death completes the process of reduction.

16. We are near to waking, when we dream we dream.

17. The imagination places the future world in relation to us either in the heights, or in the depths, or in the transmigration of souls. We dream of journeys through the universe – But is not the universe *within us*? We do not know the depths of our mind. Inward leads the mysterious path. Within us, or nowhere, lies eternity with its worlds – the past and future. The external world is the world of shadows – It casts its shadows into the realm of light. True, it all seems

to be dark and lonely and formless within us now. But how different it will appear when this eclipse is over and the body casting its shadow has moved on. We will enjoy more fully than ever, for our spirit has abstained.

19. How can a man have a feeling for a thing, if he does not have the germ of it within himself? What I am to understand has to develop organically within me – and what I appear to be learning is only nourishment – a stimulus to the organism.

20. The seat of the soul is located at the meeting-place of the world within and the world without. Where they interpenetrate each other, there it is at every point of interpenetration.

21.   The life of a truly canonical human being must be symbolic through and through. Given this assumption, would not every death be a death of expiation? More or less of course – and are there not several very remarkable inferences to be drawn from this?

22. He that seeks, doubts. But the genius can tell swiftly and surely what is taking place within him because he is not involved in his representation and consequently the representation is not embroiled in him, but his observation chimes in free accord with the thing observed, and they appear to unite freely to make one work. When we speak of the external world, when we describe real objects, then we proceed like the genius. So genius consists in the capacity to treat imaginary objects as if they were real, and real objects as if they were imagined. So the talent for representation, for exact observation, for the purposeful description of what has been observed, is different from genius. Without this talent, one's vision is incomplete, one is but half a genius, one can have a disposition towards genius, but lacking that talent one will never develop into a genius. Without genius we would none of us exist at all. Genius is necessary to everything. But what we call genius – is the genius of genius.

23.   It is the most arbitrary prejudice that man should be denied the power to be *beside himself*, to be conscious and at the same time beyond his senses. At every moment man has the capacity of an existence beyond his senses. Without this he would not be a citizen of the world – he would be a beast. True, in this state concentration, self-possession is very difficult, as it is constantly, necessarily bound up with our other states. But the more aware of this state we can become, the more vivid, powerful and satisfying is the conviction arising out of it – the belief in true revelations of the spirit. It is not a seeing, hearing, feeling – it is made up of all three – more than all three, it is a sense of immediate certainty – a prospect of my own, true, innermost life – thoughts are transformed into laws, wishes into their fulfilment. For the weak, *the fact of this moment is an article of faith*.

24. The phenomenon becomes particularly striking when we look at certain human figures and faces especially, at many eyes, expressions, gestures, as we hear certain words, read certain passages, view certain aspects of the world, life and destiny. Accidental things, a natural event, particularly the cycles of the day and the seasons, will very often yield such experiences. Certain moods are particularly favourable to these revelations. Most of them last but a moment, a few fleeting, fewest of all remaining. People are very various in this respect. The one is more capable of revelation than the other. The one has more feeling for it, the other more understanding. The latter will always dwell in its gentle light, and though the illuminations visiting the former may be but intermittent, yet they will be brighter and more various. This faculty is likewise potentially pathological when it is characterized either by too much feeling and too little understanding, or by too much understanding and too little feeling.

25. Modesty is very likely a feeling of profanation. Friendship, love, and piety should be treated secretly. We should speak of them only in rare and intimate moments, and reach a silent understanding on them – there is much which is too fragile to be thought, and still more too delicate for discussion.

26. Self-alienation is the source of all abasement, as well as being on the contrary the ground of all true elevation. The first step will be insight into ourselves – detaching contemplation of ourself – To stop here would be to go only half way. The second step must be the active glance outwards – the independent, steady observation of the outside world.

Man will never achieve any great representation, if he represents nothing further than his own experiences, his favourite themes and objects, if he cannot bring himself to study diligently an object which is quite alien and uninteresting to him. The artist who represents must have the ability and the will to represent everything. This is what gives rise to the grand style of representation, which we admire so much, and rightly so, in Goethe.

27. One remarkable characteristic of Goethe's is evident from the way he connects small insignificant incidents with more important events. He seems to have no other intention than to find a poetic way of engaging the imagination in a mysterious kind of play. Here too this rare man has caught the scent of Nature's way, and learned from her a pretty trick of art. Ordinary life is full of similar accidents. They constitute a kind of play, which like all play, ends in surprise and illusion.

Many common sayings depend on the observation of this topsy-turvy relationship – for example *bad dreams* mean good luck – news of a death means long life – a hare crossing your path bad luck. Almost all the common folk's store of superstition rests on interpretations of this seeming-arbitrary playfulness of Nature.

28. The highest task of education is – to seize the mastery of one's transcendental Self – to be at the same time the Self of one's Self.[4] Accordingly, our lack of full understanding and feeling for others is less strange. Without a complete understanding of ourselves, we will never truly come to understand others.

29. I cannot show that I have understood a writer until I am able to act in his spirit, until, without diminishing his individuality, I am able to translate, vary and change him.

30. Humour is a capriciously assumed style. This capriciousness gives it its piquancy. Humour is the result of a free combination of the Absolute and the Conditioned. Humour gives a general interest and an objective value to what is peculiar and conditioned. Where fantasy and judgment meet, we have wit – where reason and caprice come together, we have humour. Persiflage belongs to humour, but is a lesser thing. It is no longer artistic < and much more limited. Serene souls have no wit. Wit reveals a balance out of true – It is the consequence of a disturbance, and at the same time the means of restoring it. Passion has the strongest wit. Truly sociable wit has no violent resonance. There is a kind of wit which is the play of magical colours in the higher spheres. When all relationships are disintegrating, despair, spiritual death – these provide states of the most terrible wit.

Only wit can make the insignificant, the common, coarse, ugly, the immoral fit for society. They are there, as it might be, only for the sake of the witticism – their determining purpose is the joke. >

32. We are on a *mission*. We are summoned to educate the earth. If a spirit were to appear to us, we would make ourselves master of our own spirituality at once – we would be inspired, both by ourselves and by the spirit. Without inspiration, no apparition. Inspiration is both appearance and appearance given in return, both appropriation and communication.

33. A Man's life and active impact survive only ideally, in the memory of his existence. For the present there is no other means of spiritual influence upon this world. We therefore have a duty to remember the dead. It is the only way of remaining in communion with them. This is the only way God himself acts as a moving spirit among us – through faith.

36. What Schlegel characterizes so sharply as Irony[5] is to my mind nothing other than the consequence, the character of presence of mind – of the true

presence of the spirit. The spirit always appears in *strange and airy* form. To me, Schlegel's Irony seems to be genuine humour. One idea can usefully have several names.

43. Among us humans, withdrawing into ourselves means abstracting ourselves from the external world. Among the spirits, earthly life is analogously called inward contemplation – an entering into oneself – an immanent activity. In this way earthly life arises out of an original reflection – a primordial withdrawal and concentration within the self, which is as free as our reflection. Contrariwise, spiritual life arises in this world out of an eruption in that primordial reflection – the spirit unfolds itself again – the spirit emerges forth to itself – partly suspends that reflection – and in this moment for the first time says – I. We can see here how relative is the emerging from and withdrawal into the Self. What we call withdrawing is actually emerging – a resumption of the original form.

45. Where a true disposition of mind towards reflection prevails, and not just an inclination towards thinking this or that thought – there you will find Progredibility [or the potentiality for progress].[6] Many scholars do not have this disposition. They have learned how to draw inferences and conclusions in the same way as a shoemaker has learned to make shoes, without ever coming upon the underlying design or troubling to discover the first principles behind the thought. Yet salvation is not to be found by any other route. In many thinkers, this disposition of mind only lasts a short time – it grows and declines – often as they grow older – often with the discovery of a System, which they have only sought in order to be relieved of the labour of any further reflection.

51. The interesting thing is what sets me in motion not for my own sake, but only as a means, as a member. *The Classical* does not disturb me at all – it affects me only indirectly through myself – It does not exist for me as classical, if I do not assume it to be the kind of thing that would affect me, if I did not for my part intend and encourage myself to produce it, if I did not tear off a part of myself and let this germinate and develop in its own way before my eyes – a development which often only requires a moment – and co-incides with the sense-perception of the object – in such a way that I can behold an object before me in which the base object and the ideal, interpenetrating each other, form one single marvellous individual object.

58. Man appears at his most estimable when the first impression he gives is the impression of an absolutely witty idea, that is, of being spirit and a certain individual at the same time. Each one of these excellent men must seem to be as it were permeated by an airy spirit, which acts as a kind of ideal parody of the visible phenomenon.

61. The best thing about the sciences is their philosophical ingredient – like life in a physical organism. If we dephilosophize the sciences – what is left – earth, air, and water.

64. Courts of law, theatre, church, court, government, public assemblies, academies, colleges etc. are as it were the specialized inner organs of the mystical individual, the state.

65. All the actions of our life are materials of which we can make what we will – a great mind will make something great of his life – The great mind would make of every acquaintance, every incident, the first item in an infinite series – the beginning of a never-ending romance.

68. A translation is either grammatical, or transformatory, or mythical. Mythical translations are translations in the grand style. They present the pure and perfect character of the individual work of art. They do not give us the work of art in its reality, but in its ideal form. To the best of my belief, we do not yet have a perfect model of this kind, but we do encounter bright traces in the spirit of several descriptions and criticisms of works of art. It needs a mind in which the poetic spirit and the philosophical spirit have interpenetrated each other in all their fullness. Greek mythology is in some part a mythical translation of a national religion. The modern Madonna too is a myth of this kind.

Grammatical translations are translations in the ordinary sense. They require much scholarship, but only discursive talents.

Transformatory translations, if they are to be genuine, require the highest poetic spirit. They can come very close to travesty – like Bürger's Homer in iambics[7] – Pope's Homer – all the French translations. The true translator of this kind must indeed be an artist himself and be able to convey the idea of the whole in this way or that, as he pleases. He must be the poet's poet, and so enable him to speak according to the translator's and the poet's own idea *at the same time*. The genius of mankind stands in the same relationship to each individual.

Not only books – everything can be translated in these three ways.

70. Our language is either – mechanical – atomistic – or dynamic. But true poetic language should be organic and alive. How often one feels the poverty of words to express several ideas at a blow.

73. Nothing is more indispensible to the truly religious temper of mind than an intermediary to unite us with the Divinity. Man simply cannot stand in an immediate relationship to the Godhead. His choice of this intermediary must be

utterly free. The least compulsion in this respect will harm his religion. The choice is characteristic, and consequently men of cultivation will choose much the same intermediaries – on the other hand, the choice made by the uneducated is usually determined by accident. But since so few are capable of making a free choice, many intermediaries become more generally shared, whether by accident, by association, or by their special fitness. This is how national religions develop. The more independent man becomes, the more the number of the intermediaries diminishes, while their quality grows more refined – and his relationship to them becomes more various and more sophisticated – fetishes – stars – beasts – heroes – idols – gods – *One* Divine Man. We can quickly see how relative these choices are, and we will all unawares be drawn towards the idea – that the essence of the religion probably does not depend on the nature of the mediator, but consists simply of the view of it and of the relationships to it.

It is idolatry in the wider sense if in fact I regard this mediator as God himself. It is *irreligion* if I assume no mediator at all – and to that extent superstition, or idolatry – and unbelief – or theism, which can also be called the older Judaism – are both *irreligion*. On the other hand, atheism is the negation of all religion, and so has nothing to do with religion. True religion is one which takes its mediator to be mediator, regards him as it were as the organ of the Godhead, as its physical manifestation. In this respect the Jews at the time of the Babylonian Captivity had a true religious inclination – a religious hope – a faith in a future religion which they transformed fundamentally in so strange a way, and which they have maintained with remarkable persistence until the present day.

But observed more closely, true religion seems to be further divided into antinomies – into Pantheism and Entheism. I will allow myself some licence in using the term Pantheism in a different sense from the usual one – understanding by it the idea that every organ of the Godhead can be a mediator if I elevate it to make it so – just as by contrast the term Entheism designates the belief that there is only one organ of this kind in the world for us, which is the only one appropriate to the idea of mediator, and is the only one through which the voice of God is heard, and which I would compel myself to choose, for without this, Entheism would not be true religion.

However incompatible both may seem to be, their union can be brought about – if we make the entheistic mediator into the mediator of the pantheist's intermediary world and as it were its centre – so that each, though in different ways, is the necessary condition of the other.

Thus prayer, or religious thought, consists of a threefold ascending and indissoluble abstraction or assumption. To the religious mind, every object can be a temple, as the ancient Augurs intended. The spirit of this temple is the omni-present High Priest – the entheistic mediator – who alone stands in an immediate relationship to God, the Father of all things.

86. We usually understand the artificial better than the natural.

91. We are related to all parts of the universe – As we are to future and past. Which relation we develop fully, which is to be most important and effective for us depends only on the direction and duration of our attention. A true theory of this procedure would be nothing less than the long-desired art of invention. But it would be more than this. Man acts at all times according to its laws, and there is no doubt that by means of intense self-observation it is possible for the genius to discover them.

95. If the world is as it were a precipitate of human nature, then the divine world is its sublimate. Both take place *uno actu*. No precipitation without sublimation. What the former loses in agility is gained by the latter.

101. That which appears simply *still* is, in respect of the external world, that which is simply motionless. However variously it may change, its relation to the external world remains one of rest. This statement holds good for all self-modifications. That is why the Beautiful appears so still. Everything beautiful is a self-illuminated, perfect, individual object.

103. The more narrow-minded a system is, the more it will please the wordly-wise. That is why the Materialists' system, Helvetius' theory, and even Locke have received most approval from this class. And Kant will still find more supporters than Fichte.

104. The art of writing books has not yet been invented. But it is on the point of being invented. Fragments of this kind are literary seed-houses. True, there may be many a barren grain among them. But meanwhile, if only a few germinate . . .

105. < Schlegel's writings are philosophy as lyric. His [essays on] Forster and Lessing are first-rate minor poetry, and resemble the Pindaric hymns. The lyrical prose writer will compose logical epigrams. If he is utterly intoxicated with life, they will be dithyrambs which the reader will of course have to enjoy and judge as dithyrambs. A work of art can be half-intoxicated – entirely intoxicated, the work of art melts into nothing – Man becomes an animal – The character of the animal is dithyrambic – The animal is an over-plus of life – the plant is a deficient life. Man is a *free* life. >

'Monologue'
'Monolog' (uncertain date)

Speaking and writing is a crazy state of affairs really; true conversation is just a game with words. It is amazing, the absurd error people make of imagining they are speaking for the sake of things; no one knows the essential thing about language, that it is concerned only with itself. That is why it is such a marvellous and fruitful mystery – for if someone merely speaks for the sake of speaking, he utters the most splendid, original truths. But if he wants to talk about something definite, the whims of language make him say the most ridiculous false stuff. Hence the hatred that so many serious people have for language. They notice its waywardness, but they do not notice that the babbling they scorn is the infinitely serious side of language. If it were only possible to make people understand that it is the same with language as it is with mathematical formulae – they constitute a world in itself – their play is self-sufficient, they express nothing but their own marvellous nature, and this is the very reason why they are so expressive, why they are the mirror to the strange play of relationships among things. Only their freedom makes them members of nature, only in their free movements does the world-soul express itself and make of them a delicate measure and a ground-plan of things. And so it is with language – the man who has a fine feeling for its tempo, its fingering, its musical spirit, who can hear with his inward ear the fine effects of its inner nature and raises his voice or hand accordingly, he shall surely be a prophet; on the other hand the man who knows how to write truths like this, but lacks a feeling and an ear for language, will find language making a game of him, and will become a mockery to men, as Cassandra was to the Trojans. And though I believe that with these words I have delineated the nature and office of poetry as clearly as I can, all the same I know that no one can understand it, and what I have said is quite foolish because I wanted to say it, and that is no way for poetry to come about. But what if I were compelled to speak? what if this urge to speak were the mark of the inspiration of language, the working of language within me? and my will only wanted to do what I had to do? Could this in the end, without my knowing or believing, be poetry? Could it make a mystery comprehensible to language? If so, would I be a writer by vocation, for after all, a writer is only someone inspired by language?

'Dialogues'
'Dialogen' (1798)

I.

A. The new catalogue for the book fair?

B. Still wet from the printer's.

A. What a load of letters – what a monstrous waste of time!

B. You seem to belong to the Omarists[8] – if I may call you after the most thorough-going of your kind.

A. You don't intend to sing the praises of this book-making epidemic, do you?

B. Why praises? But I am certainly delighted at how the number of these articles of trade increases year by year. Their export brings only reputation, but their import brings solid profit. There are more honest and worthy ideas circulating among us than among all our neighbours put together. The middle of the present century saw the discovery of these great mines in Germany, richer than those of Potosi or Brazil, which will surely bring about a greater revolution, now and in the future, than the discovery of America. What advances we have since made in the scientific extraction, treatment, and brilliant and useful processing of their products! Everywhere we are bringing together the crude ore or the beautiful moulds – we are melting down the ore, and have the skills to imitate and surpass the moulds. And you want me to fill all those mines in? And return to the rude poverty of our forefathers? Are they not at least a spur to activity? And is not any activity worthy of praise?

A. Put like that, there is nothing to object to. But let us take a closer look at the fine art and the precious metal.

B. I shall not admit arguments against the whole enterprise which are based on the frailty and inadequacy of the individual. This kind of thing needs to be seen as a whole.

A. A whole which is made up of miserable parts is a miserable whole itself – or rather, it is not a whole at all. Yes, if it were a progression according to a plan, if every book filled a gap somewhere, and every book fair were a kind of systematic link in the educational chain! Then each book fair would mark a necessary period, and from these purposeful advances there would finally emerge a perfect road to ideal culture – A systematic catalogue of this kind – how much smaller in volume, and how much greater in weight!

B. You, and many of your kind, are like the Jews. You are for ever hoping for the Messiah, and he came long ago. Do you really believe that the destiny of man, or, if you prefer, human nature, needs to frequent our lecture-halls in order to learn what a system is? It seems to me that our system-builders still have a lot to learn from them. The individual facts are accidental – the arrangement, the conjunction of accidents is not accident, it is law – the consequence of a wise and profound design. There is not a book in the catalogue that has not borne its fruit, even if all it did was fertilize the ground on which it grew. We think we have found many redundancies [tautologies]. Where they occurred they gave life to this or that idea. They are redundant only for the whole, for us; the worst novel has at least given pleasure to the author's friends. Second-rate sermons and books for our edification have their public, their devotees, and in the armour of typography they make their effect tenfold upon their listeners and readers – and that goes for the entire catalogue.

A. You seem to overlook entirely the harmful consequences of reading, to say nothing of the monstrous cost of these articles of modern luxury.

B. My dear friend, doesn't money exist to give life? Why shouldn't it serve this need of our nature, and rouse and satisfy our feeling for thought? As for the harmful consequences, do, I beg you, consider seriously for a moment, for a reproach of that kind from you almost makes me angry.

A. I know what you are aiming at, and I have no desire to take over the real Philistine's objections, but have you not yourself complained often enough about your reading? Have you not spoken often enough of our fatal habituation to a *printed* Nature?

B. It may be that these complaints of mine have given you cause for misunderstanding – but, considering that these are usually but the expressions of a moment's ill-humour, when we speak not in general truths but partially, as mood and passion do, I was complaining more at the inescapable weakness of our nature, its inclination towards custom and easy habit; it was not an objection in principle to the world of ciphers. It is not the ciphers' fault that we end up seeing nothing but books, no longer things[9] – nor that we have as good as lost our five bodily senses. Why do we cling so strangely, like thin and meagre moss, to the printer's vine?

A. But if things go on like this, in the end we will no longer be able to study a science in its entirety – the range of the literature grows so monstrously.

B. Don't believe it. Practice makes perfect, even in the reading of books. You will learn soon enough to be a good judge of your writers – Often you need only to have listened to barely two pages of an author, and you know who you have before you. The mere title is often a pretty readable profile. And the preface too is a subtle measure of the book. Which is why nowadays wiser writers usually omit that treacherous advertisement of its contents, and the easy-going ones usually leave it out because a good foreword is more difficult to write than the book itself – for, as Lessing put it in his younger, revolutionary days,[10] the foreword is at the same time the book's root and its square. And, I would add, it is also its best review.

And the older philologists' manner of filling their works with quotations and commentaries – what was it but the child of poverty? Born of lack of books and abundance of literary spirit.

A. But I don't know. As far as I am concerned, there are even too many *good* books. I spend so much time with a good book – or rather, every good book becomes the vehicle of a life-long interest, the object of never-ending enjoyment. And why do you limit yourself to the few good and intelligent writers? Is it not for the same reason? We are now so limited that there is very little we can enjoy wholly, and in the end is it not better to absorb and assimilate one beautiful object entirely than alight upon a hundred, tasting everything, and dulling our senses soon enough with often conflicting demi-pleasures, without having profited anything for eternity?

B. You speak like a man of religion – in me, unfortunately, you have met a Pantheist – for whom the vast, immeasurable world is just wide enough. I limit myself to the few good and intelligent people – because I must. What more could I want? And so it is with books. For me there could never be enough of the making of books. If I had the good fortune to be a father – I could never have enough children – not just ten or twelve – a hundred, at least.

A. And women too, my greedy friend?

B. No. Only one. Seriously.

A. What bizarre inconsistency.

B. Not bizarre. And not inconsistent either, for there is only one spirit within me, not a hundred. And just as my spirit can be transformed into a hundred or a million minds, my wife can be transformed into all the women there are. Every person is infinitely variable. I feel the same about children as I do about books. I would like to see before me as the work of my mind a whole collection of books from all the arts and sciences. I feel the same about everything. Wilhelm Meister's Years of Apprenticeship are all we have at the moment. We should have as many Years of Apprenticeship as possible, written in the same spirit – the collected Years of Apprenticeship of all the people who have ever lived!

A. Stop, stop. My head is in a whirl. More tomorrow. Then I will be in a fit state to drink a few glasses of your favourite wine with you.

2.

A. Would you care to share your ideas further about writing and so on? I trust I can survive a lively paradoxical thrust – and if you set me going, I may give you some help. You know, once a slow mind is set in motion, its movements are all the bolder and more irresistible.

B. Of course. The more heavily a thing expresses force, the more force it can absorb – and with this remark, we have arrived at German literature, which is a striking confirmation of its truth. Its capacity is enormous. And I do not mean to offend tender sensibilities when I say that it is not easy to use it for filigree work. But that is not to deny that in the mass it resembles the ancient German warrior-troops, who would probably have vanquished ten Roman armies fighting man to man, but, I admit, were defeated in the mass by corporate discipline, rapid deployment and a general tactical view.

A. Do you think that its velocity and force are increasing, or are they still at least in a phase of equal acceleration?

B. Increasing, of course. And in such a way that the nucleus separates and refines more and more of the loose material surrounding it and hindering its motion. In the case of an entity such as literature, the force that gave the first impetus, the motive energy, increases in proportion to its acceleration, and thus enlarges its capacity. You see that this is a situation of infinite potential. There are two variables in a mutually increasing relationship, the product of which is in a state of hyperbolic progression. But to make the metaphor clearer, we have to do not with a quantity – motion and extension – but with a refining *variation* (distinction) of qualities, whose essence we call Nature. Let us call one of these variables the sense-faculty, the organibility, the faculty of animation – which then includes the idea of variability. Let us call the other the energy, order and variety of the moving powers. Think of the two in a mutually increasing relationship, and then deduce the series of their products. Richness increases with simplicity, fullness of tone with harmony, the individual and the perfection of the part with the perfection of the whole, inner union with outward separation.

A. However accurate and flattering a picture of our literary history this may be, it is a little too erudite. I can understand it only superficially – though that may be just as well – so I beg you, instead of giving an inexplicable explanation, come down from the eternal snows and talk to me as plainly as you can about certain phenomena below the tree-line, at the foot of the mountain, where you are not so close to the gods, and I do not have to fear your oracular speech.

3.

[A.] Life is very short.

[B.] It seems very long to me.

[A.] It is short when it should be long, and long when it should be short.

[B.] Which of us is alive, then? Are you not the one who dwells on the disagreeable, and flees from the agreeable?

[A.] That is what is so bad: that in this respect I am as incapable of changing as you are. The agreeable stimulates one's energy, the disagreeable inhibits it.

[B.] Well . . . and you perceive an incompleteness here . . .?

[A.] All too vividly, alas.

[B.] What is stopping you from pursuing this indication?

[A.] What indication?

[B.] That you should not expect what you desire, but should go in search of it. Don't you see that you are thrown onto your own resources?

[A.] To contain myself in patience? I've known that for a long time.

[B.] But not to help yourself too?

[A.] The sick man sends for the doctor because he cannot help himself.

[B.] But what if the doctor prescribes as medicine for his patient the exertion of his own intellect? The sick man who fails himself can only be cured by being prescribed – himself.

[A.] Don't forget that we started from the brevity and length of life.

[B.] Its application is as brief and easy as the gladness of pleasure, and as painfully slow as forebearance. The former I will give you, the latter is up to you. Moderate with reflection the current of energy flowing all too swiftly through your joy, hasten the slow progress – by regular activity.

[A.] Your prescription is not what I am looking for, after all: you are prescribing a mixture by *dilution*. I would accept half gratefully.

[B.] My dear friend, you are not a chymist, otherwise you would know that out of a true mixture, a third factor emerges which contains both elements at the same time, and is more than each separately.

4.

[A.] You are right after all. Our conversation led me to a most interesting result –

[B.] Now it is my turn to be instructed – a turn-about which comes only from true friendship.

[A.] You cleared me a way right through my doubts at the value of pleasure. I understand now that our original existence, if I can express it like this, is pleasure. Time came into being with un-pleasure. That is why all un-pleasure is so long, and all pleasure so brief. Absolute pleasure is *eternal* – outside of all time. Relative pleasure more or less one integral moment.

[B.] You fill me with enthusiasm – only a few steps more, and we will be standing on the heights of the inner world.

[A.] I know what steps you mean. Like time, un-pleasure is finite. Everything finite arises from un-pleasure. Such as life.

[B.] I will take over from you – and continue. The Finite is finite – What remains? Absolute pleasure – eternity – absolute life. And what have we to do in time, whose purpose is the self-*consciousness* of infinity? Assuming that it has a purpose, for one could well ask whether purposelessness were not the very thing that characterizes illusion!

[A.] That too – meantime, what should we try to bring about? The transformation of un-pleasure into pleasure, and with it the transform-ation of time into eternity, by means of an independent abstraction and elation of spirit, consciousness and illusion, as such.

[B.] Yes, my dear friend. And here at the pillars of Hercules let us embrace, in our delight at the conviction that it is in our power to regard life as a beautiful, inspired illusion, and as a splendid spectacle, that in spirit we can even here be in a state of absolute pleasure and eternity, and that the old lament at the transience of things itself can, and shall, become the most joyful of our thoughts.

[A.] This view of life as a temporal illusion, as drama, might become second nature to us. How swiftly then would dark hours pass, and how enchanting transience would seem.

―――――――――――――

5.

A. Dearest friend, give me a clear idea of the Prince, one that will stand the test
of scrutiny. I have been brooding long on it, but these damned princes are
not for me – they vanish in the light of my concentration. They cannot be
fire-proof, or light-proof. Is the idea of the Prince rather like a frame around
a picture of Egyptian darkness?

B. A fortunate genius has brought you to the very man, for a happy chance has
revealed to me the following great mystery – although I admit, like every
mystery, it sounds pretty paradoxical:
Princes are zeroes – in themselves they are nought, but with numbers
    Which raise them at random beside them, they are worth a great deal.

A. But my good friend, what do these hypotheses amount to in the end? After
all, one single fact truly observed is worth more than the most brilliant
hypothesis. Hypothesizing is a risky pastime – in the end it turns into a
passionate proneness to un-truth, and probably nothing has done more
harm to the best minds and all the sciences than this extravagance of the
fantasizing intelligence. This intellectual indecency wholly blunts our sense
of the truth, and makes us lose the habit of strict observation, which is the
only true foundation for extending and discovering new knowledge.

B. Like nets are hypotheses – only the fisher who casts his net far
Hauls in the catch. Was not America found by hypothesis?
Praise to hypothesis, long may she live, for she only
Stays ever-young, though oft she may be self-defeating.
And now the practical application in prose. The sceptic, my friend, has
done little, and common empiricism even less, for the extension of science.
All the sceptic does is to spoil things for the maker of hypotheses, and
unsteady the ground beneath his feet. A strange way of advancing science.
At the best a very indirect achievement. Your true maker of hypotheses is
none other than the inventor himself, for the new-discovered land already
hovers obscurely before his eyes before he has actually made his discovery.
With this obscure image in mind, he hovers above observation and
experience, and it is only after frequent and various contacts and frictions
between his ideas and practical experience that he finally comes upon the
idea which has a positive or negative relation to experience, such that both
may then be linked for ever more, and a new, divine light may illumine the
power that has come into the world.

6.

[A.] Hark'ee, it is now fashionable to talk rationally about Nature – so we too
must make our contribution. Well – what shall we do – come, answer me, do.

[B.] I have been trying for some time to think of a natural beginning for our conversation – I am pressing my natural intelligence into it, but it has dried up, and there is no more pith in it.

[A.] Perhaps some scholar has used it as a fine specimen to press between the leaves of his herbarium . . .?

[B.] I would be curious to know how he has classified it.

[A.] Probably among the cryptogamia, for there is no trace of blossom or fruit.

[B.] You see, we are already inspired by Nature – we have slipped into Nature all unnoticed. You are one of the realists – or, in plain German, you are a bluff, coarse fellow.

[A.] That is a true word – a word of consecration. I am much disposed to become one of Nature's priests.

[B.] You mean because priests have a belly as great as yours, and Nature is in truth nothing more than a vast belly.

[A.] That is true too – but the true disposition lies in the coarseness. For see, Nature is tremendously coarse, and to know her aright, you have to grasp her coarsely. Coarse sand needs coarse sieve. This proverb was made for natural philosophy, for we are to grind it finer with our intellects. Our ancestors must have had a great insight into Nature, for only in Germany has true coarseness been discovered and cultivated.

[B.] It suits our soil very well – which is why things look so barren for us now, for we have neglected our national plant and been most careless of the wealth it has to offer. It flourishes now only among common men – and that is why Nature still grows green for them. She has long ago turned her back on the finer sort of people, and would be pleased to do so for ever.

[A.] Our conversation has given me a definition of Nature – she is the essence of all coarseness.

[B.] And all the laws of Nature can be deduced from that – she is constantly, unceasingly, coarse, she grows ever coarser, and no coarseness is the coarsest. Lex continuitatis [law of unbroken succession].

[A.] She likes going straight to the point without any ado. Lex Parsimoniae [law of parsimony].

[B.] Yes – and a number of unknown laws can be developed from this fruitful
      idea. But because we are philosophers, we do not have to bother about
      pursuing this in detail. We have the principle, and that is good enough –
      the rest we can leave to baser minds.

[A.] But tell me, how is it that Nature has become so damned rare now. Art is
      actually the usual thing.

[B.] Yes, she must be, for after all she makes herself comprehensible enough,
      and is always ready to burst forth in all her nature, so she ought to be
      much more widely understood.

[A.] The man who is so obsessed by the exaggerated artificiality of art will take
      her very coarseness to be art, and so she is misunderstood everywhere.

[B.] But we are also born to Nature, and all this comes naturally to the natural
      man – so what is there left to say about it? Merely talking about it shows
      you are a dull blunderer without pith or energy, for whereof one speaks,
      thereof one has nothing. That is an axiom.

[A.] Then let us stop talking about it, for otherwise our Nature will give us the
      slip.

[B.] You are right. And then fashion might almost have played us an
      underhand trick and falsely driven us from our nature. Let us go down to
      the cellar – Nature is at home there – so that we can restore our natural
      selves.

[A.] But take care not to talk about the wine – for whereof one speaks, thereof
      one has nothing.

[B.] True, that is why you are always talking about intelligence –

[A.] Only when you talk about short ears.

'On Goethe'
'Über Goethe' (1798)

445. Goethe is a practical poet through and through. He is in his works – what
the English are in their wares – utterly simple, neat, convenient and durable.
He has done for German literature what Wedgwood did for English art. Like
the Englishman, he has a natural business sense and a refined taste acquired by

good sense. Both are wholly compatible with each other, and are closely related, in the *chemical* sense. His studies in physics make it quite clear that he is much more inclined to complete something slight, and give it elegance and high finish, then tackle an entire world, or take on something which one can be certain from the start cannot be carried out perfectly, will surely remain awkward, and resists the high polish of mastery. Even in this field he will choose a romantic subject, or something similarly intricate. His observations on light and on the metamorphoses of plants and insects[11] both confirm and demonstrate most convincingly that the perfect style for instruction is also part of the artist's range. There is a sense in which we might also, and rightly, declare that Goethe is the foremost physicist of his time, and has in fact marked an era in physics. It is not a question of the extent of his knowledge, nor would we claim that discoveries determine the stature of a natural scientist. It is rather a question of whether the scientist observes Nature as an artist observes the ancient world – for Nature is something different from living Antiquity. Nature and insight into Nature develop at the same time, as Antiquity and knowledge of Antiquity develop together. For it is a great mistake to believe that such things as ancient worlds really exist. It is only now that Antiquity is coming into existence. This is brought about by the artist's eyes and soul. The relics of the ancient world are only the particular stimulus to our creation of Antiquity. Antiquity was not built with hands. The mind produces it with the eye, and the hewn stone is but the body which acquires meaning only when imbued with the idea of Antiquity, and as its appearance. Goethe the poet has the same relationship to other poets as Goethe the physicist has to other physicists. Other poets may sometimes exceed him in range, variety or depth, but in the art that comes from cultivation, who would claim to be his equal? Where others only tend towards some end, he completes the deed. He really makes something, whereas others only make something possible – or necessary. We are all of us necessary or possible creators, but how few of us are real creators. A scholastic philosopher might call this active empiricism. We will content ourselves with observing Goethe's artistic talent and taking another look at the quality of his intellect. He casts new light for us on the gift of abstraction. He abstracts with a rare precision, but never without at the same time reconstructing the object which corresponds to the abstraction. This is nothing but applied philosophy – and so, to our astonishment, we finally discover a practical philosopher, applying his insights – which is after all what every true artist has always been. The *pure* philosopher too will be practical, although the applied philosopher does not need to devote himself to pure philosophy – for that is an art in itself. (Goethe's *Wilhelm Meister*.) True art is situated in the intellect, which creates according to a characteristic concept: only fantasy, wit and good judgment are required of it. Thus *Wilhelm Meister* is entirely a product of art, a work of the intellect. From this point of view, we see that many mediocre works of art are exhibited in the halls of art, while on the other hand many writings regarded as excellent are excluded. The Italians and the Spanish are far more talented in

matters of art than we are. And even the French are not without gifts – the
English have far fewer, and in this respect they resemble us, for we too rarely
have a talent for art, although of all the nations we are most richly endowed
with those capacities employed by the intelligence in its works. This abundance
of the requirements needed for art is what makes the few artists amongst us so
unique – so outstanding, and we can be assured that the greatest works of art
will arise among us, for there is no nation to match us in energy and
universality. If I have understood our modern lovers of ancient literature
aright, their intention when they demand the imitation of classical writers is to
educate our artists, and rouse in us a talent for art. No modern nation has
possessed an artistic mentality to such a high degree as the ancients. Everything
about them is art. But perhaps we would not be saying too much if we were to
assume that they are, or could become, the supreme artists, only in our eyes. It is
the same with classical literature as it is with ancient art: it is not a given, it is not
there already, but it has first to be produced by us. We can bring a classical
literature – which the ancients themselves did not possess – into existence only
by keen and intelligent study of the ancients. The ancients would have to take
on the opposite task – for the mere artist is a one-sided, limited being. Goethe
may not be a match for the ancients in rigour, but he excels them in content –
though that is not to his credit. His *Wilhelm Meister* approaches them pretty
closely. It is the Absolute Novel, without qualification - and that is a great deal
in our time.

Goethe will and must be surpassed – but only as the ancients can be surpassed
– in content and energy, in variety and depth – not really as an artist – and even
so, only by very little, for his rightness and rigour are perhaps more classic than
they seem.

446. Consummate philosophers easily happen upon the principle: philosophy
too is vanity – and this applies to all branches of learning.

447. *The art of living* – against *macrobiotics*.

448. the sensitive will / All stimuli *attract* – the *stimulation identifies*. Ego – Non-
ego – product. All stimuli thought into one is Ego and Non-ego. Theory of
magic. / Individual definitions.

449. *Composition in speech*. musical treatment of writing.

450. The looser, the more *sensitive* – the denser, the more *capable of rousing
sensitivity*.

[451.] All a prime minister, a prince, or any kind of director needs are *human
beings* and *artists* – a *knowledge* of character and talent.

452. Truly universal thoughts are like the country parson in the second part of *Wilhelm Meister's Apprenticeship* – They seem so familiar because they look like the general thoughts of mankind, and not like the thoughts of any Tom, Dick or Harry.[12]

453. World psychology. We cannot explain the organism without assuming a *world soul*, just as we cannot assume the universal plan without assuming a universal rational being.

The thinker who attempts to explain the organism without taking into consideration the *soul* and the mysterious bond between *soul and body*, will not get very far. Perhaps life is nothing but the result of this union, *the action of this contact.*

Light is produced by the friction of steel on stone, sound by the touch of bow on strings, spasmodic movement by the making and breaking of galvanic contact; it may be that life is likewise produced by the arousal (penetration) of organic matter.

Indirect construction. The right thing appears of its own accord, when the conditions for its appearance are present. The relationship of the *mechanical operation* to its higher *result* is absolutely the same as that of steel, stone and contact to the spark. (*free collaboration*)

Every dynamic effect is accompanied by a higher genius.
The individual soul shall become congruent with the world soul.
The world soul rules, and the individual soul rules jointly with it.

454. Of the many ways of making an *effect* or *stimulus* (by combination, impact, contact, indirect contact, mere presence, possible presence, etc.)

455. *Dramatic* narrative mode. Fairy-tale and *Wilhelm Meister*. Toujours en état de Poësie.

456. Great value of mathematics as an *active science*. Superior interest of *Mechanics.* (*the study of touch. Acoustics.*) The many kinds of touch – and tangents, active and passive tangents. Angles of contact. Rapidity of contact, or rhythmic units. Sequences and series of rhythmic units. Units of rhythmical pattern present in the line, the point, the surface, the mass. Persistent units of rhythm.

457. Foundations of geognosy and oryctognosy [that is, geology and mineralogy]. Critique of characteristic signs.

458. Theory of instruments – or *organology*.

459. Light is in any case action – Light is like life – dynamic action – a *phenomenon which reveals itself*, but only when the appropriate conditions conjoin. Light makes fire. Light is the genius of the combustion process. Like light, life is capable of intensification, fading, and gradual negation. Does it also break down, as light does into colours? The process of nutrition is not the cause, but only the consequence, of life.

460. All activity is *transition*. In chymistry, both elements transform each other in their combination. But not in what is called mechanical influence.

461. Signs of *disease* – of the instinct for self-destruction – This is so of everything imperfect – and so even of life – or rather, of organic matter. Cancellation of the distinction between life and death. Annihilation of death.

462. Might it not be so, that all the changes brought about by the mutual effect of bodies upon one another are merely changes of capacity and sensitivity, and that all chymical operations and influences have this *general unity*, in that they modify the sensitivity and capacity of every material? Thus, for example, oxygen acts in the process of combustion. All chymical elements are *indirectly congruent*. The characteristics and appearances of every substance depend on its sensitivity. All changes brought about by combination are connected with the capacity and sensitivity of the bodies. The bodies are distinguished by the variety of their sensitivity. Or could one say that bodies are most naturally classified as stimuli by the variety of their relations to *sensitivity*? All this agrees very well with Galvanism. Chymistry is already Galvanism – the Galvanism of inanimate Nature. Fire is only a *means* – a learned resource used by the Chymist. (Spontaneous combustion is Galvanization.) (Metallic calcides are still not sufficiently used in medicine.) Does heat have a chymical action? Strictly speaking, no – it only encourages galvanization.

463. Cold is an *indirect stimulation* – in healthy bodies it draws heat out. There is nothing that keeps a thoroughly healthy body so lively and active as an alternating deficiency and excess of stimulations – it is *stimulated* by the deficiency to find a *substitute* – excess moderates and inhibits its functioning, excess causes it to lower its *activity*.

The *deficiency* stimulates the healthy body to *activity*, and the *excess* to *rest*. Are not works of art the products of a healthy inactivity?

[464.] The drive to organization is the drive to turn everything into instrument and means.

465. Journals are actually the first books to be written *in common*. Writing in company is an interesting symptom giving us an inkling of a great development

in authorship. Perhaps one day people will write, think and act as a mass. Entire communities, even nations, will undertake One Work.

466. Every person who consists of persons is a person *to a higher power*, a person *squared*. In this connection one might say that the Greeks never existed, only a Greek genius. A cultured Greek was only indirectly and only in very small part his own creator. This explains the great and pure individuality of Greek art and science, which is not to deny that on the fringes they succumbed to the modernizing influence of Egyptian and oriental mysticism. In Ionia we notice the relaxing effect of the warm Asian skies, whereas in the early Doric forms we are aware of the mysterious rigour and austerity of the Egyptian divinities. Later writers have often assumed this ancient style, out of a modern, romantic instinct, and filled these uncouth figures with a new spirit; they have set them among their contemporaries to bid them pause in the giddy course of civilization, and make them pay renewed attention to these long-abandoned sacred relics.

467. In early times only nations – or geniuses – really lived. / Genius to a higher power, squared. So the ancients must be regarded in the mass.

468. To inquire into the *basis*, the law of a phenomenon etc., is to put an abstract question, that is, one directed away from the object and towards the spirit. It aims at *appropriation*, assimilation of the object. Explanation makes the object no longer alien. The spirit aims at absorbing the stimulus. It is stimulated by what is alien. Hence, it is the unceasing occupation of the spirit to appropriate, to transform the alien into its own.

One day, there shall no longer be any stimulus nor anything alien; the spirit shall, or should deliberately be able, to make itself self-alienated and self-stimulating. Now, the spirit is spirit out of instinct – a Nature-Spirit – but reflection and *art* shall make him a Spirit of Reason.

(Nature shall become art, and art shall become second nature.)

469. The point of dispute between the pathologists who base their theories on the humours and those who base them on the nerves is a common point at issue between physicists.

This dispute touches on the most important problems in physics.

The pathologists of the humours have their equivalent in the physicists who multiply materials – the 'matter-seers'; the neural pathologists in the atomistic, mechanical 'form-seers'. The true *actionists*, such as Fichte, etc. combine both systems. These last could be called creative observers, *creators of modes of seeing*. The other two are the *directly* and *indirectly* Sluggish – the Fluid and the Rigid.

The concept of action can be analysed into the concept *Matter* and *Movement* (impact). Thus the actionist can be analysed into the *Humoralist* and the *Neurist*. They are his closest elements, his *most intimate* components.

470. Similarly between historical geognosy and oryctognosy on the one hand, and philology on the other.

471. Sciences can be analysed into sciences, senses into senses. The more limited and definite, the more practical. Of the inclination of scholars to universalize their science. Various objects come into being in this way. An object, [so] that various senses become one.

472. Presentation of an object in *series* – (series of variations, modifications, etc.) For example, as Goethe presents the persons of Wilhelm Meister, the beautiful soul, Nathalie. In self-reflection – in things at first, second and third hand, etc. An historical sequence is of this kind, a collection of engravings from the crudest beginnings of art to its perfection, and so on – of forms, from the frog to Apollo etc.

473. Religious, moral, spiritual, moral *crimes* etc. Poetry is the true and absolute reality. This is the heart of my philosophy. The more poetic, the more true. Is the beautiful neuter? / On general concepts. Are they neutra, combinations, or *quid*? Facility and popularity. / Transforming the fiscal sciences into poetry. / Critique of previous physicists. / J. W. *Ritter*.[13] Concept of erudition. / A *universal encyclopaedia* is the best handbook. / What is more like life? Life-mass like Candlemass? A mass of life, like a mass of light? / Animals as attributes of the gods. / The treatment of astrology by Theophrastus[14] and the astrologists. / Murhard's History of Physics.[15] Reticulation. / The mathematical nature of analogy. / On the *surface*, as synthesis. / On experiments / Time and space – treated with greater liveliness – / Nature – things born – Suggestion of procreation / Astronomical geognostic division of bodies into luminous and non-luminous. / Electrometric electricity – absolute – relative. / Essay on theorists and the *use* of speculative sciences.

'Studies in the Visual Arts'
'Studien zur bildenden Kunst' (1799)

475. On the sensations of *thinking* in the *body*.

476. *Ancients*. The Madonna. / Man is a self-endowed historical individual. Stages of mankind. When mankind has reached the highest stage, the higher will reveal and conceal itself spontaneously. / Aspect of the history of mankind – the masses – nations – societies – individuals. / Elevation of mechanics. Fichte's intellectual chemistry. Chemistry is the *passionate ground*. Chemistry is the

crudest and first formation. / *Descriptions of paintings etc.* / On *Landscape painting* –
and painting against sculpture in general. / *Everything must be amenable to being
mathematically squared and resistant to being squared at the same time.* Use, practice is
infinitely graded – so is measurement. Landscapes – *Surfaces* – *Structures* –
Architectonic. Cavernous *Landscapes.* Atmospheres. Cloudlandscapes. The entire
landscape should form *An Individual* – Vegetation and inorganic nature – Fluid
Firm – *Masculine* – *Feminine.* geognostic Landscapes. Nature Variations. / Must
not sculpture and painting be symbolic. The picture gallery is a store-room for
every kind of indirect stimulus for the poet. / *Necessity* of all works of art. / Every
work of art has an Ideal a priori – has a necessity within itself to be there. Only
this way is a true criticism of painters possible. Suite of madonnas. Suite of
heroes. Suite of wise men. Suite of geniuses. Suite of gods. Suite of men. We are
compelled by the ancients to treat them as holy relics. Particular kinds of *souls*
and *spirits.* Who dwell in trees, landscapes, stones and paintings. A landscape
must be looked at as a dryad or an oread. A landscape must be felt like a body.
Every landscape is an ideal body for a particular *kind of spirit.* / The Sonnet. /
The *Joke.* / Feeling for *Antiquity* – roused by the Ancients.

477. The poet borrows all his materials, except images. / On Friedrich *Schlegel* –
etc. / Character, meaning.

478. Eternal virgins – born wives. / Fichte's apotheosis of Kant's philosophy. /
Thinking about thinking certainly teaches one to get thinking in his power –
because we learn thereby to think how and what we will. / Innermost,
furthestmost, infinite universe – Analogy with outside – light – gravity.

479. Do all humans have to be human beings? It is possible for beings quite other
than human to exist in human form. / Virtuousness in the educator is the
indirectly positive principle in education. / *universal writer's dexterity.* / On the
wide thinkers – and the deep thinkers – e.g. [Friedrich] Schlegel and Fichte. /
Trivializing the divine, apotheosizing the base. / We are past the time of
generally valid *forms* – / Influence of the sculptural material upon the figure –
and its *effect.* / Might not the stronger and more attractive effect of rarer and
more delicate materials be *galvanic*? / *Compulsion* is a stimulus for the mind –
compulsion has something absolutely stimulating for the mind. / Medicinal
application of happiness and unhappiness. / On neutralization – complicated
diseases – local pain – reproductive system. / All doubt, all need for *truth* –
dissolution – Knowledge is the consequence of *crudity* and *over-education* –
Symptom of an imperfect constitution. Hence all scientific *education* aims at
dexterity – practice – All scientific *healing* aims at the *restitution* of health where
there are no scientific needs.

480. Revolutionizing and adaptation of mathematics. / Letter on art and
antiquity to Schlegel[16] sen. *Gedichte* / Letter to F[riedrich] S[chlegel]. / Fichte's

synthesis – true chemical compound. In suspension. | Individuality and generality of humans and diseases. | On necessary *self-limitation* – infinite versatility of the cultivated mind – it is possible to draw oneself out of everything, twist and turn everything at will. | The *powerful geniuses*. | Headings of the main masses in letters etc. | On the *inks* – and the *tone* – analogously moral. | On the right condition of dialogue. On the experimental genius. | The essential businessman has less need of knowledge and skill than of historical spirit and culture. | Spiritual metre. | On mechanics. | Learned conferences – their purpose. | Marriages are mostly divorces. | Mimicry in musical *notation*. | Wit in the great | Experimental religion and philosophy. | What effect on one has ordinary intercourse in Brown's sense.[17] | Stimulus *becomes* capable of stimulation – etc. Physiology. | Concept of neutralisation. Is the Neutrum the highest – negative neutrum positive neutrum and synthesis | On the transformation of history into tradition. The latter is the higher.

481. Everything visible cleaves to the Invisible – the Audible to the Inaudible – the Palpable to the Impalpable. Perhaps the Thinkable to the Unthinkable –. The *telescope* is an *artificial, invisible organ*. | *Vessel*. | The imagination is the marvellous sense which can *replace* all senses for us – and which is so much ours to command. If the outward senses seem to be ruled entirely by mechanical laws – the imagination is obviously not bound to the present and to contact with external stimuli.

482. Herder's *Plastik* p. 7.[18] They taught the man who was born blind and who recovered his sight to recognize his touch with his eyes. He often forgot the meanings of the symbols for his tactile feeling until his eye grew practised in regarding figures in space and coloured images as the letters of previous physical sensations; it became accustomed to associating the one rapidly with the other and reading the objects around him.

483. The unity of the picture, the form, the graphic composition rests upon firm proportions, like the unity of musical harmony. | Harmony and melody. |

484.
Space	Visual arts	Sight	Surface	
Time	Music	Hearing	Sound	
Energy	Poesy	Feeling	Body	Herder[19]

485. Our *body* is *part* of the *world* – or better, a member: it already expresses the *independence*, the analogy with the whole – in short the concept of the microcosm. This member must correspond to the whole. So many senses, so many modi of the universe – the universe entirely an analogy of the human being in body, soul and spirit. The former the abbreviated form, the latter the extended form of the same substance.

I should not and will not on the whole act arbitrarily upon the world – that is why I have a body. By modifying my body, I modify *my* world. By not acting upon the *vessel of my existence*, I likewise indirectly shape my world.

486. The tree can turn for me into a flame burgeoning – man into a flame speaking – beast into a flame walking.

487. Everything perceived is perceived in proportion to its repulsive power. Explanation of the Visible and the Illuminated – by analogy to sensible warmth. Likewise with sounds. Perhaps also with thoughts.

Part 3
Tieck

Ludwig Tieck

(1773–1853)

Ludwig Tieck, probably the most productive author of the German Romantic period, excelled as poet, novelist, dramatist, critic, translator, and as a scholar of Shakespeare and of Spanish, Italian, and English literature, as well as old German literature. Tieck's best known works include the novel *Franz Sternbalds Wanderungen* (1798), the comedy *Der gestiefelte Kater* (1797), known in English as *Puss-in-Boots*, the drama *Genoveva* (1800), and the lyrical poems, the *Magelone Lieder* (1809). Amongst the literati in Germany and England he was well known as one of the two most prominent Shakespeare scholars of his time. During his visit to England in 1817 he succeeded in making a profound impression on no less an encyclopaedic mind than S. T. Coleridge with his acquaintance with Shakespeare's plays, of Shakespeare's contemporaries and predecessors, and with his first-hand knowledge of European languages and literature generally.

The vast range of Tieck's criticism, quite different from the theoretical style of Friedrich Schlegel or the systematic philosophizing of his friend Solger, falls into several major categories: the Shakespeare criticism, translation and scholarly work on Shakespeare's contemporaries and predecessors; Tieck's joint productions with Wackenroder: *Herzensergiessungen eines kunstliebenden Klosterbruders* and *Phantasien über die Kunst*; the old German literature researches; reviews and articles on contemporary writers; the 'Rahmengespräche' in *Phantasus*, which Coleridge prized so highly and which are often commentaries on Tieck's own writings; the *Dramaturgische Blätter*, or the collection of articles for the Dresden *Abendzeitung* between 1821 and 1824 on drama primarily; the material in the Köpke reminiscences; and finally letters, particularly the Solger–Tieck exchanges. Tieck's Shakespeare researches may act as the background for his entire critical corpus; his appreciation of Shakespeare informed and influenced his critical practice from an early age. His youthful essay, 'Shakespeares Behandlung des Wunderbaren' (1793, published 1796 as the preface to his translation in prose of *The Tempest*) was an enquiry into the relation of 'das Wunderbare', the supernatural, to reason and experience. Like his interest in Shakespeare, the category of the 'Wunderbare' continued to fascinate Tieck throughout his life as a central part of his aesthetic concern, playing an important role in his late novels especially. The influence of Jacob Boehme is not unrelated to this preoccupation, and is expressive of Tieck's temperament (in distinction from other of his Romantic fellow writers) and of his interest in the intuitive, the revelatory, the fantastic and the imaginative. In Tieck's Shakespeare criticism, some of the major themes of Romantic theory emerge: (1) the relation of reader and text; (2) romantic irony; and (3) the emphasis on aesthetic effect instead of overt content, so that the style and method constituted the meaning of a work of art rather than its 'Weltanschauung'. The other major Shakespeare criticism includes the *Altenglisches Theatre* (translations and prefaces, 1811), *Über Shakespeares Sonette* (1826), *Vier Schauspiele von Shakespeare* (translations, 1836), and *Das Buch über Shakespeare*, put together by Henry Lüdeke out of fragments from Tieck's papers (Halle, 1920). Much of

Tieck's other criticism can be found in the *Kritische Schriften*, 4 volumes in three (1848–52), edited by himself. Of particular interest are, first, his article on Heinrich von Kleist, second, the essay 'Goethe und seine Zeit', and his 'Shakespeares Behandlung des Wunderbaren' (1793), the latter in *Ausgewählte Kritische Schriften*, ed. E. Ribbat (Tübingen, 1975), 1–38.

The first selection follows the German text from *Kritische Schriften* (hereafter *KS*), III, 90–4; the second from *KS* II, 184–5; the third from *KS*, I, 207–8 and 274; the fourth from *Tieck Schriften* (*TS*), I, viii–xi; the fifth from *TS*, VI, xxvii–xxix; and the sixth from *TS*, V, 280–2.

'Tony – A Drama in Three Acts by Th. Körner'
'Tony – Drama in drei Aufzügen, von Th. Körner' (date uncertain)

This drama is based on a tale of Heinrich von Kleist which, in spite of occasional flaws in the language, can be considered a masterpiece (see, in the second volume of his stories, 'The Betrothal in St Domingo').

Only a few people realize how difficult it is to create a genuine drama from a really good story or novella. More often than not, the opposite view is put forward, namely, that more than half of the dramatic writer's work has already been done in good novellas. Indeed even Shakespeare has, in some measure, those old writers of the novella to thank for his fortune and fame. Those people who hold this opinion fail to consider that Shakespeare did not choose one single novella as a model for his works, that he preferred traditions like that of the Menaechmi[1] or partially successful novels (in 'As You Like It') and fabulous folk tales (in 'The Merchant' among others). Only in his youth did he choose a novella, one by Boccaccio[2] ('All's Well') and this comedy borrowed from the Italian author is certainly not one of Shakespeare's finest. His contemporaries plundered the works of Boccaccio. Bandello[3] and Cervantes[4] and other considerable talents mutilated the magnificent creations of these poets and dragged them into disgrace more often than they succeeded in bringing unexpectedly to life a new dramatic work out of these perfect creations.

This error has then already led other men of talent astray, and yet, to seize and understand it is so simple. How magnificent, how graphic, how gripping the final songs of the *Odyssey* are, how deeply moving, how awesome the demise of the suitors: all is resolved into speech and appears to approximate to drama. Yet how strange must the attempt appear to take Homer at his word and imagine that one is composing as a tragic dramatist the return of Odysseus simply by transcribing words. Transformed entirely into drama, everything that in the epic poem arouses fear and excitement in us would appear cold, lifeless, plodding.

How excellent is Boccaccio's 'Griselda'! Perhaps the most accomplished of his novellas. It is difficult to read it without tears, and it too seems, while still in Boccaccio's hands, to take on the contours of a real drama of its own accord. But let the poet try to do the same and he will find that, of all the beautiful things which move him so deeply in the story, he can use virtually none, that it is quite impossible to deck oneself out in this way with the finery of a hero from an earlier time; rather that on the contrary he must win for himself and be clad in armour which is quite new, which has its own special lustre and which that writer of novellas, in his turn, could never have been allowed to acquire without mistaking his own vocation.

The painter who can really paint will not wish to make colour copies of bas-reliefs from antiquity, and no sculptor will have any use on his marble tablets for Raphael and Michelangelo, and least of all for Titian or Correggio. Yet this error has also brought much confusion into the world.

One will hardly go far wrong if one turns this last proposition right around. For the dramatic writer his own free invention is the easiest thing to transform, fable, tradition and history adopted from elsewhere much more difficult, but something that can already lay claim to the name of a work of art in some other area the most difficult of all. That which produces an effect in narrative can never produce the same effect in drama. And indeed why should it? After all, the dramatist has at his command, if he knows the advantages of his genre, entirely different effects which far surpass those of the narrative writer, however skilful he may be and however well he may measure up to his material. Yet if the dramatist cannot achieve creative mastery over his own field, chosen as the arena for his wondrous feats, if he doubts his own power and looks with envy on another's territory so as to bring back from there something that could enliven the lifeless elements of his work, then the result will always be a frontier war in which the dramatist is bound in all events to be the loser. To give examples is too much of a business but anyone with any discernment will find them ready to hand.

Many admirers of Shakespeare took great offence at a certain Mrs Lennox[5] when she devoted a book specifically to the purpose of comparing the great man's poetic works with those older stories and novellas and of proving that the celebrated man had, like some bungling young lad, merely spoilt them by recasting them in a way that lacked rhyme or reason, and occasionally even morality. On every page she is of the serious conviction that the ironic dramatist really did not possess the ability to understand those stories. For those who know Shakespeare her foolish book is instructive enough since, without her knowledge or intention, she constantly touches on the essential difference between the epic and the dramatic poem.

That Shakespeare's wanton energy so often tore out from the body of those stories the strongest and best members, those which were intended morally or seriously, and made the fool or the gossip speak where sententious phrases or oaths of love and faithfulness were expected – it was just this fact that made his poem into drama. His discovery of indispensable motifs, interesting figures, and the wealth of ideas contained in what seemed unobtrusive and peripheral was precisely the reason why he came to be the source of wonder for his contemporaries and of astonishment for posterity. The other poets had read those little stories just as he had, indeed more so, they had a more precise knowledge of the old models and believed that they too possessed critical sense, and yet he alone succeeded, by the magical power of alchemy, in transforming that dull lead into gold.

If, then, it is certain that the dramatist can make no use of those powers which make the narrative writer excel as a narrator, then let him consider whether, if he does have to discard so much, enough still remains for it to be worth his while transferring the given material into a new element: and let him consider, further, whether the inventiveness at his command is sufficient to replace what has been lost with new splendours, four and fivefold, splendours which would only have crushed the narrative artist – or made him look foolish.

It could appear, if the reader does not fully understand me, that my goal in all this were one solitary form of drama. Yet this would run so counter to my view that I should rather state, once again, that each play must have its own particular form: that in the vast mass of these works there can, and must, also be some which apparently approximate to the epic at certain points, is understandable and justifiable.

In the story time and place must be continually evoked, all the more so because it is set in a distant period or land. The circumstantial detail makes of the excitement which captivates the heart something gentle and artistic. The unfolding of the plot, the unforeseen incidents and characters, often allowed to contradict the beginning, the way the main action is connected with minor details and its resolution by some incalculable twist of chance, all this can lend the story charm and marvellous character. But all these magical effects must disappear in the face of the dazzling nearness of the present into which the dramatist whisks his action, leaving it right before our eyes. The remoteness of time and its slow passage completely disappear, as does the foreignness of the setting because both, in the real poetic work, are completely absorbed into the present. But here too every work of art has its own rule, which can never become universal. It is just as foolish to want to frenchify *Lear* as it is to want to give Racine and Corneille an English form – and thereby martyr them.

This insight, which offers itself freely to anyone with an open mind, nevertheless still tortures the critics of all nations because they consider that time and place play a real and active role, whereas in fact each one of us (assuming he is not without poetic sense) has surely been so taken in by a dream that on first waking up he was still under the illusion for a few seconds that the evening of the previous day had receded by at least seven or eight yeaars.

From 'Goethe and his Time'
'Goethe und seiner Zeit' (1828)

'Since the name of Cervantes has now been mentioned,' the orthodox person continued, 'I suppose his *Don Quixote* is the only book in which caprice, delight, playfulness, gravity and parody, poetry and wit, the wildest inventions of the imagination and the most bitter realities of life are all raised up to the level of a true work of art. Here the consummate poem is encircled from without by moderate limits laid down by the most clear-headed reason, and the poetic necessity which from its central point governs and directs all, pervades every part of the work, however small or peripheral, with such powerful radiance that one does not become aware at any time of that necessary limitation imposed by everyday reason, as all here appears to be good humour, wilfulness and extreme lightheartedness. In Ben Jonson's comedies, which are also supposed to proclaim a madcap humour and to know no restraint in their comic power, the external limitation on reason is so visible in every line that all the internal energy of the poem, however exuberantly it may well up, is weighed down by the written word almost to the point of impotence. It appears that, in the ancient world, Aristophanes' works are as artistically correct within as they are encircled without by reason. I say it appears thus. For even if I think I understand individual aspects, only after I have consulted all the commentators, interpretations and treatises, of which I'm sure I have read any of significance, will understanding of the whole be mine. And the former sort of understanding without the latter is reduced, in actual fact, to mere incomprehension or misunderstanding. No author of the ancient world awaits the time of his resurrection as this rogue – and true poet – does.'

'If we are willing to be sincere here and to admit our lack of insight,' the paradoxical one continued, 'we will come to the conclusion that in all places and ages there is little understanding of art to be found. That which delights and excites the crowd is precisely always something random, entirely incidental to the thing itself, and so too it is due to chance, whim and satiety whenever the crowd drops its celebrated genius or idol again. Art, truth, and real, immortal fame do exist but only a few people can grasp the highest and proclaim it to others. How many untenable opinions and errors about Goethe, Schiller and Jean Paul circulate in our fatherland, how badly greatness is misunderstood, how often falseness pursued and how frequently can people be found, not merely among the weak minds, who will revere that which is insubstantial and petty. For that reason, only the man who can open himself fully and enthusiastically to the poet should pronounce as a critic, but even here I might be misunderstood because in too many people a fire that blazes up only to die down as quickly has to take the place of real enthusiasm and inspiration.'

From 'The Old English Theatre'
'Das altenglische Theatre' (1811)

(1)

The Italian verse form had come over to Spain and almost replaced the indigenous form when one of the greatest poets, Cervantes, painfully aware of how far removed from life poetry had become in the epic 'miracle' stories of Amadis[6] and his successors, and out of love for poetry and the miraculous, thought up the most daring piece of fun designed to reunite poetry and life whilst yet remaining aware of their disharmony. His *Don Quixote* which, both consciously and unconsciously, set the tone for the whole age, is the reflection of an unfathomable mind, for which parody is always genuine poetry, so that one cannot tell whether the poetry in this work is perhaps not to be taken throughout as parody, since one is tempted to say that the whole work is illuminated by such radiant wit that there is no certainty at any point as to whether one is seeing clearly or merely being dazzled.

Just as Cervantes, with great understanding and the most delicate and graceful touch, was trying to provide poetry in its orphaned state with a safe course and steady support in real life, so that profound man Shakespeare sought, around the same time, to give poetry a secure and, as it were, everlasting foundation in the earth. In the South all poetry had inclined towards evaporating into fantasy, in the North it had tended from an early stage to be swallowed up in the common, the everyday and the indifferent. Shakespeare's unfathomable mind married poetry with these, its most extreme opposites, and gave it the moral strength and boldness which is needed to portray and express Fate and which we can never admire in him enough. He draws a magic circle of the most painful irony around his fantasies, which may not step outside it and which now appear to us to be as jolly as they are sad, as grand and powerful as they are pinched and cramped. In no less puzzling a way than with Cervantes, we are gripped in his presence by a feeling of anxiety because we sense a mystery which causes us at every moment to forget the lively good humour of the Southern poet. It is from this poetic realm that all subsequent understanding and misunderstanding has come, and Cervantes' works, and in a still more encompassing way those of Shakespeare, will have to remain for us the central vantage point from which we can survey the past and understand the present and the future.

(2)

Searches were carried out and more witches found. Middleton wrote a play, *The Witch* and it enjoyed much success.[7] A few years later Shakespeare presented his *Macbeth* to the theatre, making use of his predecessor and indeed borrowing several features from his play, including a brood of witches. He took it in his own way and created a truly great scene. Heywood,[8] a man whose talent brought him easy success and who wrote a number of plays including many excellent ones, took a story, said to have happened at that time in the county of Lancaster, and, having lent it a mischievous and humorous tone, put it on the stage when it was still the latest gossip of the ordinary people. Time-worn tales recur here and will do for evermore: such as that of the lady being changed into a horse or the witch who has been changed into a cat having her paw cut off, only for it to turn out to be a hand. Heywood presents his strange story in all good faith, as if he believed it himself, but you can nevertheless feel in the whole and each of its parts how far above his subject he remains, although it would be unfitting, having once chosen this most contemporary story, to make his scepticism too obvious by heavier irony.

From the preface to *Kaiser Octavianus*
Vorwort zu *Kaiser Octavianus* (1804)

Magelone had been written early in 1797 and around the same time *Puss-in-Boots* was also written, and enjoyed almost universal praise. That the theatre can make fun of itself I had learnt – early on from Holberg whose *Melampe* and *Ulysses* were always very dear to me. Fletcher and Ben Jonson tried the same thing in their own way, only with more acerbity and pedantry. It had been given to me to see good theatre from my earliest childhood and to grow so accustomed to excellent acting, nature and truth that when I was older quality seemed to me to be indispensable and perfection to be near at hand. Not even the ordinary man, not even the thoroughly poetically minded man, can go on enjoying what he sees for ever without, sooner or later, justifying his enjoyment to himself, praising what is of better quality and criticizing what has missed the mark. Every man who does not merely seek to pass the time of day in the theatre will weigh up one thing against another, enlighten himself, and, if he has the skill or a strong conviction, will wish to bring others too (that is, the general crowd) around to his opinion. Yet the sources from which criticism springs are highly varied. We have seen, and continue to see every day, how the philosopher, without feeling for art and poetry, devoid of experience, often ignorant of the basic foundations of art, tries to direct and fashion according to his own system even those things for which he has least understanding. If this school governs things for a time even its fancy phrases will come to dominate and no doubt even influence individuals who consider themselves poetically talented to write according to its demands and notions. In this way poetry runs the risk of degenerating into pretence and verbal tricks and puzzles instead of gaining in depth, scope and detail. If even the most profound philosopher, provided he has artistic feeling, is unable to learn something new from an authentic work of poetry, then the work just cannot be called authentic. However, when the scholar is indeed dealing with such a work, he will need time in order to pronounce upon it a true and reliable judgment. The artist, with his inspiration, sees and uncovers new forces at work. There appear new relations, different conditions, trains of thought which until now were foreign to us, and in just the same way new aesthetic rules are created in the work itself, or those already familiar to us are subjected to a surprisingly new application. To feel these things with simplicity and truth devoid of artificiality, to make them one's own, and to recognize the essence of each work of art is a gift not commonly found: for if one is familiar with art history and with one's contemporaries one can have the boldness to assert that real feeling for art is found only very rarely. Talent, even dazzling talent, is more common and often acts as an obstacle to such feeling and insight. Yet nothing is as disruptive of these as the habit of seeking a knowledge of the creations of art on the basis of prematurely created philosophical principles. The mind then loses the ability to take the works in with any emotion and heightened feeling and to experience them in a similar way to the poet or artist himself. The fact that for years we have regressed more than we have progressed in what is termed 'aesthetics' is proved by the reception given to Solger's work *Erwin*. This writer combined both artistic feeling and philosophy: and yet neither lovers of art nor thinkers paid his book much attention. On the other hand, some of the things tried by the latest school of philosophy are proof of how easily you can cook up any and every conclusion you wish: such an arbitrary method would have no difficulty in discovering, by use of its first principles, the heights of perfection in insignificant nothings.

From the preface to *Wilhelm Lovell*
Vorwort zu *Wilhelm Lovell* (1793–6)

Thus in this instance irony pure and simple, when things are inverted so that bad is labelled good and good bad, as in the frequent practice of Swift and others (including even Rabener)[9] – this irony was completely misunderstood by a man who ranked himself among the leading minds of his age. How then shall the higher form of irony in Aristophanes or even Shakespeare be grasped by the mass of readers? For what are ordinary readers, who are after all only at a lower level, to make of Socratic irony or the irony declared by Solger to be indispensable to every work of art, if many professional philosphers (so one might think) have hardly read a Platonic dialogue right through, let alone Solger's *Erwin*? Over the whole of a Platonic dialogue (take just the *Symposium*) hovers a higher intellectual irony than is communicated even in Socrates' apparent ignorance. And how can critics or philosophers hope to find a name for that final touch which brings a poetic work to perfection, the guarantee and highest proof of genuine inspiration, that ethereal spirit which, however much it penetrates into the depths of the work with love, nevertheless hovers disinterested and unconstrained over the whole – that whole which can be created and grasped from this height alone? If we are not to call this concept irony, following Solger or Friedrich Schlegel (as the latter already hinted in *Athenäum*), then let those with insight invent for us another name. Yet it will no doubt be better to retain this appropriate designation, which Schleiermacher too has already defined so excellently in his masterly introductions to Plato's dialogues.[10] If, however, it should be the case that those philosophers have never yet experienced for themselves what Solger seeks to describe and explain, then of course they are no better off than so many of those subordinate readers. It will do them no good (if they have never truly felt and enjoyed a genuine work of art) to read *Erwin* right through or to educate themselves by reading the many letters left by Solger, that profound thinker, since on the contrary it almost seems as if they think Solger is demanding that the poetic work should negate its own existence by means of this irony.

'Final Conclusion' to *Puss-in-Boots*
'Völliger Schluss' von *Der gestiefelte Kater* (1797, revised 1812)

Clara and Augusta had enjoyed this reading immensely, Rosalie had not laughed as much and Emily had remained almost solemn, finding fault in the fact that the theatre wished to parody the theatre and thereby play with the play. 'It is a circle', Willibald said, 'which returns to its starting point and where the reader is no further on at the end than he was at the beginning.' 'And what is wrong with that?' Manfred asked 'As the theatre is born, so too is mockery of the theatre, as we can already see in Aristophanes: he can barely desist from being ironical about himself, something which other forms of poetry and even more so art are less prone to, since comic theatre is actually based on the ambivalence of the human mind, on the mysterious contradiction within us. The strange ambition of the theatre to put before us a story as lifelike as possible has been the object of Shakespeare's irony more than once in tragedy, where he claims his play to be true and by contrasting truth and the theatre denigrates the latter as deceit and feeble imitation. He must have been very sure of what he was about not to fear that dispelling of the illusion which almost all modern textbooks on art prophesy will happen when mention is made, on stage, of the theatre.'

'Willibald', Augusta said, 'behaved very discourteously towards us and the readers the whole time, and I hereby declare to him my extreme displeasure, unless he makes good his misdeed by means of a similar comedy which shall, as far as possible, be yet more childish and foolish.' Willibald bowed in silence, and Emily continued 'Neither can I approve the kind of joke which actually names certain people and treats them comically on stage, for why should a convivial mood create animosity between people?' 'If that happens,' Manfred said, 'then the mood is probably not convivial: and yet comedy and art have not been able to get by easily without personality, and as long as the portrayal is not aggressive, spiteful and accusing, I see nothing in it that could get in the way of innocent pleasure. It is natural that imagination exaggerates in creating such pleasure, since otherwise the portrayal it gives would either not be poetic or be no portrayal at all, and it is for this reason that we enjoy Aristophanes' caricature of Socrates:[11] I also believe that if we want a truthful picture of this famous man we must translate the descriptions given by the comic poet into reality in addition to those of Xenophon and Plato, in order to glimpse more than just a venerable shadow of him. Art has no power to enthral unless the truthfulness of the picture can be seen through the caricature. But I'll break off there and start my own reading: I hope that the humanity of our Emily will not be able to level the same criticism I've been discussing at my own play, even if my friend may once again discover that circular line so criticized for only leading back to itself.'

Part 4

Solger

Karl Solger

(1780–1819)

Karl Solger, close friend of Ludwig Tieck and major theorist of aesthetics, was involved in a work on the religion and mythology of ancient peoples, influenced by his early enthusiasm for Spinoza and Schleiermacher, when he decided finally to write up in dialogue form his aesthetic philosophy. In *Erwin. Vier Gespräche über das Schöne und die Kunst*, finished in 1815, Solger began from Schelling's position that 'art is to the philosopher the highest concern', but then deviated from Schelling in insisting that art is the propaedeutic to philosophy, and plays a crucial role in the education of man. Like Schiller and Fichte before him, Solger was deeply concerned with the 'Bildung des Menschen'; he claimed that the philosopher's true role was to show men the way to raise themselves from ordinary life to a knowledge of reality in that life. Art for Solger was alone the means of opening the way to this ascent toward self-cultivation and knowledge. Both the influence of Plato and that of Solger's contemporary Schleiermacher can be seen in Solger's philosophy and in his choice of the dialogue form as the only adequate means of genuinely communicating his insights to his fellow man – a goal of the highest importance to these 'Symphilosophen', who rejected the abstract and inaccessible style of philosophizing for one more intelligible to a wider readership. Solger's aesthetic lectures, published posthumously by his student K. W. L. Heyse in 1829, discuss in lecture style many of the problems Solger grappled with artistically in *Erwin*.

Solger's aesthetic philosophy remained to his bitter disappointment almost unknown to his contemporaries outside his immediate circle of friends until, after his death, Tieck and Raumer published his *Nachgelassene Schriften* in 1826, and won him the attention and admiration of Goethe and Hegel. Both men quickly published appreciative reviews of the new edition of Solger's work; Hegel's article, in the *Berliner Jahrbücher für wissenschaftliche Kritik*, recognized Solger's contribution to the laying of the first speculative foundations of aesthetics, and particularly praised his analysis of allegory and symbol. After Hegel's pronouncements, Solger was seen as the main development between Schelling's 'Identitätsphilosophie' and Hegel's dialectic. Just over a decade after these reviews, Kierkegaard named Solger the 'metaphysical knight of Negation' in *The Concept of Irony* (1841).

Hegel, in his Solger review, insisted that Solger's aesthetics bore little if any relation to that of the school of romantic ironists, and denied any relation between Solger's concept of irony and that of Schlegel and Tieck. Both Hegel's and Kierkegaard's different comments raise the issue of the extent to which Solger's aesthetics are related to Romantic irony. Twentieth-century judgments, as for example those by Oskar Walzel and Ingrid Strohschneider-Kohrs, tend to reject Hegel's claim, recognizing a close affinity between Solger and Friedrich Schlegel's concepts of irony and art, while insisting on the divergence of both from A. W. Schlegel's popularized versions, especially on irony and tragedy. Solger's own extensive essay (1819) on A. W. Schlegel's 'Lectures on Dramatic Art and Literature' reveals his disagreement with *this* Schlegel and clarifies his own position, particularly on tragedy (an essentially Hegelian conception of tragedy). At the same time the essay indicates close links with the Romantic concept of irony, of which A. W. Schlegel is hardly a representative (a distinction which Hegel failed to make, it seems). Nevertheless, his dialectical method and his abstract style will continue to link Solger with Hegel while his aesthetics link him with Friedrich Schlegel, as well as the English Romantic theorists such as Coleridge.

Solger's other most important writings include his correspondence with Tieck on art and mysticism – involving discussions of both irony in relation to enthusiasm and the allegory/symbol distinction included in part of this anthology. His essay 'Über Sophocles und die alte Tragödie' is of interest, particularly in connection with Solger's translations in verse of Sophocles, published in 1801. Goethe himself highly valued Solger's article on his *Wahlverwandschaften*, published first in *Nachgelassene Schriften*, where numerous discourses on philosophy, religion, and mythology are also to be found.

The text follows the German of *Erwin. Vier Gespräche über das Schöne und die Kunst*, edited W. Henckmann (München, 1971), 218–29, 350–5, 368–73, 378–81, 386–95. The following points should be noted about the translation of these selections from *Erwin*. First, 'Anschauung' has in the main been translated as 'intuition', though occasionally its meaning has been rendered by 'perception'. 'Phantasie' has been translated as 'Imagination'; 'Dasein' as 'existence'; 'Erkenntnis' as 'cognition'; 'Wesen' as 'nature', 'essence' or 'reality'; 'Darstellung' as 'representation' and 'Gegenstand' as 'object', or sometimes as 'subject matter'.

From *Erwin*, or *Four Dialogues on Beauty and Art*
Erwin. *Vier Gespräche über das Schöne und die Kunst* (1816)

On the Symbol

So in our view, I said, the symbol would be a thing of the imagination which, as such, would be the presence of the idea itself in existence.[1] But what distinguishes the idea from any subordinate cognition?

The unity of the universal and the particular.

Correct. And if we go on to make a further distinction between idea and symbol (not because each of them is in itself something different, but because our mode of cognition requires us to differentiate the relations of one and the same essence), should we not then give to this unity of the universal and the particular the name of symbol,[2] when we consider it from the point of view of the particular, but the name of idea, preferably, when we consider the unity from the point of view of the universal?

Certainly, he said. This is the best way for us to establish this distinction.

It is also certain, Erwin, I continued, that *all* art is symbolic in this sense – but only in this sense. The symbol is neither an arbitrary sign, nor yet an imitation of an original, from which it would be absolutely different, but the true revelation of the idea. For in revelation our innermost cognition is so closely intertwined with the apparently accidental external appearance that it is utterly impossible to separate them. So if someone were to ask us if the choice of the particular external object were *necessarily* given by means of the idea, and if they were to put it to us that artists will often select and then reject their subject matter, what would be our reply?

The same, I should think, rejoined the young man, as we gave to the question as to how far art could be learned – or something of that kind.

I would think so too, I said. We would remind him of our representation of the holy realm of the imagination: the moment the soul's activity emerges from the perfect light of our innermost being, this light also is already clothed in form and matter, and in this sense, at whatever point you may envisage in the transition from centre to surface, you always have the complete symbol – the specific thing which is at the same time the eternal, universal thought of the light itself. The artist does in fact create this real thing out of his essential nature. But according to all we have learned so far, is not this essential nature at the same time also his real existence, which, regarded as 'given', and as coming from without in accordance with the relations and connections to other things on the dark surface, appears but accidental? For scarcely do we conceive this activity and creativity as in process of emerging, before it is already 'given' existence, because only in existence and through existence is it an activity of beauty. So anyone who looks merely at the process of creation will not acknowledge any subject matter to be a subject for art, if it did not arise from the free invention of the artist; and equally, on the other hand, anyone who, approaching the object from outside, comes upon it as already given, will regard it as accidental, because it will seem to him just one among all the thronging confusion of individual things. And there is no doubt that both types of spectators break apart art and symbol, and are speaking of entirely different things. If the artist chose his subject arbitrarily, it would be nothing but an image for a thought he had contrived; if it were thrust upon him by the blind necessity of accident, that would be an isolated fact without essential meaning or content. By contrast, art tells the truth just because the highest idea always appears to the artist in a real form and not otherwise, that is, because his subject matter is not chosen; nor does it freely emerge, but, by a mysterious inevitability, it is present both within him and without. This is why in true art traditional kinds of subject matter are so prevalent: they have a living existence in popular belief, and they surround the artist from his birth. So it is scarcely possible even to say that for the artist the world of imagination and the real world are one and the same; for the realm of imagination is itself reality – but in its essential and truly higher existence. This can perhaps be seen most clearly in truly poetic fairy-tales, whose first priority is often to present this unity as actual, present life. The most ordinary and everyday things fuse with the most marvellous, and the poet unites both, as if they were all located in one and the same world.

This peculiar nature of the symbol, observed Erwin, is no doubt the source of the inextricable contradictions into which it is possible to fall if we try to distinguish what was presented to the artist as a given fact in the ordinary meaning of the word, and what arose in his imagination.

And that, I rejoined, is because an attempt of that kind is entirely illegitimate, and can at the very least never lead to any insight into the work of art. For in the true symbol the external object has merged itself with the light of the inward essence, and is entirely one with it, so that this inner light is not to be found by itself in a particular part, nor even in the inner core of the thing, but equally over its entire external surface; and one could well say that it is the task of the artist to turn the inwardness of things into their outwardness.

Since I paused a little after these words, Erwin looked rather mischievously at his friend Bernhard and said, Bernhard, will you not take this opportunity to re-establish your old claims, now that Adalbert has declared so clearly that the artist turns inwardness into outwardness?

I would probably have done so myself, Bernhard replied, if I had not noticed, as I did recently when we spoke about the sublime, that though I could certainly make use of the expression, I would soon get caught up in a train of thought which was alien to my views. For I can see that we are talking not about pure cognition of the essential nature of phenomena, but about a world which, as Adalbert presents it, is supposed to float in the middle between the light of inwardness and the darkness of the surface.

And not only that, I interrupted. Have you not heard that the world of art is all-embracing? That it excludes neither the divine light which on first emerging assumes corporeal form, nor the particular body still charged with that light?

All the more strange, said Bernhard. And all the less appropriate to my argument. I have followed you up till now, and understood your symbol to unite idea and appearance, as it were giving equal rights to each – which certainly does not accord with my other views on appearance. I could not possibly ascribe the same truth to appearance as to idea.

Yes, resumed Erwin. I must confess that I too understand the symbol as Bernhard did. And yet you maintain that absolute Divinity and particular objects in reality are both taken up into the realm of art, and necessarily so. But this does not seem to accord with our conception of the symbol so far.

But, I replied, who bade you set to work so mechanically and connect the idea to the particular merely in the middle? Bear in mind, as I have just said, that the Godhead itself is something real, just as each individual thing is something eternal and essential.

That is my view too, he rejoined, with deep seriousness, for it is all too easy to lose the right path in this strange region we have entered. And yet always above me hovers the vague suspicion that we could attain perfect knowledge both of the place where idea and appearance saturate each other utterly, metaphysic-ally and in reality, divinely and terrestrially, and of the place where the creative activity is as it were extinguished.

I am delighted to see from your remarks, I replied, that you have kept entirely to the right path. For when we were first identifying the symbol, we chose those terms for it which best served to distinguish it from other, related things. That is how it has come about that we have been regarding it from one aspect only. For you are not wrong to observe that everywhere in the symbol idea and appearance saturate each other, although I cannot agree with your remark that creative activity is extinguished in this.

True, he said. I should not say that it is extinguished, rather that it is wholly present in it.

That sounds better, I responded. But is not this activity itself the beautiful? And have we not observed that it must pass over into the real world if beauty is to be realised?

Indeed, he said. But this realized activity is art, is it not?

And is art, I rejoined, then so very different from the symbol? Rather, is not the symbol, as you will have perceived, completely present only in the work of art? For what is found in art must also be in the symbol. Consequently the symbol must not only appear as the consummate work of our powers, but also as the life and activity of those powers itself. Do you see that?

I certainly see that all this is a real consequence of the whole argument, he said. But I do not entirely understand what you mean by it.

What I mean, I answered, is that as far as creative activity is concerned we had still not entirely removed our conception of art from the refuge of the common view, where it is still lurking. For as long as we regarded the work of art as a symbol, as we did before, or as a real thing in which idea and appearance were one, we still did so with the silent reservation that we were pushing imagination, as a living activity, into the background, and cutting it off from existence. But now let us also summon forth imagination into the light of day and of real existence: how will it appear to us now, as it fills that holy realm? Will it not emanate out into reality as a divine energy, bursting forth from the light of the Holy of Holies? And on the other hand will it not soar up out of individual created things, purifying them and raising them to the light? And will not the divine *pneuma*, as it lives and moves and has its being in this holy world, be itself a work of art and the present actuality of the beautiful?

At this Erwin said, Now my insight into the inmost soul of the world of art has been marvellously extended. Yes, this is the only way beauty has passed wholly into reality. But I do not know how to carry this inner intuition, whose truth touches me so deeply, over into appearance. For I still require the outward form of a completed work in which this life-giving energy appears to me, and this, I fear, will make me revert to the old view of the symbol.

This, too, I replied, will resolve itself the moment you remember that even when we require the form of a real existence, we must free ourselves entirely from the bonds of sense-perception and gaze only with the eyes of the imagination. For this form seen by imagination is the real object, something that we perceive in our ordinary experience by every other cognitive means except the senses, that is, by energy, cause, will and the very inwardness of things. That activity itself then, that is, the dynamic life of the imagination as a whole, must at the same time also be its own revelation in the form of an object. Only now this whole activity seems to be filled with matter or object, whereas earlier in the symbol the object seemed to burst with energy. Now do you understand me more fully?

In general, I understand the train of thought so perfectly, he said, that I am quite convinced this is the only means by which the world of the imagination becomes complete in itself and a true world filled not merely with its own existence but also with its own creative power. But it would make me very happy, if you were to make it clearer to me how exactly to apply this to experience.

First, I said, I will have to explain it to you more fully in terms of our previous train of thought; for examples applied to philosophical subjects before the fundamental principles are completely clarified tend only to confuse. So in our earlier argument, when we considered the beautiful, as it lives in art, as symbol, we found it filling that whole world of the imagination from the beginning as a fully perfected existence, saturated with its own energy and activity. It was, you will recall, the idea in its full reality, appearing not only as a complete and definite presence, but enclosed within this presence by its own perfection, without any necessity or effort. That is why here the highest perfection of existence is united (in a way that can never occur in the ordinary world of appearance) with that veiled beatitude in which the inner relation of idea and appearance does not unfold gradually, but is immediately there as the most complete contentment in present actuality. But it will obviously be a very different matter if in this world, taken as a whole, we consider activity or creativity itself. This too cannot be present in art without an object or an actual form. But will there not have to be a striving and an efficacy present here in each form by which it takes into itself its opposite? For an activity can be known only by its effect in some particular direction, and this direction is still the governing and determining factor, even when such activity steps forth in a particular guise. Seen in these terms, if the essence of the Godhead clothes itself in form, it can do so only by actively lowering itself into existence, and through its omnipotent and eternal activity uniting the world of the individual and the particular with itself. Similarly, the individual can partake of this life only by lifting itself up in longing and aspiration to the splendour of the Divine. Whatever can enter the world of appearance only in this way includes within itself the perfect aspiration towards something other, and this dynamic effort and aspiration, already carrying the object of its striving perfected within itself, revolves it with all its powers from out of itself. If you would protest that in this scheme each one refers to another, or means the same thing as the other, I will concede the point, but only if you bear in mind that we cannot be speaking of a meaning in the sense ordinarily assumed by the understanding – even you would at least grant that. In order, however, to choose a particular term of art that corresponds to symbol, let us give the name of allegory to this kind of appearance of the beautiful in art where the beautiful constantly refers, in the way indicated, to something other.

Then according to this, said Erwin, allegory would be a relationship comprehending the entire realm of art, and not that subordinate mode of representation which we usually tend to understand by it, and which, if I am not mistaken, comes very close to being a mere sign.

I see there is no need to warn you against this misunderstanding, I responded, for you have rightly noted it yourself. Just as the symbol is commonly confused with the image, so the allegory is commonly confused with the sign.[3] It is childish and unworthy of art to try to indicate an idea by means of some external similarity, and still more ridiculous to treat a general concept as a particular personality as the French so often do. And that is what is usually called allegory. Certainly the truly allegorical work always says more than is to be found in its limited presence, but nothing more than it carries within itself and develops dynamically out of itself. This is why allegory is also given what is granted to the symbol: a comprehensible lucidity within and a completely delimited form without. On the other hand, its meaning penetrates the imagination in its innermost and outermost being all the more deeply, while neither the serene, unclouded light of the Godhead nor the multiform external surface of things is inaccessible to it. The inward being and acting of the divine powers, which the symbol veils in bodily form, are brought to light by allegory, and with conscious pleasure it penetrates that blissful state, still veiled, of the beautiful.

Now, said Erwin, I believe I have grasped the whole train of thought correctly, and, I beg you, give me the examples you promised.

Examples which would be adequate to my argument, I said, must doubtless be of the kind in which both aspects of the representation by art of the beautiful, namely symbol and allegory, would be fundamentally and completely revealed. For each must include in itself a whole world of art. You will recall that Anselm's argument recently led us to a paradoxical position in which the Godhead appeared on the one hand as a universal and eternal necessity of nature, but on the other hand as freedom and personality. On closer reflection you will discover that precisely in that paradox are to be found the most perfect examples. If you like, we might first consider in this light how the Greeks represented the Divine.

That would fulfil my warmest desire, he said.

Then turn your thoughts first, I continued, towards that perfect necessity of the universe, harmonious and coherent in itself, as it was in the beginning. Now this contains within itself no variety, no change, no contingent particularity, nor can it ever become for itself the object of art, because it cannot assume any definite form. That is why the moment we speak of its existence in terms of that pure universality, we conceive it first as the negation of all particular existence, as the opposite of the ordered world, as chaos. It does not enter the artistic imagination as form until it has been transformed by various particular tendencies into individual persons, and this – that the original universality can only become actual in particularity – is the basis of polytheism. But what is the essence of the symbol, if not this inner, indissoluble fusion of the general and the particular into one and the same reality? Through this marvellous fusion alone is it possible for the general tendencies into which the idea disintegrates to become not mere forms or concepts, but living, fully rounded persons. In the Greek gods, the bliss that consists in the unity with the universal coincides perfectly with the activity which is the attribute only of particular, impersonated, dynamic beings. This is also why their particular deeds, being the perfect expression of their nature, can be subjected to moral judgment. This coexistence of so many worlds in individual beings is the true nature of the symbol. And that in fact is what the symbol is: necessity and the eternal universe itself in its existence and in its reality – which after all has always been the aim and purpose of art. For in that view of the world which regards the universe and necessity as prior and original, creative activity vanishes as something in itself because it has from the beginning been bound up in existence by necessity. Where everything is from time immemorial already complete and eternal, there is no longer any possibility or need for an originating or perfecting power. But at the same time as real existence emerges out of the division of this universe (by contradiction and opposition into heaven and earth, active and passive, begetting and bearing), everything is already populated by real, separate persons from whose individual actions necessity shines forth; and real existence now recedes as a universal into the dark profundities of the universe. For this very power which with impartial rigour presses in upon the infinite variety of temporal existence, and subjects even the gods as individuals to the bondage of the law, at the same time makes their deeds perfect and infallible; and in so doing it fills their life with that untroubled serenity which repeatedly stirs our admiration and our longing. And just as this power, as it creates and determines, cannot endure anything accidental or inadequate in their appearance, it also gives the gods in their reality a thoroughly definite, limited form, perfect and full of life. So if anyone, led astray by the general characteristics in the personalities of these gods, looks underneath for general concepts (applying what is commonly thought of as allegory), he is on the wrong path, for each divinity contains an entire world of meaning within itself. We also note that in ancient art, the more the gods appear to signify quite separate concepts – Aphrodite, for example, or Ares, or others of that kind – the more they actively and effectively influence the affairs of men and the temporal world, so that they do not degenerate into general forms, but still remain thoroughly rounded persons.[4] On the other hand, there are gods, above all Zeus, who are more in control of the overall management of the world. This in itself makes them perfect as individuals, and they are able to give themselves up to a blissful serenity virtually indifferent to the tumult of the world. This is the symbolic world of ancient art, which in the symbol itself includes all tendencies in their universality. But where necessity is conceived by itself, without this fusion with the world of the individual, or where mere temporality appears without the indwelling power of the whole, there comes about a separation of the two extremes in whose interpenetration the symbol consists, and its kingdom hath an end. In this example, I hope, you will recognize what has been said about the nature of the symbol.[5]

Indeed, he answered. Now at last I understand how the symbol can be a wholly individual thing, and at the same time the Divine itself.

On Humour

Consider once again what we have just said about emotion: that each single feeling should have the capacity to become comprehensive and change the entire meaning of man's life with its power. That is to say, every thought he had of the great and good would sink into this feeling and be merged into it, just as the lover, if he is so minded, will discover all that is noble, perfect, and divine in his love. But it is a different matter if all that is divine appears to him only in the realm of perception and feeling, with the result that the nature of his imagination is constantly disrupted, fragmented into a thousand different tendencies of sensuous drives and feelings, whereas on the other hand everything he has perceived and felt has any value for him only because it suggests the divine nature appearing in it. Is this not the extreme instance of its kind, and can we not take it to be the absolute opposite of the state in which the imagination creates itself and everything out of the idea of the Godhead?

Indeed, it is so.

Well, Erwin, this is what we usually call humour – to use a word from the country where it is most widespread.

This word is supposed to mean something so significant? he said. I always thought it meant something much more limited.

But what, then? Surely not just an external, individual idiosyncrasy, a habit which has grown on a man out of inertia or partial foolishness? This was already refuted most emphatically by Ben Jonson.[6]

No, not that. But I was looking for it more in particular passions and inclinations and in all the things that go to making a character, which – so I thought – all assumed a very one-sided and limited tendency in the humour, and could not go beyond it.

That is just how Ben Jonson wants to correct the prevailing opinion, but even that is not enough. For what could this one-sidedness of our merely temporal, personal part, or the limited tendency of all our impulses and inclinations, possibly have to offer to art? They do not even have much to offer as external subject matter, because they can give rise only to the eccentric, and we have already observed that this is not suitable for art. So humour is certainly not to be found in mere one-sidedness and limitation – as the humorous poets demonstrate. For there is to be found in their works an infinite variety of perceptions, passions and impulses such as no other genre has to offer. But it is a very different matter if the Divine reveals itself only by means of this variety. And if we look for help in a comparison with the first aspect of the imagination, remember how there divine beauty emerged from the innermost essence and still had to assume a particular form and presence. The Godhead stood there in all its purity – something real, and yet above the temporal world, and even above earthly beauty. But in humour, its presence and particularity is that of the real world itself, just as in ancient art, in the sensuous realization of the figures, the Divine is nothing but the idea of the individual thing. But it is because of the coherence and homogeneity of modern art and its all-prevalent reference to a common unity that, vice versa, every perception and feeling appears as the real life of that divine spirit, in all its variety – only that the spirit has entirely lost itself and infinitely individualized itself in that variety. And so the spirit is known only as the innermost soul of the universal driving force, as the essential nature which alone can make the impulse universal; and for that very reason, the spirit does not step outside the impulse, but is felt and perceived by it in the most various ways in every kind of material and matter apprehended by the senses.

This, said Erwin, would certainly explain that reversal whereby in humour the most sensuous and secular often contains all the force and significance of the Divine.

This is often, I said, how what I have just been describing manifests itself. It is also why our own Friedrich Richter, who characterized his own art with such wonderful insight, called humour the sublime turned upside-down, or a finite applied to the infinite.[7] However, this reversal is only partly how it is manifested, and could not be undertaken if there were not in the imagination necessarily a realm where all finite things are derived by our feeling from a divine driving force. This driving force, however, because it is confronted only with the variety of phenomena, will appear to be of the same kind as the finite matter which feeds it. This force is the means by which we see the temporal world quite in the ordinary way, but at the same time in an entirely different light, for the light of true being and of the imagination has passed into it. This is why everywhere objects appear customary and familiar to us, but at the same time, if we regard them by the measure of ordinary sense-impressions, they seem distorted, strange, jostling grotesquely up against one another. And because we are accustomed to ascribing such peculiarities in the world of the individual to the peculiarity of one single cause, we shift this on to the manifestation of a limited and one-sided personality, when we should in fact do the complete opposite, and recognize that this peculiarity derives from the absolute essence of all personality, whose light is refracted in the individual in such a peculiar way. For what strikes us first in humour is just this inexhaustible totality of the sensuous, the common and the low, and I cannot give you a better example than Jean Paul's *Blumenstücke*, which my argument explains perfectly.[8]

This, Erwin joined in, is a characteristic of humour which has always struck me as very curious, and I was thinking of it to myself just now when you were talking about sensuous representation in the art of the ancients. For this does not go nearly as far into individuality and temporality as humour does, which elaborates down to the finest detail of appearance, as it might be under a magnifying glass.

From this, I said, you will see how indispensable to humour too is shaping, fashioning, or in other words the externalizing tendency, and how yet again this externalizing tendency has solid ground to offer. For without this detailed elaboration of the sensuous material, the driving force, which should be completely bound and embodied, would hover unfinished in the air, and become a prey to base fancy, which endeavours to employ it for the representation of general and empty thoughts. This can be seen in Jean Paul sometimes, when he philosophizes too grandiosely, or falls into a rapture – which is just what makes these passages vague and airy-fairy.

Allow me to make another observation, said Erwin at that point, which I might otherwise forget. It seems to me that this is where the two extremes are very sharply contrasted. At the point in ancient art where the act of shaping begins, in the creation of divine figures, the reflective imagination is most apparent; but in modern art, at the point where the reality is traced back to the thought, it is the elaboration of detail that is most prominent. Tell me if I have grasped this contrast correctly.

Quite correctly, I replied. But you have run ahead of yourself somewhat into a comparison which we really should not set up until later. But in the meantime let us note that it is this very development of detail which also brings about this complete disappearance and dissolution into thin air. For there is nothing there to cohere as a whole, although it has all been conceived from the standpoint of the idea. This, as Jean Paul has also observed and argued, is because in humour the intention of the representation must never be directed solely towards the individual detail, for its very elaboration dissolves it into nothing, but towards the whole and the universal. But when he adds that it is not the individual who is made ridiculous, but the entire finite world, his account is obviously too limited.[9] For it cannot be a matter of the absurd alone, but rather of a state in which the absurd and the tragic are still bound up in each other and not yet distinct. The divine, which has descended entirely into the cycle of things earthly, cannot be set against the temporal world in such a way as to give rise to a purely tragic effect. But as far as the low origin of the ridiculous is concerned, it is characteristic of that very elaboration of detail that even the highest and the noblest will blend with it – indeed it must transform itself into the highest and the noblest. So in this case too the low and the beautiful are not to be apprehended as pure opposites. For in humour everything is to be found in one great flux, and everywhere opposites flow into one another, as they do in the world of common appearance. In humour, whatever is ridiculous or comic needs only an admixture of dignity or emotion to turn it into melancholy; and there is nothing sublime or tragic which its worldly or even low form could not turn into triviality or absurdity. Everything is equally significant and equally insignificant, and what is represented is by no means simply the finite, as Jean Paul argued, but at the same time the idea itself.

But it is terrible, said Erwin, that humour should turn everything to nothing, including the idea.

That is why, I said, its expressions are not infrequently sick. And yet, on the other hand, it is almost the only thing in the modern world which will protect art, sensuous art most of all, from degenerating into mere gross flattery of the senses. But as for its universal destructiveness, this offence is already nullified, first because the real world in all its detail must be represented with love, and so in a certain sense must continue to be; but still more because we are protected by the idea, which is eternal and indestructible, and rises like a phoenix from its descent into the temporal world as a pure and purified yearning. For after all, Erwin, everything had passed over into that impulse, and even though it has now annihilated itself in these nullities, it is still nonetheless the universal and perfect driving force, and after this purification the only object left to it is the eternal itself. But now, it is true, the eternal can no longer assume a sensuous form as a divinity, so it transforms itself utterly into this impulse and makes its annunciation through it alone. So although we are left with a great emptiness after the universal destruction, it is still the emptiness of the pure blue heavens, and through this the impulse towards the Divine takes flight, fully conscious that, being divine itself, it bears its own achievement within it. This, my dear Erwin, says more or less everything we need for our purposes about the aesthetic judgment of humour and the entire sensuous aspect of art.

On Wit (1)

You understand it quite correctly, I said. The understanding attaches itself to the actual and the particular, and it can surely do this only by means of opposites; for in the realm of the particular its business is to compare and contrast. But as long as this happens gradually or partially in a sequence of divisions and combinations, actuality still remains ordinary appearance. This appearance is counteracted by the artistic intelligence as it reveals immediately that reconciling intuition as present in the relationships and contrasts which originate out of or terminate in that intuition. The understanding is then united with this self-contradictory intuition; and its subject matter, which at first appeared only as particularity, is revealed in an unexpected way to be the intuition realized, and to be essentiality. The ability of the intelligence to bring this about, my dear Erwin, is what we usually call wit.[10]

I am astonished, said Erwin, that you are so ready to explain the nature of wit, for it is usually regarded as so inexplicable that many think this is its definitive characteristic. And besides, what you say sounds very strange to me. According to this, we are to believe that the things which wit compares should always coincide with essential characteristics and traits, but in fact it mostly raises comparisons that are accidental and one-sided – which, after all, is the source of the rule that we should not push our scrutiny of witty comparisons too far.

This law, I replied, can have any meaning only if it is intended as a warning that we should regard wit as a process of the ordinary understanding. For anyone who embarks on the infinite number of ordinary associations between individual ideas and concepts will certainly move further and further from an understanding of wit. Without the presence of the intuition (which is achieved only by enthusiasm), without a mind filled with perceptual intuition and its essential content, there will be no wit, but only a false wit, just as there is such a thing as a false reflection.

What, he cried, you want to banish entirely that kind of wit which plays with sense-impressions and which delights us so often in our everyday life, and you would admit only that quite rare sort which aims at the idea?

That is not what I mean, Erwin. What I call false wit is the kind that has no intuition at all, such as should leap forth like a hidden spark from the depths of our mind at the reconciliation of opposites in the intelligence. A practised intelligence, one-sidedly intent upon it, will easily produce the reconciliation, but it does not strike the flame which must both consume and transfigure everything; instead, the opposites lie side by side, flat and lifeless, so that when they meet there is not so much a reconciliation as a breakdown, and we recognize this false wit from the flaccid coldness which is its true inward characteristic. There cannot be any external characteristics, as you will see yourself. I could give you many examples of such cold and joyless witticisms, hammered together with much ado; but you will no doubt notice for yourself how many of those slight works of our time which intend to be comic have nothing but the intention. The case is just the same with what I have called false reflection: it puts forward some lifeless concept or ghost of the imagination, which it will even call the ideal, and elaborates on it with oracular profundity. You will not have to go far to find examples of this in most recent sonnets and canzoni, and in those novels which only imitate Goethe's quiet lucidity.

Now I understand what you mean by false reflection. But what relationship can we establish now between the low wit of the senses and the higher wit?

Let us rather reject entirely, I said, the insulting label 'low' for anything that is true wit. But you will not doubt for a moment that there must be a wit of the senses, when you recall that sensuousness and imagination are as it were the two poles of the self-same art. Art must be just as intensely alive in its sensuous intuition as it is in the idea; and the perfect convergence of the particular, picked out by the intelligence in its sensuous intuition, replenishes sensuous intuition and raises it through opposition to the condition of the essential and the beautiful. What you earlier pointed out, that accidental characteristics of things are often compared, is true only if we examine things according to the laws of the ordinary understanding. For the imagination it must always be the idea which is consumed and renewed in the oppositions, and if this takes place by way of ordinary sensuous intuition in accidental appearances, it will necessarily produce a comic effect, as everything we have agreed about the comic will surely prove. What makes this wit of the senses so delightful, then, is the happy consciousness that even in the most extreme contradiction and in the most external surfaces of things, however crassly the colours clash, the fundamental intuition is at one with itself.

I can see how this is based on the same principles as the comic, he said. But surely the higher or more serious wit would be more difficult to understand?

And yet, I said, at its innermost root it is no different. Only you must distinguish correctly how we arrived at our analysis of wit and the comic. We worked out our idea of the comic in the course of our discussion of the beautiful, as it manifests itself, and we analysed it into its components of idea and appearance. But wit, we agreed, is a kind of working of the active artistic intelligence, which runs through the entire realm of art; but in a certain direction. So it certainly cannot be restricted only to that area where the comic alone is to be found; it can equally have a tragic or a sublime effect, when it plunges the entire world of appearance, with all its oppositions and contradictions, into the intuition of the idea. This aspiration towards universality and totality (which cannot, as you saw, attend the wit of the senses, because there the whole appears in each detail) is what distinguishes universal wit, or, if you will, the wit of the ideal. You will encounter it in many of the great modern works, in which reality is elaborated and decorated in the most varied ways by a fine intelligence in order to sacrifice it in its universal and all-pervasive contradictions to a fate which rules over all. Now at least you will have an idea of the range of wit as well, and from this you will recognize that it is by no means a one-sided faculty of the intelligence, appearing only in the particular, but the intelligence itself as a whole, seen from a certain point of view.

I am deeply taken with the truth of your explanation, he said, although I shall find it rather difficult to break away from the usual way of thinking about wit, which we tend to recognize only in a single, unexpected stroke or flash.

Then, I continued, I shall add something for your further enlightenment. True, it seems to be a peculiarity of wit that we should perceive it only as a single spark that leaps suddenly over intermediate steps. But that characteristic really derives from the nature of the beautiful in general; for it is by means of beauty, remember, that we perceive the idea immediately, in the outermost surface of things, without intermediate stages or step-by-step connections. This comes as a surprise in wit because wit proceeds from the external variety of the surface inwards – which is otherwise only possible to the ordinary understanding by way of gradual ascent. This is why, unless it has a living intuition as its foundation, wit, and most especially false wit, can turn into empty and decorative play or mere silliness. But this characteristic by no means excludes the possibility that, as long as art is alive in the element of wit, the intelligence can invent the most varied chains of association, by which a stroke of wit can be conducted like an electric current through an entire world, as it re-energises the immediate connection to the inner intuition in every link of the chain at the same time. This is what you will learn best of all from the great masters of this manner, such as Shakespeare or Cervantes. That is why a far greater wealth of intentional connections is actually possible in poetry of wit than in what we called the poetry of reflection. For in contemplative art, every particular is already to be found in the idea, where it is absolutely of the same kind; and the idea contributes its entire universe to the reality of each particular that emerges from its depths. So if on the one hand in ancient art the intelligence creates complex sequences, as it does particularly in lyrical works such as Pindar's odes and the tragic choruses, it is all a development of the One itself, necessarily given. The wit of modern writers on the other hand must first create that eternal content for each particular standpoint out of the manifold world of appearance, and this can happen only when wit conceives that eternal content both as an individual thing in its external relations, and yet at the same time as unmediated and in its true nature. Hence, in this contemplative kind of art, the beautiful usually appears more independent of those involvements and external interests than our common passions could accept. But this is exactly what in fact is also brought about by wit; and you might say it does so even more completely, because it takes hold of the particular, interested, passionate involvements themselves, including one-sided moral attitudes, and submerges them in the intuition. If we give to the origin of these involvements the name of sentimentality, as many people do, then it is the true business of wit to annihilate this trivial affection. And the sentimentally minded are often very put out that it should so ruthlessly destroy the tender niceness of their feeling. But wit thereby first endows beauty with its true nobility and the high detachment that it must preserve unaltered in the midst of all the one-sided interpretations reflected back upon it by the variety of the world around. But I fear I will go too far and lose my way on these topics, so I will ask whether you have a clearer understanding now of this view of wit.

Yes, said Erwin. I now have a general overall grasp of the faculty which you call artistic intelligence, and which fuses the idea with the actual appearance in two opposite directions, by means of reflection, and of wit.

On Wit (2)

You seem to have understood it excellently, I said. Now you will see still more easily that the workings of the imagination or the emotions can also not be conceived practically and actually without wit.

I think I have already noticed that, he replied. For here too, if it were not for the wit which uncovers the intuition that is the basis of their connections and relations, we could not become conscious of how the essence of things is contained in particular appearances that transform themselves to become the expression of the idea, or call forth the idea by means of feeling.

That is exactly how you should think of it, I said. Just as according to the aims of ancient art essence and appearance were always indeed symbolically united in activity itself, here, on the other hand, the two stand in an allegorical opposition that can be reconciled only by wit. Wit draws together the individual relationships of things, and nullifies these relations *qua* individual by absorbing them into the intuition as essentials. Many have explained wit as being the mere comparison of individual things in their interconnections; but this is in fact the very opposite of what wit really is. For them the finite remains simply finite; its connection to the infinite remains incomplete and the intuition of essence infinitely distant. True wit annihilates all that with a single blow, by discovering in every connection the essential intuition whereby things converge. Wit connects what is present and individual in things with this intuition, and in so far as presentness and individuality are for simple existence accidental and sporadic, it is only through this process of the wit that existence is unified. This procedure is exactly the same, whether the intuition belongs to the sensuous intuition or to that of the idea. For alike in emotion and the reflective imagination, wit unites sensuous appearance and idea perfectly, and makes them the centre of art. In our view, with respect to emotion, merely sensuous feeling must, by means of wit, become truly essential feeling. That is, it must become an appearance of the idea itself and converge with it perfectly. With respect to the reflective imagination, the idea becomes at the same time sensuous intuition, in that wit relates only the present and the actual to intuition. From this you will see that through wit the inward essence of art is everywhere present.

Now I understand, said Erwin, that this omnipresence of art is possible only through the activity of the intelligence detected just at that transition from idea into actuality where the one transforms itself into the other. But wit is still more difficult for me to grasp than contemplation. For in contemplation, the essence out of which actuality proceeded was assumed; wit, on the other hand, seems entirely destructive, and, taking its starting point in appearances, it expands into formlessness and vacuum. For I still don't see clearly where the idea embodied in some particular form (which is after all the only mode of relation to individuality for the idea) comes to us from.

But Erwin, I cried, where does the particular come from in contemplation? Is not the particular form of the idea given in so far as wit discovers the form precisely in the particular and the real? Is the particular form not to be produced as idea out of the particular, and is it not on the contrary always and from the start present in the artistic intelligence? Surely you remember that only that connection made by the intelligence that is also endowed with all the richness of intuition can be called wit? And now intuition bursts forth into the particular, and from this lightning-flash there spreads a light in which the idea appears present for the first time, and the particular appears simultaneously annihilated and transfigured in the idea. Hence wit cannot relate and connect actuality at all unless wit already carries the inward intuition with it – the goal it makes everything aim for – the end for which it relates and connects. And here we have the essential distinction between wit and contemplation, for in contemplation everything necessarily proceeds from sensuous intuition. If we gave the name of representation to this unfolding of the essential nature by means of forming and amplifying, aided by contemplation, then now we must contrast this activity with the *trans*forming and relating of particularity by the reflective imagination and emotion, which is possible only by means of wit. Let us distinguish this by the name of portrayal.

It would be a good thing, he replied, if usage were to establish these terms as you have defined them; also, I seem to see the sense of taking them from the fine arts, for representation is a term chiefly appropriate to sculpture, and portrayal to painting.

That is not a bad remark, I said. But remember, these terms refer only to how the subject matter of intuition is treated, and how intuition proceeds by the two possible tendencies of the intelligence, while these tendencies still remain strictly separate. And this will not satisfy you, I suppose?

Certainly not! I have already asked you – though it was too soon then – how the intelligence reaches a unity with itself. Nevertheless, I admit you could not answer that until we had seen how the intelligence, pursuing each of its two tendencies, that of the imagination and that of the senses, combines the elements of the beautiful in the same way and into the same unity. But for the moment these tendencies are still separate, divided – which is surely most striking – between ancient and modern art. And it seems to me all the more difficult to unite the two, since each artistic world has attained in itself a certain perfection, or at least an inner harmony. So I am all the more curious now to see how you will place the key-stone on the whole arch.

You know, I said, we have always been most successful when we have moved forward step by step. It will doubtless be our best procedure here too if we first observe how contemplation and wit pass into one another in ancient and modern art. Would you agree?

Certainly.

Let us take contemplation first. Where, do you think, must it come close to wit?

Obviously at the point where it goes as far as splitting up the idea into actuality in all its variety for the senses, and thereby dissolves the idea into appearance. This is what seems to me to happen in the comic.

Then you do recognize correctly that it is always the case that art perfects itself only at the actual threshold where essentiality and finiteness are one. This is in fact how the contradiction arises between idea and nullified appearance; and this, if we look at it entirely from the aspect of appearance, is what creates the comic effect. So a kind of wit seems to be present here which does not appear to be brought about by the activity of the intelligence, but seems to emerge from the thing itself, in so far as its representation loses itself in that very division otherwise united by the relational activity of the intelligence. Hence too the comic wit of the Greeks is of a very special kind, and often very foreign to our own aspirations, for it arises merely from the powerful representation and elaboration of what is very low and vain indeed. And to be honest, we must admit that this is why so much in Aristophanes is no longer fit for our taste. Nevertheless, wit cannot be restricted only to the comic, either in reference to

Greek literature or anywhere else. For did we not expressly remark earlier that releasing the idea into nullity by means of contemplation was absolutely essential to the tragic?

Indeed we did, and so we concluded that there was also a tragic wit among the ancients, which likewise proceeded only from a very powerful and direct representation.

That is doubtless how it is; nor will you fail to recognize it if you recall the bitterness in Aeschylus, and the sharp and irreconcilable contradictions in his work, which often tear the idea apart, and in this way perfect the tragic effect. These examples should make it quite clear to you. Otherwise, as you will see from them, it lies in the nature of representation itself that these dissonances remain unresolved, without the annihilating effect of wit.

Yes, to the extent that the representation has to be pushed as far as pure actuality. And representation as the appearance of the idea cannot be conceived without wit.

Perfectly correct. But you will no doubt be able to declare even more firmly of wit that it cannot exist without contemplation. For at an earlier stage in our discussion you were demanding a definite form of the idea for wit.

So I did.

So you felt then that wit must already be endowed with the essential intuition, if it is not to become mere false wit and resolve into a nullity of nothingness. True, however, this general intuition of the idea does not receive its definitive form until wit brings back to it specific forms of individuality and actuality. The idea cannot come into existence, but it can be given form by conceiving a specific particularity as one with it; and so the contemplation is given which will find this particularity in the idea.

So much is certain. But this seems to me to be really suitable only to the wit of the senses. For from the beginning there must be given in the reflective imagination a form of the Divine to which it can relate everything actual.

When you regard wit as if it took hold of only the crude exterior of low appearance, my dear Erwin, you forget sometimes what we have otherwise agreed on, perhaps most completely when we discussed the reflective imagination. It is rather a function of wit, as it was previously in a different sense a function of allegory,[11] as it were, to bring the Divine as such face to face with appearance, so that both become one. This assumes that each is somehow destined in advance for the other, a destiny which can be understood only in terms of their original unity, which we acknowledged much earlier, and which forms the entire basis of our account. If you simply look at wit, and how it grasps the contradictions and unites them, then the essence is already caught as a specific form in these contradictions, just as in allegory essence was also subject to the relationships. But if you turn to look at the unity of intuition in which the opposites are acknowledged to be present, then wit itself is also at the same time contemplation. But one cannot exist without the other. Even should the Divinity be assumed in a definite form, even this is not contrary to our meaning, as long as actuality is represented as in contradiction to the Divinity and yet at the same time one with it, and as long as this representation is made only by relationships and opposites, and not by means of unfolding and development.

On Irony

I think, Erwin replied, that not long ago you said in this context that we had considered the activity of the intelligence too much in terms of mere present existence. No doubt you meant that we should at the same time also maintain its whole activity present in us as idea, which with particularity changes into nothingness. At the same time that particularity is perpetuated in the idea itself. Only I am not in the least clear myself how this contradiction is to be grasped from both sides at the same time.

At last, I cried, you have penetrated to the true centre of art, which is where I wanted to guide you. You know that contemplation cannot exist without wit, nor wit without contemplation, for the simple reason that both, proceeding in different directions, and in reciprocal relation to each other, arise from the self-same root! This is the moment of transition in which the intelligence merges both types of intuitions, the general and the particular, completely into each other. And since each stands in a relationship of pure contradiction to the other, they are also bound to cancel each other. You must take care not to believe that in this transition the particular becomes merely an expression, as they say, of the general, and nothing more.

Indeed I must, he replied. But I confess that during your developing account of imagination and the senses I could reassure myself by thinking that the appearance is taken up in the idea, or that the idea is imprinted in the appearance, both in an identical way, without giving a thought to the essential contradiction between the two, the one being essential, the other nullity.

That was because, in our step-by-step approach, I said we had not yet mentioned the function of the intelligence, which after all is the means for imagination and sensuousness to turn into real activity. Even with the intelligence, you certainly could not relinquish this contradiction entirely.

Indeed, he said, you have drawn my attention to this from time to time.

So now, I went on, immerse yourself entirely in the thought that a particular which was nothing but the expression of the idea – whether we understand this as Anselm did, or Bernhard[12] – would be nothing but an unheard-of impossibility; for in that situation it would have to cease to be either particular or actual. So if the idea passes into the particular by means of the artistic intelligence, it does not only impress itself upon it, nor does it merely appear as temporal and transient; the idea actually becomes present actuality, and since nothing exists apart from idea, it becomes nullity and transience itself. And we cannot help being seized by an immeasurable grief when we see what is most glorious of all dispersed into nothing on account of its necessary earthly existence. Yet we can blame only absolute perfection as it is revealed to temporal cognition. For the merely earthly (when we perceive *only* it) holds its elements together by means of interaction in an endless state of coming into being and passing away. Now this moment of transition in which the idea itself necessarily perishes, must be the true realm of art: the place where wit and contemplation, each striving against each other simultaneously to create and destroy, must be one and the same. This then is the place where the spirit of the artist must draw all tendencies together in one all-embracing glance. This penetrating glance, that hovers over everything, annihilating everything, we call irony.

I am astonished, said Anselm at this point, at your boldness in resolving the entire nature of art into irony, for many would regard this as infamy.

Don't attack me, I replied, with the insipid and false religiosity which the poets of the day support with ideals concocted by themselves, and which they use so sturdily to push widespread sentimentality and hypocritical self-deception concerning religion, patriotism and art one stage further into the emptiest nonsense! I tell you, anyone who has not the courage to grasp ideas themselves in all their transience and nullity is, at least for art, utterly lost. But there is of course also a *false* irony, just as there is *false* wit and *false* contemplation, and I must take great care to avoid this being imputed to me. False irony arises, however, when emptiness is lent an apparent existence in order to destroy it the more easily, either consciously – and then it is an ordinary joke – or unconsciously, when we believe that we are about to seize hold of the truth – and then it certainly can lead to a profligacy in art. This is the so-called benevolent philosophy of life which we find in old Lucian and in many of his modern imitators,[13] among whom I do not like to see it. It is a philosophy which succeeds in proving from the common way of the world that there is no such thing as virtue or truth, that nothing noble or pure exists, and that for man, the more hopefully he aspires towards higher things, the deeper he plunges into the filth of sensuality and baseness. But how could it demonstrate this so successfully if it did not combine this enterprise with that other sickness which has long been our enemy: the foisting of empty ideals upon us in place of the true ideas! But it is in fact easy to expose the vanity of these false images arising out of a deluded imagination. Consequently, false irony is itself, without knowing it, two-fold in nature. For it can annihilate only that to which it had lent merely an apparent existence anyway.[14] This is far from being our kind of irony. For whoever has grasped the heart of our irony will thereby be able to possess in this life true being and the divine idea.

I think I understand you, said Erwin, even if it may cost me much labour to keep my understanding ever alive within me.[15] Precisely by means of this nullity of the idea as earthly appearance, I think, we will be able to recognize it as actual, and recognize what appears to us to be the phenomenal world as the idea in existence. For reality and temporal existence have here interpenetrated each other in the same original unity, and the loss of the one is the gain of the other. But both interpenetrate each other by the continual activity of the artistic intelligence, which is at all times one with itself and yet flashes back and forth between the two.

Truly, I cried, my dear Erwin, you outstrip my expectations. And only now am I convinced that it was not base sensuality which first inspired you. Through your urgent aspiration to come to know something higher in actual things as such, though they persisted in showing you only their disintegrating external forms, the true irony dawned upon you. Now you seem happily to avoid the one thing I thought it was still necessary to warn you against. At least, I assume you do not mean that the earthly, for its part, should be raised by the magic of art to a universal perfection and an unchangeably fixed essence?

Not at all, he replied. Otherwise it would become an undifferentiated intuition. Rather, reality must pulse through all that is mortal: for reality's very existence is after all art, and earthly things themselves, in their coming into being and passing away, must be the idea in its living presence, which indeed comes into being and passes away concurrently with them. Through its transience as earthly thing, which pervades its entire existence, the idea is determined, and sensuous intuition completes itself in it; while actuality, by means of *its* ever-recurring existence, is the ever-present unfolding of that essential intuition.

Art, then, my dear Erwin, I said joyfully, is all existence and presence and reality; that you clearly understand. But art is the existence and the presence of the actuality of the eternal essence of all things, and this is effected only by means of the intelligence, unified and yet working actively between both sides. So there is no longer any need for us to enquire anxiously how it is possible that the essence of art should still remain the same everywhere, despite the imperfection of its temporal existence; for now we know that it is only in this imperfection – indeed, in the very nullity of appearance – that essence really *is*. This is why, when we look at everything merely under the aspect of mortality, we are seized by melancholy, and the beautiful reveals itself to us only as the embodiment of some veiled, higher archetype – not merely as the most transient of all things, but as that thing consisting of pure transience and nullity alone. If we penetrate more deeply into reality, this very temporality becomes for us a living reality and a continuous revelation of the living presence of the Godhead. Now do you also see that art is the only route by which truth and genuine, eternal content may enter into our life of temporal appearance, as far as that life exists independently?

This, he said, is not even a consequence drawn from what we agreed about irony, but only another way of putting it. Only there is still something, Adalbert, which prevents my joy from breaking forth untroubled, and I would like to ask you about it.

What is it?

That ancient and modern art still seem to be going separate ways.

What is wrong with that, as long as irony is present in both?

But it is present in each in a very different way.

Yes, in ancient art it is present more unconsciously, and, like wit, lies in the things themselves. On the other hand, in modern art the irony bears the consciousness within itself, and perhaps this is why it does not appear so easily as a natural presence in the objects represented by modern art, and is not always able to keep false ideals at bay. But in the mature works of ancient art, irony does come into consciousness, as it does in Sophocles' *Oedipus at Colonus*, which is entirely the product of this consciousness. However, in modern art at its highest, irony is embodied in the objects too, and even in the ordinary course of affairs. This is to be seen most clearly in Shakespeare. The great works of each kind grow richer then as that central core of irony radiates forth from them in its own peculiar nature, even though the growth and aspirations of each type of art had to attain it from a different side. For in Sophocles' drama there appears the natural subject matter furnished by tradition, only represented as such out of the depths of profound contemplation, quite as if its complexity and ultimate effect had been brought about by a freely considered transformation into the idea. Oedipus' innocence counts for nothing before the natural laws which annihilate him, and yet his transgression of these laws leads him to a miraculous transfiguration. Similarly, the basic genius of Shakespeare's complicated situations arises entirely from his innermost soul and from his own particular world view, and it leads towards nothing less than the course of the world itself. And this encounter in an unknown predetermination of consciousness is the very thing that produces, in what is without consciousness, such a strong and shattering effect. The greatest power of his genius reveals itself when Shakespeare conceives an historical subject matter as if entirely given. On the summit of art, then, opposites must be so reconciled that the thought of one-sidedness will no longer lay hold of us.

But one of the two, said Erwin, is bound to predominate, and then, it seems to me, the conscious is better than the unconscious.

But, I asked, can there be the one without the other? If irony did not lie embedded in the very existence of things, and if it were not already contained in the mere contemplation of their existence, would it not be an arbitrary, false irony? Moreover, how would irony be recognized in this actuality, if the intelligence had not annihilated the actual and related it to the idea?

So really, he replied, both tendencies would always have to be present concurrently, or at least the one would always have to lose itself in the other.

In fact, I said, both are always present concurrently where true art is present; and as the intelligence brings the one to perfection, so it also includes the realization of the other. For without this, as you will easily understand, it could never attain to irony and hence to the essential centre of art. For that centre is present only when both tendencies interpenetrate each other, hovering at the midpoint between them. One may still ask whether the intelligence might be able to ascend from this centre toward both tendencies in equal proportion. If so, it would produce an art never before imagined, which would consciously create the unconscious, and simultaneously create out of the unconscious consciousness. There is surely no longer any need for us to doubt the possibility of such an art, now that we have convinced ourselves that the unchangeable essence of art is only there where the nullity of actual existence is co-present. For art, precisely while shaping existence, can dissolve it continually with its accompanying irony and at the same time lead existence back to the essence of the idea. Whereas it usually treats the present individual item as subject matter, it would now have to develop the ironical standpoint itself as immediate existence. And because the ironical standpoint has exactly the same attitude to both tendencies, and is present and real everywhere at the same time, this can take place with equal truth towards both sides. This art would be the first to unite perfectly freedom with necessity and contemplation with wit, and thus realize its entire scope from the purest concept of art. But perhaps our temporal weakness makes that unattainable in real life, and it is reserved for only the Godhead itself, or, it may be, for an imitation of the Godhead's actions – which may be granted us only if we reach a higher world. For as I gaze on this centre between both tendencies of the self-fulfilling intelligence, the radiant circle of the true, eternal universe opens out before me. For I have again touched the innermost root of the soul, the talisman which reveals its eternal essence in which its whole existence is transfigured into a full, unified and completed life. Again I glimpse them, those forms and figures, full of the divine essence, and my feelings are very different from when I first gazed into this realm: I am filled with the joyful hope that I may be on the brink of emerging from that dream into a true awakening. For everything I gaze upon now is nothing other than the world around me itself, and all the doubts and contradictions that it recently involved us in are now banished utterly by means of the consciousness of art. I see that the entire soul is implanted in each body by an eternal, perfectly shaping art, and if its existence risks becoming solidified in its abstract concept, the vital inward warmth of that art nevertheless penetrates to its outermost form in the innumerable expressions of life. Each thing, then, loses its own individuality of being in unending mutual involvement and the reciprocal influence of things, and this is at the same time painting incarnate, which allows the inner focal point of that same light to stream through all things and involve all things in its common light. All the external relationships of things, number, measure, time, and space, ultimately resolve themselves into the harmony of the world's movement, which builds in rapid transformation an edifice ever firm and ordered and plays to perfection a living music whose harmony is heard by the highest intelligence. But even as I am losing myself in the totality, the present life-producing workings of that totality merge from all directions and meet in my own human individuality. Gazing toward the absolute human and personal essence, which pours itself with all its strength into our existence, I catch a glimpse of that transfiguration of this existence in the splendour of epic poetry. But even if the contradictions of my present life tear apart the union of the essential and the particular, they both still strive, rising and sinking, towards the purest unity and harmony in the flights of lyrical poetry. Finally, completely accomplished, rounded into blissful perfection, my life and its every moment is revealed to me when I grasp fully its immediate presence by means of dramatic art, even as in the nullity of my being the essence of the Godhead constantly reveals itself as my own intensest existence. Should not this, my friends, be the ultimately true and perfect art, which realizes the intelligence of God as an actual, living art, whose works we, with our ordinary understanding, bring together only as the scattered limbs of the artist? And it is this divine intelligence which has the same kind of effect within us, and teaches us in the productions of our mortal, earthly poets a full understanding of what indeed our true existence is. In short, we could well say that our present, real existence, recognized and lived in its essential nature, is art, and that everywhere we will find irony, the most perfect fruit of the artistic intelligence, and central core where essence and actuality interpenetrate each other as presence. In irony, intelligence is one and the same with that two-fold self-creating, self-limiting intuition, and that is why here too the divine universe, of which I am granted a glimpse, is revealed in all its clarity. Once again I see the sacred figure of wisdom standing in this bright gateway to perfect knowledge, and it was none other than she who appeared to me the first time also. From this place, she intimates to me, goodness and bliss are to be found in all directions; and in return for her revelations, she demands an oath, with a wave of her luminous hand, that we will not rest here. For if we did, everything she has shown us might vanish again. Rather, we must strive further with her along all the other paths towards the goal which will reveal itself only when all those paths meet again in the centre of the divine universe. Shall we all swear the oath?

Of how Erwin swore that oath with solemn feeling, and how the other two joined him as a witness of the seriousness of their purpose, I will be silent, for what I set out to tell is, as far as I am able, for the time being, accomplished.

Part 5

Tieck–Solger Correspondence

Tieck–Solger Correspondence

In these extracts from the letters of Tieck and Solger to one another, the concepts of mysticism, symbol, and allegory are explained, and provide a gloss, in a conversational and more fully accessible style, on the section in *Erwin* on the symbol. The extracts also hint at the interconnections among these concepts and their connection to the theory of irony only touched upon by Solger at the end of *Erwin*. A few words here about Solger's unique concept of the relation of allegory to symbol may be of use to the general reader.

For Solger, as for Coleridge, the symbol enacts the permeation of finite reality by the ideal; it is the finite representation of the idea, or, the existence of the idea, that is, the idea realized. It is neither a sign nor an image of truth, nor a datum of perception, but rather the mental activity itself of creative consciousness momentarily realized. In the symbol, Solger distinguishes two aspects or moments of realization: first, the symbol 'in the narrower sense', by which he means the symbolic activity (of the realization of the idea in finite form) as completed. The second aspect of the symbol is called allegory, or the moment of the representation of the mental activity itself of creative consciousness still not completed, but yet in the process of completing itself. In the letters he gives only general examples of works or writers whom he considers as chiefly allegorical or symbolical, where specific examples might have more clearly elucidated his meaning. But Solger clearly seeks here and in the first extract from *Erwin* to rescue the word 'allegory' from the misuse into which it has fallen, partly in order to establish the desired distinction of moments within the concept of the symbol as a whole that is usually ignored. For Solger, however, all art is symbolical in the general sense of the word, but within that compass two distinguishable types of symbolical art exist, namely the two moments mentioned above, symbol 'in the narrower sense', and allegory.

Mysticism Solger describes as the 'inner life' which inspires and fills all art, whether symbolical in the narrower sense – that is, tending toward the sensuous and concrete – or allegorical, tending toward the spiritual. He admits that he means by 'Mysticism' what Tieck means by 'Poesie', and that allegory can be understood as conscious, and symbolical (in the narrower sense) as unconscious mysticism. Allegorical art points from appearance toward reality, while symbolical art (in the narrower sense) points from reality toward appearance. Allegory is not subordinated to symbol; both are rather basic forms of the representation of the interpenetration of essence and existence.

Solger and Tieck are sometimes confusing because they use the terms 'allegorical' and 'symbolical' in their negative, degenerate senses, as 'Schein', or false, pretended allegory or symbol. That is, both allegory and symbol can be presented by authors in form only, without the living essence of the mystical or poetical to give them their genuine spirit. Such degenerate allegory becomes a mere play of the understanding with abstractions, while degenerate forms of symbols are mere imitations of nature. Thus Tieck and Solger often use the term 'allegorical' in *contrast* to truly mystical poetry, instead of as a type of mystical poetry. The context does not always make it exactly clear how the reader is to interpret or evaluate the term.

The English text follows the German of *Tieck and Solger. The Complete Correspondence*, ed. Percy Matenko (New York and Berlin, 1933), 468–9, 476–7, 485–6, 493–4, 509–10.

Mysticism and Allegory

Solger to Tieck, 3 August 1818

I still owe you an answer on many questions, especially regarding *Parsifal* and the difference between mysticism and allegory. If only I could be brief and concise! I still find, as I say, that *Parsifal* is more allegorical than mystical. Of course it's true that both belong together, and mysticism is the actual core of both allegory and symbol, which two things I consider, as you know, to be the forms through which the eternal represents itself in art. Now mysticism consists in the recognition and representation of the immediate presence of the eternal in allegory and symbol, as in reality generally, and the highest form of mysticism would in my opinion be the one which grasped the whole of reality as revelation, without any further interpretation or reference back to concepts or productions of the imagination: a way to this goal is opened up for us by Christianity, or rather this mysticism is itself Christianity. But where do we enjoy a perfect understanding of the eternal and guard it in ever-present contemplation? We feel a constant urge wherever possible to draw it into our presence by means of *individual* symbols or to lend it meaning by allegory. Now even where this urge prevails we are still left with an ideal which is distinct from the real. We want before us only that which possesses meaning, and for this precise reason must separate it again from the meaning itself. We are unable to make both coincide completely, as they do in true revelation and mysticism. Yet for the very reason that all religion rests solely upon that living presence of God within actual existence, every allegorizing representation becomes at once something incidental to religion, ethical, perhaps, or physical etc.: and this seems to me to be the case in *Parsifal*. In that work everything finally becomes so full of meaning that reality itself, devoid of meaning, is reduced to nothing and thus the living awareness of our eternal relationship to God is also dissolved into a meaning or connection. This is, no doubt, not very intelligible? More soon!

Mysticism

Tieck to Solger, 10 November 1818

Just for a change I have been very well for some time (I don't count mere pains) and have, what's more, made use of this good health to busy myself. I have developed our all too brief conversation about mysticism a good deal in my own mind and think I now understand you better: this understanding is also indispensable for me as regards *Erwin*. Quite naturally the 'Titurel'[1] is for you also merely allegorical, and probably so will be everything else too that has been attempted in this style since Dante. I also now include Calderón's *Sibyl of the Orient*;[2] it is thoroughly allegorical, and I have convinced myself of that fact even more since I have now read a number of his sacramental autos,[3] many of which are great and highly poetic works, many of which are arbitrary and some (especially the 'Loas' or prologues) often crassly allegorical or childish. The mind of Calderón is one of the strangest of all phenomena: there is barely a trace of the great reason which makes Shakespeare so heavenly and so authentically human, none of that magnificent naïveté which I am always compelled to admire in Lope;[4] but for all that he is the most thoroughgoing mannerist (in the good sense) I know. Nature, love, passion, religion, and all those other prejudices (which, having risen up from their primordial and most natural foundation into a higher and lighter element, make up man's humanity in addition to his reason) have, in spite of Calderón's extreme arbitrariness, splendid depth, vitality, and fire, and acquire thereby a different though not a higher kind of necessity. But I would say that what I feel I must now call mysticism is what I searched for all along in Shakespeare and in art, albeit unconsciously: I called it art (and such it is, after all) and to my shame I'm now forced to realize that the actual mystics led me astray for some time from the more accurate view of things, a view I was closer to earlier on (as is so often the case in life: the passage about this in *Puss-in-Boots*[5] has always been most true of me). Only now do I fully understand why Novalis called J. Boehme arbitrary,[6] why he wished him to be regarded as an allegorical poet whose manner and thoughts one could continue oneself, whose vision of nature and everything else one could share and whose style of writing one might even take up, given the same great talent: of course that is true, just as Calderón's autos can be perfectly well imitated and even transferred to philosophical subjects, and until now only the lack of an acquaintance with these autos has kept our modern poets from making mystical, religious and philosophical poems as if using Peschek's book of tables: compared with this all the guilt and 'fate' tragedies are really only trivialities.

Mysticism and Irony

Solger to Tieck, 22 November 1818

We now seem to be in complete agreement as regards mysticism. It's another part of my philistinism that I rate all excursions into the spectacular (and everything which parades its name around) below that which really is there – that which all men think they have known for a long time but simply don't understand and thus consider to be the everyday norm: Shakespeare, for example, only really has their approval because, in the first place, he represents real life with such psychological accuracy and, in the second place, because he appears to go to the extreme limits of all that is stirring in human nature. The fact that he can achieve both these things only because he also portrays in every case the deepest, unyielding foundation of all, they do not understand. Now as for my philistinism one could admittedly say that if we only ever wanted to understand what is well-known and taken as given, we wouldn't get far with such pedantry: if something new is to be done, there must be fluctuations and specific directions. Yet I don't wish to do away with these either: only they must not disappear into a void, but must always remain in and return to the sphere of what exists eternally. Neither is allegory to be discarded, any more than symbolism is, but both must be full of mysticism. The latter is the inner life, the former are the forms it takes. Mysticism is, when looking to the real world, the mother of irony, when looking to the eternal world, the child of enthusiasm or inspiration. What I call mysticism, you called poetry: I call it the same, I call it religion too in as far as it is conscious and unconscious of itself.

But what I call mysticism 'for itself' is the living and immediate insight which it enjoys into itself at all levels, the development of which is – philosophy.

Mysticism

Tieck to Solger, 17 December 1818

If you were here you would probably now talk with me at somewhat greater length about the mysticism of poets, a thought which occupies me day and night, since what I have really been striving for since my youth and the reasons for my worship of Shakespeare have only now become clear to me. I became acquainted with Dante late. I almost always hated the spiritual and Christian poets like Milton, but above all Klopstock[7] in his *Messiah*. In Milton the allegory of sin and death, which people have tried to criticize, is precisely what is good, the descriptions of paradise and the state of innocence are beautiful, some of Satan's feelings have grandeur, and God the Father and the hierarchy, the disputation in heaven, the decision of Christ to die for the world, and all that goes with it, are most stupid. What can be said about the *Messiah*? Neither epic nor descriptive, nor evangelical nor polemical nor catholic nor allegorical, least of all mystical: rather, enlightenment at its drabbest, humanity, unpoetic psychology which is highly mannered into the bargain, no arousing of pity, terror, hatred or love – mere inflated words trying to be great thoughts – and all of it, if I look at it as a Christian, most unchristian, indeed anti-christian. You may find this wrong: in every form of art I have a turning point of hate which is an indispensable support for my love. In poetry this has always been Klopstock, along with Wieland[8] who provoked distaste in me rather than hate: in painting Rubens, in music the modern frivolity and effeminacy, in architecture the empty imitation of the Greek, and the same in sculpture. Actually it is here of course more a case of vacuity yawning at me than of some power like that of

Rubens or Klopstock arousing my hate. I am still busily reading Calderón and as many Spaniards as I can get hold of. Calderón is a perfect mannerist, and in his way great and beyond improvement, but it still seems to me uncertain whether Lope is not the greater poet, even if he may have brought only little or nothing to completion. But Calderón too has his great weaknesses.

Allegory and Symbol

Solger to Tieck, 11 January 1819

In art, and especially in poetry, we must just be clear about the difference between conscious and unconscious mysticism. But of course I think I have already written to you about that before now.[9] Allegory in art is based on conscious, symbolism on unconscious mysticism, and both have their limit, beyond which allegory becomes a mere game of the intellect and symbolism imitation of nature. At this limit, irony and inspiration are both extinguished at once. Irony then becomes an instinctual struggle against what is true and eternal. Therefore the poetry of common sensuality is always polemical at the same time, as in the case of Kotzebue[10] and Wieland. Inspiration becomes sensual pleasure or worldly wise conceit, the latter especially prevalent in the ethical, spiritual and generally philosophizing works of this species (or should I say 'specious'). So this would be the turning point of love and hate, as you call it: for it is natural that whatever confronts us with animosity and antagonism should also transform our love, which always remains love as long as the true domain of poetry is its home, into hate. With regard to Milton and Klopstock I actually agree with you completely, and if I would not like to call my attitude towards the latter hate, then it is at least distaste. Milton will always be the better of the two, because he knows how to portray things: this gift raises his work from the level of rhetoric to poetry, in spite of the author's intentions. Klopstock has no such gift and has for that very reason hit on what I would call the desperate type of rhetorical ode-making which has without doubt caused untold confusion in the hearts and minds of our German people. When I read these bombastic odes, to a riding horse, an ice skate, a system of grammar and so on, I feel as if I were right next to a madhouse. At this point of course not only all mysticism but also all allegory ceases. Where I still contrast allegory with mysticism is when it begins to loose itself from the centre and to dissolve the work in a one-sided way: when it may, then, still be poetry in the full sense but is already directed completely towards width and breadth, thus preparing a possible separation of its real constituent parts. Now it is this kind of thing that I already perceive in the poems about the Holy Grail, the starting point of our initial observations on this topic. This tendency contains the seed of what causes orders and secret societies to split off from the main body of the Church and State, and what is commonly called mystical because most people become aware of the principles only when they are about to lose them, or already have lost them. Calderón is also caught up in this dissipating effect of allegory, and that is exactly why he tends so much towards mannerism. I don't know enough of his work to give a rounded judgment, and with all my present obligations it is also not possible for me to read much of it now.

Part 6

Jean Paul Richter

Jean Paul Richter

(1763–1825)

Jean Paul, novelist of dream and fantasy literature, essayist, and reviewer, was a close friend and admirer of Herder; while warmly received by the Romantics he preferred to make his name apart from the Romantic School, though sharing many of their approaches to literature and criticism. Jean Paul is perhaps best known for his novel, *Hesperus* (1795), which won him a fame in his own day rivalled only by Goethe's *Werther*.

Jean Paul was well known in England to Crabb Robinson and Thomas Beddoes, and felt a particular affinity to English culture. He was influenced by Hartley's philosophy of associationism and Laurence Sterne's ironic, witty, style in *Tristram Shandy*, as well as by Fielding and many other English writers and critics. Not surprisingly, his analysis of the faculties is in important respects similar to that of his English contemporary, S. T. Coleridge. He distinguished 'Einbildungskraft' (Coleridge's 'fancy') from 'Phantasie' (creative imagination). The first was related to memory and association; the second was the faculty that makes parts into a coherent whole, which, like Coleridge and Shelley, Jean Paul insisted was necessary both to perception and to art. He also discussed the relation of instinct to judgment or reflectiveness in the two different types of genius which he distinguished from talent. Like Coleridge, he was aware of the role of the unconscious in creativity, and insisted furthermore that what appears to be spontaneous can in fact be attributed to our own unconscious activity.

Jean Paul maintained that good criticism must be based upon the 'analytic power of taste' and the 'synthetic power of good sense'. Like the other Romantics, he recommended beginning with the literary artifact (rather than with literary history or generalization), and then seeking to derive the principles embodied in it. Jean Paul's terminological differences from Friedrich Schlegel, Solger, and others ought not to be allowed to obscure the similarities of their insights. Jean Paul tends to use 'irony' for 'common irony' – sarcasm, satire, or hyperbole – and 'humour' for 'high irony', that is, the true Socratic-Platonic irony. Indeed, in the *Athenäum Fragment* 305, Friedrich Schlegel virtually defines 'humour' as 'irony'. Jean Paul, Friedrich Schlegel, and Solger all differ from A. W. Schlegel in insisting on the close relation of irony and tragedy, and on the affirmative and positive nature of irony, which appears purely negative and destructive only to those who misunderstand it. Solger best explains this 'positive negation', or 'cancellation', in *Erwin* (see above, and also the Introduction, for discussion). These three writers also shared the view that the paradoxical relation of play and seriousness was essential to their 'irony–humour' concept, as was the idea of self-criticism or self-parody. Like Solger, Jean Paul was deeply interested in the 'Bildung des Menschen' (cultivation of the human being) – the *School for Aesthetics* was originally written allegedly as a series of lectures for aesthetic education; Jean Paul however viewed his book as a work of art in the true Romantic tradition of criticism as poetry. While emphasizing practical criticism over theoretical aesthetics, the *School* nevertheless derives principles of criticism about the unity of art, the role of the spectator, the mental experience of aesthetic response, and the psychology of language as art.

Jean Paul's other major publications include the novels *Die unsichtbare Loge* (1793), *Siebenkäs* (1796), *Titan* (1800); a study of immortality, *Das Kampaner Tal* (1797); a collection of essays, *Herbst-Blumen* (1810); and a theory of education, *Levana* (1807).

The reader is referred to the German critical edition, *Jean Pauls Sämtliche Werke*, edited by Eduard Berend (Weimar, 1927–44, Berlin, 1952–63), and organized into three sections: Part 1 contains material published during Jean Paul's lifetime, Part 2 manuscripts, and Part 3 letters. Also useful is the *Jean Paul-Bibliographie*, ed. E. Berend, revised J. Krogoll (Stuttgart, 1963).

The *School for Aesthetics* (*Vorlesungen über Aesthetik*) was first published in 1804; an enlarged second edition appeared in 1813, and in 1825 Jean Paul added the extension 'Kleine Nachschule' to the work. The English text is taken from *Horn of Oberon. Jean Paul Richter's School for Aesthetics*, translated by Margaret Hale (Detroit, 1973), 28–32, 35–43, 88–102, 120–34, 179–85.

School for Aesthetics
Vorlesungen über Aesthetik (1804; revised 1813 and 1825)

On the Poetic Faculties

§6. *Reproductive Imagination*[1]

Reproductive imagination is the prose of creativity or imagination. It is only an intensified and more vividly coloured memory, which animals also have, for they both dream and fear. Its images are only fallen leaves wafted from the real world; fever, neurasthenia, drinks can so condense and materialize these images that they pass from the inner world into the outer and there stiffen into bodies.

§7. *Creativity or Imagination*

But imagination or creativity is higher; it is the world-soul of the soul and the elemental spirit for the other faculties. Accordingly a great imagination can indeed be drained and diverted towards particular faculties, such as wit, judgment, etc., but none of these faculties can be extended into imagination. If wit is the playful *anagram* of nature, then imagination is its *hieroglyphic alphabet*, which expresses all nature in a few images. Whereas the other faculties and experience only tear leaves from the book of nature, imagination writes all parts into wholes and transforms all parts of the world into worlds. It totalizes everything, even the infinite universe. Hence its poetic optimism, the beauty of the figures who inhabit its realm, and the freedom with which beings move like suns in its ether. Imagination brings as it were the absolute and infinity of reason closer and makes them more perceptible to mortal man. To do this it uses much of the future and much of the past, its two creative eternities, because no other time can become an infinite or a whole. Not from a room full of air, but only from the whole height of an atmospheric column can the ethereal azure of a heaven be created. [. . .]

Imagination practises its cosmetic power already in life; it throws its light into the distant rainy past and surrounds it with the splendid rainbow or arch of peace, which we never reach. Imagination is the goddess of love, the goddess of youth. For the same reason that a life-sized head in a drawing seems larger than its original, or that a landscape engraved on copper promises more by its limitation than is held by the original, every memory of life shines in its distance like a planet in heaven; the imagination compresses the parts into a closed and serene whole. It could just as well compose a *gloomy* whole; but it places Spanish castles in the air full of torture chambers only in the *future* and only Belvederes in the past. Unlike Orpheus we win our Eurydice by looking back and lose her by looking ahead.

§8. Degrees of Imagination

We want to accompany the imagination through its various degrees to the point where it creates poetically under the name of genius. At the lowest level it only receives. There can be no simple reception without production or creation, since every man receives poetic beauty only in parts, like chemical elements which he must compose organically into a whole, in order to contemplate it. Hence anyone who has ever said, 'That is beautiful,' has some imaginative creativity, even if he is wrong about the object. And how could a genius be tolerated or even exalted for so much as a month, not to mention thousands of years, by the multitude so unlike him, if there were not some understood family resemblance? Many works are like the *Clavicula Salomonis*; people may be reading them casually, without any intention of calling up an apparition, when suddenly the angry spirit steps out of the air before them.[2]

§9. Talent

In the second stage of imagination several faculties are prominent, such as acumen, wit, understanding, and the mathematical or historical reproductive imagination, while the faculty of creative imagination is minimal. This stage is that of *talent*, whose inner being is an aristocracy or monarchy, while that of the genius is a theocratic republic. Strictly speaking, talent, not genius, has instinct or the one-sided direction of all faculties; as a result it lacks the poetic reflectiveness by which the human being is distinguished from the animal. The reflectiveness of talent is only partial; it is mere separation of the inner from the external world, not that high separation of the self from its own whole inner world. The melodramatic *speaking voice* of talent drowns out the double choir of poetry and philosophy, which requires the whole singing voice of a man, so that talent is heard by the audience below as the only distinct music.

In philosophy mere talent is dogmatically exclusive, even mathematical, and hence intolerant. (True tolerance is present only in the man who mirrors all mankind.) The talented person numbers the doctrinal constructs and says he lives at number 1 or 99 or the like, while the great philosopher dwells in the wonder of the world, in that labyrinth of countless rooms half above, half below the earth. The talented philosopher, as soon as he has got his philosophy, naturally hates all philosophizing; for only he who is free loves free people. As he is only *quantitatively*[a] different from the multitude, he can completely amaze, please, dazzle, enlighten, and be all to the multitude, *timeless* within the *moment*. For however high the man of talent may stand and however long his measure, every other man need only apply himself as a yardstick to the man of talent to know at once his size. But the *fire* and *tone* of quality cannot be measured by the yardstick and scales of quantity. The poetry of talent affects people by particular strengths: by imagery, fire, abundance of ideas, or charms. Though such a poem is only a transfigured body with a Philistine soul, it deeply stirs the multitude, which easily recognizes limbs but not spirit, charms but not beauty. All Parnassus is full of verses which are only bright prose spread out upon verse as if on Leyden jars, or poetic petals which like botanic petals are simply juxtaposed leaves around a stalk. Since there is no image, no trope, no single thought produced by genius which talent may not also arrive at in its highest inspiration, except the poetic whole, talent may for a while be confused with genius. Indeed talent often blooms as a green hill next to the bald alp of genius, until it is destroyed by posterity, as every dictionary is by a better one. Men of talent, differentiated by degree, can destroy and replace one another; but geniuses, as genera, cannot. Images, witty, acute, profound thoughts, powers of expression, all charms in time change, as with polyps, from *food* into *colouring*. At first a few imitators steal, then the whole century does; thus the poem of talent dies in its diffusion like a talented philosophy which has more results than form. On the contrary, a whole, a spirit, can never be stolen; it lives on, great and young and alone even in a plundered work (in Homer, for example, or in Plato, repeated by rote). Talent has no excellence which cannot be imitated, as may be seen in the work of Ramler, the philosopher Wolff,[3] and others.

§10.　*Passive Geniuses*[4]

Allow me to call the third class feminine, receptive, or *passive geniuses*, or perhaps spirits written out into poetic prose.

I might describe them as being richer in receptive than in creative imagination, as commanding only weak subordinate faculties, and as lacking that reflectiveness of genius in their work which springs from the harmony of all faculties, and of great ones. But I feel that such definitions are either only systematizations of natural history according to stamens or teeth, or inventories of chemical analyses of organic corpses. There are men who, provided with a higher sensibility than that of the strong talent but with less strength, receive the great world-spirit into a holier, open soul, whether in their external life or in the inner life of poetry and thought. They cling and remain true to this spirit like the delicate woman to the strong man, disdaining mediocrity, yet when they want to express their love, torment themselves with broken and confused organs of speech and say something other than they wished. If the man of talent is the artistic actor and an ape happily miming genius, then these suffering borderline geniuses are the quiet, earnest, upright protohumans of the forest and the *night*, to whom destiny has refused speech. As animals are for Indians the mutes of the earth, they are the *mutes* of heaven. Let every man, whether inferior or superior, hold them sacred! For these very men are the mediators for the world between the common people and the genius. Like moons they cast upon the night the reconciling light of the sun.

They apprehend and comprehend the world and beauty with philosophical and poetical freedom. But when they themselves want to create, an invisible chain binds half their limbs and they create something other or smaller than they wanted. In their perceptions, they rule over all their powers with reflective imagination; in their invention, they are bound by a secondary faculty and yoked to the plow of mediocrity.

Why are their days of creation unsuccessful? Either their *reflectiveness*, which shines so brightly on the creations of others, becomes night above their own creations; they become lost in themselves and, despite all the levers in their hands, lack a standing place on a *second* world from which they could give motion to *their own*. Or their reflectiveness is not the genial sun whose light *generates* life but a moon whose reflected light *cools*. They give form to the materials of others rather than to their own and move more freely in foreign spheres than in their own, just as *flying* is easier than *running* for a man in a dream.[b]

The passive genius is unlike the man of talent, who can make us see only parts and bodies of a world but not world spirit, while for just this reason he can be compared to the genius, whose first and last distinguishing mark is contemplation of the universe. Nevertheless the world-view of the passive genius is only a continuation and development of the view of another genius.

I want to seek a few examples among the – dead, although, because of the inexhaustible mixtures and mezzotints of nature, examples always spill the colour outside the design. Where in philosophy does Diderot belong, and where in poetry Rousseau?[5] Evidently to the feminine border geniuses, although each produced more than he received, the former in poetry and the latter in philosophy.[c]

In philosophy Bayle indeed belongs to the passive geniuses. But Lessing – as much his kin as his superior in erudition, freedom, and acumen – where does he, with his thought, belong? In my diffident opinion he is an active genius more as a man than as a philosopher. His versatile acumen dissected more than his profundity[6] established. Even his most ingenious conceptions had to be confined as it were in a coffin of Wolffian formulas. Without, of course, being like Plato, Leibniz, or Hemsterhuis, the creator of a philosophical world, he was nevertheless the prophetic son of a creator and consubstantial with him. Although endowed with the freedom and reflectiveness of a genius, he was a passively free poetic philosopher, whereas Plato was actively free. Lessing resembled the great Leibniz in that he let the rays of every other system pass into his own solid system, as the brilliant diamond, despite its hardness and density, allows the passage of every ray of light, and even holds sunlight fast. The ordinary philosopher resembles cork – flexible, light, porous, but incapable of transmitting or retaining light.

Among creative writers Moritz[7] should stand at the head of the feminine geniuses. He apprehended reality with a sense for the poetic, but he could not form any poetic life. Only in his *Anton Reiser* and *Hartknopf* is the rosy *midnight glow* of an overcast sun, if not a bright *aurora*, diffused over the veiled earth; but nowhere does his sun rise as a bright Phoebus, showing *heaven* and *earth* at once in splendour. How often Sturz,[8] on the contrary, cools us with the lustre of his magnificent prose, which has no new spirit to reveal, but only illuminates corners of the world and the court. When one has nothing to say, the style of the Diet and the Imperial gazette is better than the ostentatious, crowned, squandering style which has itself heralded: 'He comes!' For an official style can at least be interpreted as self-parody. Novalis and many of his models and eulogizers also belong among the men-women of genius, who think that in conceiving they are producing.

Such border geniuses can attain a certain height and freedom through years of cultivation and like a dissonant stroke on the lyre become ever more tender, pure and refined as they die away. But one will notice in them the imitation of the spirit, as one does the imitation of parts in talent.

Let no one distinguish too boldly. Every spirit is Corinthian brass, fused out of ruins and known metals in some unknown way. If peoples can grow straight upward and to a great height against the wall of the present, why not spirits, against the past? To mark off spirits is to change space into rooms and to measure the columns of air above, whose capitals cannot be separated from ether.

Are there not spiritual hybrids, first of *periods*, then of *countries?* And as two periods or two countries can be related at two poles, are there not extremes of both bad and good? The bad I will pass over. The German-French, the Jewish-Germans, the Papists, the Grecizers, in short the spiritual mediators of the lack of spirit are at hand in too glaring numbers. Let us turn rather to the geniuses and half-geniuses! As a mediator between *countries* we can cite Lichtenberg, whose prose is an intellectual link between England and Germany. Pope is an alley crossing between London and Paris. Voltaire binds the two cities from the opposite direction on a higher level. Schiller is, if not the chord, still the dominant note between British and German poetry, on the whole a Young raised to a higher power and transfigured, with a preponderance of the philosophical and dramatic.

As a mediator between *periods* (which, of course, become *countries* in turn),

Tieck is a fine baroque, flowering hybrid of ancient and modern Germany, although he is more closely related to the genial receivers than to the givers. Wieland[10] is an orange tree bearing French blossoms and German fruit at the same time. Goethe's tall tree puts down its roots in Germany and extends its canopy of blossoms over the Greek climate. Herder is a rich, blooming isthmus between the Orient and Greece.

Now, following the regular course of nature, in whose fords and ferries the stream can never be distinguished from the shore we have finally arrived among the active geniuses.

On Genius

§*11.* *The Multiplicity of Its Strengths*

The belief in an instinctive, single faculty of genius could only arise and endure through a confusion of philosophical or poetic genius with the artistic instinct of the virtuoso. Painters, musicians, even the mechanic, must be endowed with an organ which supplies reality to them both as object and as tool of their artistic presentation. The predominance of one organ and one faculty, e.g., in Mozart, works then with the blindness and certainty of instinct.

Anyone who locates genius, the best thing the earth possesses, the awakener of slumbering centuries, in a 'marked strength of the lower psychological faculties', and who can imagine a genius lacking in understanding, as Adelung[11] does in his book on style, certainly is lacking in understanding. Our age presents me with every possible challenge to battle with sinners against the holy ghost. Shakespeare, Schiller, et al. distribute all the individual faculties among their individual characters, and often they must be within a single page witty, discerning, understanding, rational, fiery, learned, everything just so that the splendour of those faculties can shine like jewels, not like a candle-end lighting up poverty! Only the one-sided talent gives a single tone like a piano string struck by the hammer. Genius is like a string of an aeolian harp; one and the same string resounds in manifold tones in the manifold breezes. In genius[d] all faculties are in bloom at once, and imagination is not the flower, but the flower-goddess, who arranges the flower calyxes with their mingling pollens for new hybrids, as if she were the faculty of faculties. The existence of this harmony and of this harmonizer is demanded and guaranteed by two great phenomena of genius.

§*12.* *Reflectiveness*

The first is *reflectiveness*. It implies at every level a balance and a tension between activity and passivity, between subject and object. At its lowest level, which distinguishes man from animal, and waking from sleeping, it demands an equilibrium between inner and outer worlds. In the animal the external world swallows up the inner; in the man moved by passion, often the inner swallows up the external world. Then there is a higher reflectiveness which divides and separates the inner world itself into two parts, into a self and its realm, into a creator and his world. This divine reflectiveness is as far from the common kind as reason is from understanding, for these are their respective parents. The ordinary active reflectiveness is directed only outward, and is in the higher sense of the term always outside, never within itself. Its possessors have awareness rather than self-awareness, which is like a man's double contemplation of his complete self by facing one mirror and turning away from a second. The reflectiveness of genius differs so much from the other kind that it often appears as its very opposite. Like a burial lamp, this eternally burning lamp within is extinguished, if *outside* air and world touch it.[c] But what are the means of attaining it? Equality presupposes freedom more than freedom presupposes equality. The inner freedom of reflectiveness is secured and granted through the alternation and movement of great faculties, so that no single faculty can by dominating become an inferior self. The self is excited and calmed in such a way that the creator is never lost in the creation.

The poet, like the philosopher, is therefore an eye. All his pillars are pier-glasses. His is the free flight of a flame, not the explosion of an emotion-sprung mine. The wildest poet can therefore be a gentle man; one need only look into Shakespeare's heavenly clear face or, even better, into his great dramatic epic. Conversely, a man can be sold in the slave market of the moment every minute, yet raise himself gently and freely by writing poetry. Thus in the storm of his personality Guido Reni[13] rounded and curled his mild heads of children and angels, like the sea which despite its currents and waves breathes a calm clear dawn and sunset towards heaven. Only the foolish youth can believe that the fire of genius burns like that of emotion, as the bust of Bacchus is passed off for the bust of the soberly poetic Plato. Alfieri,[14] who was always moved to the point of vertigo, found at the expense of his creations less repose within than without himself. The true genius is calm from within; not the upheaving wave but the smooth deep mirrors the world.

This reflectiveness of the poet, which we are inclined to presuppose also among philosophers, confirms the kinship of the two. In few poets and philosophers does it shine as brightly as in Plato, who was in fact both, from the clear-cut characterizations of his dialogues to his hymns and ideas, those constellations of a subterranean heaven. If we consider the reflective playful criticism with which Socrates dissects the eulogy to love in the *Phaedrus*, which condemns all our rhetorics, we can comprehend why twenty beginnings of the *Republic* were found after his death. The repose of genius is like the so-called 'unrest' or balance wheel in a watch, which works only to *moderate*, and hence to maintain the motion. What did our great Herder with his acumen, profundity, versatility and breadth of vision, lack in order to become a higher poet? Only the ultimate aspect of similarity to Plato; his steering tail-feathers (*pennae rectrices*) should have been in more just proportion to his flight feathers (*remiges*).

It is a misunderstanding and a prejudice to infer from this reflectiveness any limits to the poet's enthusiasm. For he must simultaneously cast flames upon the least detail and apply a thermometer to the flames; he must in the battle heat of all his faculties maintain the subtle balance of single syllables and must (to use another metaphor) lead the stream of his perceptions to the debouchment of a rhyme. Inspiration produces only the whole; calmness produces the parts. After all, does the philosopher, for instance, offend the god within because he tries to mount one vantage point after another as best he can in order to look into his inner light? Is philosophizing about the conscience without conscience? If reflectiveness as such could become excessive, then the reflective man would indeed be inferior to the senseless animal and the unreflective child; and the Infinite One, who although incomprehensible to us, cannot be anything which he does not know, would be inferior to the finite!

A certain understanding and judgment must, however, precede and underlie that misunderstanding and prejudgment. For according to Jacobi[15] man respects only what cannot be imitated mechanically; but reflectiveness always appears to imitate, wilfully and hypocritically to simulate divine inspiration and feeling and hence to cancel them out. Illustrations of an evil presence of mind need not be sought in the thought, poetry, and activity of the vacuous solipsists of the present day; the ancient learned world offers us a wealth of examples, above all in the field of rhetoric and the humanities, with their insolent cold instructions for presenting the finest feelings, like reflective skeletons taken from the grave. With self-satisfaction and vainglorious coldness, for example, the old pedagogue selects and moves the necessary muscles and tear glands (according to Peucer or Morhof)[16] in order to have a lachrymose mourning face for the benefit of the public when he looks down from the school window in making a threnody on the grave of his predecessor, while he complacently counts every drop with a rain gauge.

But how is divine distinguished from sinful reflectiveness? By the instinct of the unconscious and the love for it.

§13. *Human Instinct*

The greatest power in the poet, breathing the good or the bad soul into his works, is precisely the unconscious. Therefore a great poet like Shakespeare will open up and distribute treasures as invisible to him as the heart in his body. For divine wisdom is always completely *immersed* upon the sleeping plant and animal instinct, and is *expressed* in the mobile soul. In general, reflectiveness does not see sight, but only the mirrored or dissected eye; and the reflection does not reflect itself. If we were completely aware of ourselves, then we would be our own creators, unlimited. An inextinguishable feeling within us places something dark, which is not our creation but rather our creator, above all our creations. So we come before God, as he commanded on Sinai, with a veil over our eyes.

If one dares to speak about the unconscious and unfathomable, one can undertake to determine only its existence, not its depth. In the following discussion, happily, I can plough with the Pegasi of Plato and Jacobi, although for the sake of my own seed.

Instinct or impulse is the sense of the future; it is blind, but only as the ear is blind to light and the eye deaf to sound. It signifies and contains its object just as the effect does the cause. If the secret were revealed to us, of how an effect which is necessarily given entirely and simultaneously with its cause nevertheless only follows the cause, then we would also understand how the instinct at the same time demands, determines, knows, and yet lacks its object. Every feeling of a deficiency supposes a relationship to that which is lacking and thus supposes its partial possession.[f] But only a true deficiency makes possible the impulse toward it, only distance allows direction. There are spiritually organic mutualisms, just as there are physically organic mutualisms; freedom and necessity, for example, or willing and thinking presuppose each other.

There is in the pure self as much a sense of the future, or an instinct, as there is in the impure self and in an animal, and its object is at once as remote as it is certain. Otherwise in the very heart of man the general truthfulness of nature would have lied for the first time. This instinct of the spirit – which eternally anticipates and demands its objects without consideration for time, because they exist beyond it – is what makes it possible for man to pronounce and understand the words *earthly*, *worldly*, *temporal*, and the like. For only that instinct gives them meaning through their opposites. If even the most ordinary man sees life and everything earthly as only a *piece*, as a *part*, then only a perception and assumption of a *whole* within him can posit and measure this partition. Even for the most ordinary realist, whose ideas and days crawl along on caterpillar feet and in caterpillar rings, something inexpressible limits the breadth of life. He is impelled to proclaim this life to be a game, confused and bestial, or painful and deceptive, or an empty *pastime*. Or like the older theologians, he compares it with a vulgar comic prologue to the heavenly, earnest play, or with a childish school for a future throne. He thus considers it the opposite of the future. In earthly, even earthy hearts, there is already something alien, like the coral islands in the Harz mountains which the earliest waters of creation may have deposited.

It matters little what names or attributes one assigns this supramundane angel of the inner life, this death-angel of the worldly in man. It is enough to recognize him in his disguises. Sometimes he shows himself to men wrapped deep in guilt and flesh as a being whose *aspect* but not *actions*, *horrifies* us. We call the feeling a fear of ghosts. And the common people say simply, 'The *shape*, the *thing* makes itself heard.' Indeed, to express the infinite, they often say simply: 'It.' Sometimes the spirit manifests himself as the infinite one and man prays. If this spirit did not exist, we would be content with the gardens of the earth. But he points out to us the true paradises in deep heavens. He draws aside the rosy sunset before the romantic realm, and we see into glimmering moonlit lands full of nightflowers, nightingales, sparks, fairies, and gambols.

He it was who first gave mankind religion – fear of death – Greek fate – superstition – and prophecy[g] – and thirst for love – belief in the devil – romanticism – the whole embodied spiritual world – as well as Greek mythology, the deified physical world.

What will the instinct, divine even in an ordinary soul, now develop into and accomplish in a soul of genius?

§14. *The Instinct or Material of Genius*

Since the other faculties are more elevated in a genius, the heavenly faculty must be raised above them all, like a transparent pure ice cap above the dark earthly Alps. It is this brighter splendour of the supernal drive which casts that light called reflectiveness through the whole soul. The momentary victory over the earthly, over its objects and our penchants for them, is a characteristic of the divine in a war of destruction without possibility of treaty. As something infinite, the moral spirit in us recognizes nothing outside itself as great. When everything has been levelled and made equal, a reflective survey is easy.

It may now be easier to settle the dispute whether poetry requires matter or reigns only with form. Certainly there is an *external mechanical* matter with which reality, both external and psychological, surrounds and often encumbers us. Without the refinement of form this is a matter of indifference to poetry. It is nothing at all. It does not matter whether the empty soul celebrates a Christ or his betrayer, Judas.

But surely there is something nobler than the cycle of everyday experience. There is an *inner* matter, an innate, involuntary poetry as it were, for which the form provides not the foil but the frame. The so-called categorical imperative (the image of form, as the external act is the image of the external matter) only shows the psyche the fork in the road but cannot harness for her the white horse which overtakes the black. The psyche herself can indeed guide and train the white horse but cannot create it. The case is the same with the Muses' Pegasus, which is ultimately the white horse, only with wings. This inner matter constitutes the originality of genius which the imitator seeks in mere form and manner. At the same time it generates the equality of geniuses, for there is only *one* divinity, but there are many kinds of humanity. Jacobi finds the philosophical profundity (but not acumen) of all times to be *concentric*; similarly poetic geniuses are like stars, which when they first rise seem to be far apart, but when on high, at the zenith of time, draw close together. One hundred lights in a single room produce only a single concentrated light but one hundred shadows (imitators). The imitator repels, even embitters us not by a theft of witty, figurative, sublime thoughts from his model – for not infrequently his thoughts are his own – but by his miming, often involuntarily approaching parody, of what is holiest in the original, the innate. This adoption of the Holy of Holies from another cannot replace parental warmth. The imitator therefore expresses his warmth for the secondary matters, for which he has more affinity, and multiplies there his embellishments – the colder, the more decorated. Thus the cold sun of Siberia is encircled all day with many secondary suns and rings.

The heart of the genius, which all the ornamental and auxiliary faculties only serve, has and presents a single genuine distinguishing mark, namely an original view of the world and of life. Talent presents only parts. Genius presents the whole of life, down to individual aphorisms, which in Shakespeare often speak of *time* and *world*; in Homer and other Greeks, of *mortals*; in Schiller, of *life*. The higher kind of world-view, constant and eternal in author and man, remains invariable, while all individual faculties can change and sink in the lassitudes of life and of time. Indeed, even as a child the genius must have assimilated the new world with feelings different from those of others and have spun from these the web of future flowers in another way, because without the earlier difference none would be thinkable in the adult. *One* melody runs through all the stanzas of the song of life. The poet creates only the external form in the tension of the moment; but the spirit and matter he carries through half a life, and either every one of this thoughts is a poem, or none is.

Like every spirit, this world spirit of the genius animates all the members of a work, without inhabiting a single one. It can make the charm of form superfluous through its own higher charm; the genius of a Goethe, for example, would still speak to us in his imperial prose as well as in his most careless poem. When a single sun is up, it can show time with a pin as well as with an obelisk. This is the spirit which never offers proofs,[h] but only itself and its point of view; it then relies upon kindred spirits and looks down on those that are hostile.

Fate thrusts a deformed form upon many a divine soul, like the Satyr's body on Socrates; for time rules over the form, not over the inner matter. Thus the poetic mirror with which Jakob Boehme[17] reflected heaven and earth hung in a dark place; and the glass had lost its foil in some places. Thus the great Hamann[18] is a deep sky full of telescopic stars; many nebulae there no eye can resolve.

For this reason many rich works have seemed to the stylist (who digs only for bodies, not for spirits) as poor as the majestic, lofty Swiss mountains seem to a miner in comparison with deep mines. The stylist says he can draw and extract little or nothing from works of this kind; which is as much as if he complained that he could gain with and from friendship nothing more than *friendship* itself. There can be philosophic works, like some by Hemsterhuis and Lessing, which inspire us with philosophic spirit without disposing their matter in separate philosophical paragraphs. This same reflective Lessing, who earlier had thought rather than sung about poetic objects, received the poetic whitsun spirit only in his *Nathan* and his *Falk*, a pair of works which the common critic, who prefers *Emilia Galotti*, tolerantly attributes to his old age. Of course, the poetic soul shows itself, like ours, only in the whole body, not in the single toes and fingers it animates, which a collector of specimens would tear off and hold out to view with the words: See how the spider's leg is twitching!

§15. *The Ideal of Genius*

If the ordinary man feels virtuous, then like every Christian in the past, he links by his faith this gross life directly to a second ethereal life after death. This fits the gross life as spirit does the body, yet is so little tied to it by *pre-established harmony*, *influence*, and *opportunity* that at first the body alone appears and governs, and only afterwards the spirit. The further any being stands from the centre, the greater the space he sees between the radii. A mute, hollow polyp, if he were to express himself, would surely find more contradictions in creation than any human seafarer.

And so one finds among the common people the inner and the outer world, time and eternity, as moral or Christian antitheses. In the philosopher these appear as a continued contrast, only with an alternating destruction of one world through the other; in the better man they appear as an alternating eclipse, like that which governs moon and earth; in the Janus-head of the man who faces opposite worlds, now one pair of eyes is closed or covered, now the other.

If, however, there are men in whom the instinct of the divine speaks more clearly and loudly than in others; if it teaches them to contemplate the earthly (instead of the earthly teaching them to contemplate it); if it provides and controls the perception of the whole; then will harmony and beauty stream back from both worlds and make them into *one* whole, for there is only *unity* before the divine and no contradiction in parts. That is genius; and the reconciliation of the two worlds is the so-called *ideal*. Only through *maps of heaven* can *maps of earth* be made; only viewed from above (for the view from below eternally divides heaven with the broad earth) does the whole sphere of heaven appear, and the sphere of earth itself will swim therein, small perhaps, but round and shining. For this reason, mere talent, which always degrades the divine world to a satellite or at most to the saturn-ring of an earthly world, can never round out any universe ideally or replace or build it with parts. When the old men of prose, petrified and full of earth[i] like men physically old, let us see poverty, the struggle of everyday existence or even its victories, we begin to feel as cramped and troubled at the sight as if we actually had to experience the adversity. One actually does experience the picture and its effect; their pain and even their joy lack a heaven. They trample down even the sublime in reality: love, friendship, and the grave, for example (as their funeral orations show), or the process of dying, this life between two worlds. In the wound-fever of reality, let us avoid those who would inoculate a new fever into the old by painting our wounds with their prosaic poetry, who make true poems necessary as antidotes to their false ones.

When, on the contrary, genius leads us over the battlefields of life, we survey them as freely as if glory or patriotism marched before us with flags fluttering behind; and next to genius poverty takes on an Arcadian form, as for a pair of lovers. Everywhere genius makes life free and death beautiful; on his sphere, as on the sea, we catch sight of the driving sails before the heavy ship. Like love and youth, he thus reconciles – indeed he weds – helpless life with ethereal sense, as at the edge of still water the real tree and its reflection seems to grow from a single root toward two heavens.

On Humorous Poetry

§31.   Concept of Humour

By our definition romantic poetry, as opposed to plastic poetry, delights in presenting the infinity of the subject in which the object-world loses its limits as in a kind of moonlight. But how will the comic become romantic, since it consists merely in contrasting the finite with the finite and cannot allow any infinity? The understanding and the object-world know only finitude. In the romantic we find only that infinite contrast between the ideas (or reason) and all finitude itself. But suppose just this finitude were imputed and lent as *subjective* contrast to the idea (infinity) as *objective* contrast, and, instead of the sublime as an applied infinity, now produced a finitude applied to the infinite, and thus simply infinity of contrast, that is a negative infinity.

Then we should have humour or the romantic comic.

And so it happens in fact; and the understanding, although the atheist of an absolute infinity, must here face a contrast extending into infinity. To prove this, I will further differentiate the four components of humour.

§32.   Humorous Totality

Humour as the inverted sublime annihilates not the individual but the finite through its contrast with the idea. It recognizes no individual foolishness, no fools, but only folly and a mad world. Unlike the common joker with his innuendoes, humour does not elevate individual imbecility but lowers the great. It does so like parody, but with a different goal: to set the small beside the great. Humour raises the small like irony, but then sets the great beside the small. Humour thus annihilates both great and small, because before infinity everything is equal and nothing. 'Vive la bagatelle', the half-mad Swift cries sublimely, who at the end of his life preferred both to read and to compose bad works, because in this concave mirror foolish finitude, the enemy of the idea, appeared to him most tattered. In these bad books which he read and wrote, he enjoyed his own thoughts. The common satirist may on his travels or in his reviews pick up a few genuine examples of tastelessness and other faults and fix them on his pillory, to throw a few salty conceits at them instead of rotten eggs. The humorist, however, would almost rather take individual folly into protection, while taking the constable of the pillory together with all the spectators into custody; it is not civic folly but human folly, the universal that touches him within. His thyrsus-staff is no baton and no scourge; its blows are accidental. In Goethe's *Annual Fair at Plundersweilern* one must seek the goal either in specific satires on drovers, actors, and the like, which is absurd, or in the epic grouping and scorn of all earthly activity. Uncle Toby's campaigns do not make Toby himself or Louis XIV alone ridiculous; they are the allegory of all human hobbyhorses. There is a child's head kept in every man's head as in a hatbox, which at times still pops out into the open air despite any number of inner cases, and which in our old age often appears by itself with silver hair.

This totality can be expressed not only through the great antithesis of life itself but through its symbolic parts; in Gozzi, Sterne, Voltaire, or Rabelais, for example, the world-humour succeeds not *by means of* but *in spite of* its contemporary allusions. The unique Shakespeare stands out here with his gigantic limbs; behind the mad mask of Hamlet and some of the melancholy fools, he carries on this ridicule of the world to the highest degree. Cervantes, whose genius was too great for a lengthy joke about an accidental derangement and a common simplicity, draws perhaps with less awareness than Shakespeare the humorous parallel between realism and idealism, between body and soul, in the face of the infinite equation; and his twin stars of folly hover above the entire human race. Swift's *Gulliver*, in style less humorous, in spirit more so than his *Tale of a Tub*, stands high on the Tarpeian Rock from which the author cast down the human race. In simple, lyrical, self-contemplative outpourings, Leibgeber[19] paints his world-humour without ever touching or blaming the individual. His friend Siebenkäs does this much more, and I would therefore ascribe to him more whimsy than humour. Tieck's humour stands before us pure, engaged in broad survey, even if too much modelled after others and in need of a greater abundance of wit. Rabener,[20] on the contrary, scourges many a fool in the electorate of Saxony, and the reviewers scourge many a humorist in Germany.

If Friedrich Schlegel is right in maintaining that the romantic is not a species of poetry, but that poetry must always be romantic,[21] then the same is even more true of the comic; all comic poetry must become romantic, i.e., humorous. In their burlesques, dramas, parodies, and the like, the students of the new aesthetic school show a higher comic world spirit which is not the denunciator and gallows priest of individual fools, even though this world spirit is often expressed rudely and roughly enough when the student still sits in the lower classes with his imitation and his written examination. But true taste is offended far more by Bahrdt, Cranz, Wezel, Merkel,[22] and most of the contributors to the *Universal German Library*,[23] whose comic attractions represent mostly false tendencies, than by Tieck, Kerner, Kanne, Arnim, Görres, Brentano, Weisser, Bernhardi, Franz Horn, Stephan Schütze, Ernst Wagner, et al.,[24] whose comic blisters and grease spots and freckles are often only excesses of the right tendency. As self-parodist of his own parody, the false mocker with his presumptuous pretensions is much more repulsive to us than the false sentimentalist with his modest pretence of moving us. When Sterne was first exported to Germany, he created and trailed a long watery comet-tail of what were then called humorists (now unnamed) who were nothing but jolly complacent blabbers; I would gladly allow them the name of humorist in a comic sense, as I would allow the same name in a medical sense to the Galenists[25] who locate all ills in vapours (*humores*). Although Wieland in his poetry is a genuine comedian, in his prose romances and especially in the notes to his *Danischmend* and *Amadis* he has strayed far into the Galenist academy of humorists.

Humorous totality takes many forms. It is expressed, for example, in the structure of Sterne's periods, which bind with dashes not parts, but wholes. It will be expressed in any generalization from something which is strictly true only in a particular case; for example, in Sterne, 'Learned men, brother Toby, don't write dialogues upon long noses for nothing.' The common critic suffocates and materializes the truly humorous world spirit by contracting and confining it in partisan satires. Because he does not possess the buttress of the comic, namely the world-scorning Idea, this insignificant critic must consider the comic unfounded, even childish and purposeless, and almost laughable in its laughter; secretly but enthusiastically he must prefer the specious whimsy of Müller from Itzehoe[26] to the humour of Shandy, in more than one respect. Although Lichtenberg praised Müller (who may deserve it for his *Siegfried von Lindenberg*, at least in the first edition), and also, like a funeral orator, praised the Berlin wags and fireflies of his day too highly, and although he was somewhat constrained by a British and mathematical one-sidedness, he was still raised by his humorous faculties higher than he really knew. With his astronomical view of worldly activity and with his witty superabundance, Lichtenberg might perhaps have been able to show something better to the world than two wings in the ether which indeed move, but whose feathers are stuck together.

This totality of humour, furthermore, explains the mildness and tolerance of humour tówards individual follies, because such follies in the mass are less significant and less harmful and because the humorist cannot deny his own kinship with humanity. The common mocker recognizes and reckons up only individual, abderitic[27] traits of both vulgar and learned existence, because they are alien to himself. He is narrowly and selfishly aware of his own superiority. And fancying that he rides as a hippocentaur through onocentaurs, he delivers from his horse that much the wilder a capuchin sermon against folly, like a matin and vesper preacher in this insane asylum of the earth. O what a difference between him and the man who simply laughs at everything, without excluding either the hippocentaur or himself!

But in the context of this general mockery, how is the humorist who warms the soul distinguished from the persifleur who chills it, since both laugh at everything? Shall the humorist, rich in feeling, be a neighbour of the cold persifleur who shows off only his lack of sensibility?[k] Impossible. The first is distinguished from the second as Voltaire from himself or from the rest of the French, by the annihilating idea.

§33. *The Annihilating or Infinite Idea of Humour*

This is the second component of humour as inverse sublimity. Whereas Luther calls our will a *lex inversa* [law of inverting] in an unfavourable sense, humour is a *lex inversa* in a good sense, and its descent to hell paves its way for an ascent to heaven. It is like the bird Merops, which indeed turns its tail towards heaven but still flies in this position up to heaven. This juggler, while dancing on his head, drinks his nectar *upwards*.

When man looks down, as ancient theology did, from the supernal world to the earthly world, it seems small and vain in the distance; when he measures out the small world, as humour does, against the infinite world and sees them together, a kind of laughter results which contains pain and greatness. Whereas Greek poetry, unlike modern poetry, made men cheerful, humour, in contrast to the ancient jest, makes men partly serious; it walks on the low *soccus*,[28] but often with the tragic mask, at least in its hand. For this reason not only have great humorists been very serious men, as said before, but the best come from a melancholy people. The ancients loved life too much to scorn it humorously. An underlying earnestness is indicated in the old German farces by the fact that the devil is generally the clown; even in the French farces a *grande diablerie* appears, a buffooning quadruple alliance of four devils. This is a significant idea! I can easily think of the devil, the true reversed world of the divine world, the great world-shadow which marks off the contours of the lightbody, as the greatest humorist and 'whimsical man!' But as the *arabesque* of an arabesque, he would be far too unaesthetic; his laugh would have too much pain; it would be like the colourful flowery garment of the – guillotined.

After all intense pathos man naturally craves humorous relaxation. Since no feeling can desire its opposite, but only its own mitigation, there must be a transitional element of seriousness in the jest which pathos seeks. And this is found in humour. Even in Kalidasa's Sanskrit drama *Sakuntala*, as in Shakespeare, there is a court jester, Madhawya. In Plato's *Symposium* Socrates argues that the genius of tragedy is the same as that of comedy. The Englishman adds to his tragedy a humorous epilogue and a comedy. Similarly in the Greek tetralogy the serious trilogy was followed by a satiric drama (Schiller began with it),[1] and the parodists began their song after the rhapsodists. In the old French mysteries, when a martyr or a Christ was to be scourged, the old tenderness and goodness of heart interpolated this advice: 'Here let Harlequin come on and speak, to cheer things up a bit again.' But would anyone ever want to be let down suddenly from the height of pathos to Lucian or Parisian persiflage? Mercier[29] says: 'For the public to watch the sublimity of a Leander without laughing, it must be permitted to expect as sequel the comic Bajazzo, with which it can kindle and thus release the laughable matter won from the sublime.' The observation is fine and true; only what a double degradation of the sublime and of humour at once, if the former relaxes and the latter stimulates! A heroic poem is easy to parody and to transform into its opposite; but woe to a tragedy which does not continue to have its effect even in its parody! One can travesty Homer, but not Shakespeare; for the trivial is indeed destructively opposed to the sublime, but not to the pathetic. When to accompany his travestied *Ariadne on Naxos* Kotzebue[30] proposes the music which Benda wrote for the serious play by Gotter,[31] he forgets that the festive earnestness of such music, armed with the powers of pathos and the sublime, would not serve but would conquer his burlesque. Like a serious goddess it would hurl the comic Ariadne more than once from a greater height than that of Naxos. Much more sublimity arises from a simply low style, as in Thümmel's *Universal Tragedy or Paradise Lost*,[32] and everyone feels truth and untruth, the divine and human nature of man, working there with equal force.

In the title of this chapter I called the Idea 'annihilating'. This is demonstrated everywhere. In general, reason dazzles the understanding with light (e.g., by the idea of an infinite divinity), as a god dazzles, prostrates, and forcibly subverts finitude. Humour does the same; unlike persiflage, humour abandons the understanding and permits it to fall down piously before the Idea. Therefore humour often delights even in contradictions and impossibilities, for example in Tieck's *Zerbino*, in which the *dramatis personae* finally believe themselves to be merely fictive nonentities, thus drawing the audience themselves onto the stage and the stage under the press jack.[m] Hence comes that fondness of humour for the emptiest conclusions, while the serious closes epigrammatically with the most important, for example, the conclusion of the preface to Möser's *Defence of Harlequin*[34] or the pitiful conclusion of the funeral oration (by Fenk[35] of myself) on a prince's stomach. Thus, for example, Sterne several times speaks lengthily and reflectively about certain incidents, until in the end he concludes: 'All the same, 'tis not a word of it true.'

Something similar to the audacity of annihilating humour, an expression of scorn for the world, can be perceived in a good deal of music, like that of Haydn, which destroys entire tonal sequences by introducing an extraneous key and storms alternately between pianissimo and fortissimo, presto and andante. Scepticism is also similar to humour; according to Platner[36] it arises when the mind's eye surveys a frightful mass of conflicting opinions around it. It is a kind of psychic vertigo which suddenly transforms *our* own rapid motion into an *external* one affecting the whole steady world.

A third analogy appears in the humorous feasts of fools of the Middle Ages, which with a free hysteronproteron, an inner spiritual masquerade innocent of any impure purpose, reversed the worldly and the spiritual, inverted social ranks and moral values, and reduced all to one great equality and freedom of joy. For such life-humour, our taste is not so much too refined nowadays as our disposition is too corrupt.

§34. *Humorous Subjectivity*

In both its serious and comic forms romanticism is the ruler of subjectivity, as opposed to classic objectivity. The comic itself consists in the alternating contrast of the subjective and objective principles. We have defined the objective principle as a desired infinity; this I cannot conceive and posit *outside* myself, but only within myself, where I ground it upon the subjective principle. Consequently I place myself in this breach. But I do not assume the standpoint of another, as I do in comedy. Rather, I divide my inner self into the finite and infinite factors and let the latter proceed from the former. People laugh then, saying, 'Impossible! Much too mad!' Quite so! For every humorist the self plays the first role; when he can, he even introduces his personal circumstances upon the comic stage, although he does so only to annihilate it poetically. The humorist is both his own court jester or quartet of masked Italian comedians and at the same time their prince and director. The reader must at least bring no hatred but some love for the writer's persona, whose semblance must not be made into being. The best reader of the best author would be one who could thoroughly enjoy a humorous lampoon on himself. Readers must show as much open hospitality towards every poet, especially the comic poet, as conversely militant reserve towards the philosopher, to the advantage of both. Even in physical reality hatred with its web closes the entrance to the lightly winged jest; a good-humoured, open reception is still more necessary for the comic poet, who with his assumed artistic distortion cannot cheerfully animate his personality, if it is weighed down and reinforced by the prosaic, hating personality of his audience. When Swift pretends to be crafty and arrogant and Musäus[37] pretends to be dumb, how shall they expect to produce a comic effect on the disaffected reader who meets their semblance with belief? The comic writer wins obliging love only if he can gain a certain confidence which he, as the ever new portrayer of ever new deviations, needs far more for reconciliation than does the serious poet of millennial feelings and beauties. This readily explains why the initial public did not really want to laugh at the higher comic works at which later centuries would laugh continuously, but faced them stupidly and seriously, while a common joke sheet of the day fluttered about from hand to hand, from mouth to ear. Cervantes, for example, had to denigrate and attack his *Don Quixote*, which was at first neglected, so that the multitude would praise it; he had to write a critique entitled 'El Buscapies' or 'The Rocket', so that he himself would not vanish like a rocket into the ether. Aristophanes was robbed of the prize for his two best plays, the *Frogs* and the *Clouds*, by a long forgotten Amipsias, who had on his side figurative Frog and Cloud choruses. At first Sterne's *Tristram Shandy* was received as coldly in England as if he had written it in Germany for Germans. A writer in the *German Mercury*, which usually spares everything of any vigour and indeed even lends it further wings, passes the following judgment on Musäus' *Physiognomic Journeys* (first volume): 'The style is à la Schubart[38] and is meant to be funny. It is impossible to get through, etc.' You wretch, who can still annoy me after so many years in this second edition, because I unfortunately excerpted your stupidity word for word to benefit aesthetics! Next to this wretch, did not a twin brother in the *Universal German Library* with similar incisors graze in Musäus' flowerbeds and root up the flowers of the very man who has genuine German humour, that paternalistic smile at oneself, whose good nature sweetens away any alien admixture of sentiment as a comic element?[n] More *exempla sunt odiosa*.

We return to humorous subjectivity. The pseudo-humorist is so disgusting, because he tries to *appear* to parody a nature already his own. Unless a noble nature reigns in the author, nothing is more awkward than to entrust the comic confession to the fool himself. When (as in Le Sage's mostly vulgar *Gil Blas*)[39] a vulgar soul, now penitent, now father confessor, vacillates arbitrarily between self-knowledge and delusion, between remorse and shamelessness, between indecisive laughter and seriousness, he puts us as well in this intermediate condition. In *Chevalier Mendoza* Pigault le Brun[40] becomes even more repulsive through his vanity and his bald and hackneyed lack of faith; even in Crébillon's[41] acerbity something higher is reflected than his fools. How great does the noble spirit of Shakespeare appear when he uses the humorous Falstaff as commentator of his wild life of sin! How Falstaff's immortality blends as mere weakness and habit with his fantastic folly!

Just as reprehensible as the pseudo-humorist is Erasmus' self-critic, Folly: first, she is an empty, abstract self, i.e., a non-self; and second, instead of lyric humour or strict irony she recites only from the primers of Wisdom, who shouts even louder from the prompter's box than Columbine herself.

Since in humour the self is displayed parodically, several Germans dispensed twenty-five years ago with the first person pronoun 'ich' in order to emphasize it the more strongly through linguistic ellipsis. A better author has struck out the first person again in a parody of this parody, with thick, conspicuous strokes; he is the delightful Musäus, whose *Physiognomic Journeys* are true picturesque excursions of Comus and the reader. Soon afterwards the suppressed 'I's rose up again from the dead *en masse* in Fichtean aseity,[42] egoism, and a din of vowels. Why do only German jests have this grammatical suicide of the first person pronoun, but neither the related modern languages, nor the ancient? Probably because we are too polite, like the Persians and the Turks,[o] to have a first person before respectable people. For a German is glad to be anything except *himself*. While the Briton capitalizes his 'I' in the middle of a sentence, many Germans still write theirs small at the beginning of letters and wish in vain for a small italic *i* which would barely be visible and which would be more like the mathematical dot above than the line below. While the Briton always adds the 'self' to 'my', and the Frenchman 'même' to 'moi', the German only seldom says 'I myself' (*Ich selber*), but gladly 'I for my part' (*ich meines Orts*), which he hopes no one will interpret as unusual pomposity. In earlier times he never named himself from foot to navel without begging pardon for existing, so that he always carried about the polite half fit for company and church on a pitiful plebeian half as if on an organic pillory. If he boldly introduces the first person, the German does so when he can join it to a smaller one; the headmaster of the high school says modestly to the students 'we'. In addition, only the German possesses 'he' (*Er*) and 'they' (*Sie*) as forms of address; he can always thereby exclude the self which 'thou' and 'you' imply. There have been times when perhaps in all of Germany no letter passed through the mails containing the word 'I'. More fortunate than the French and British, whose languages allow no pure grammatical *inversion*, we Germans make the grammatical into a spiritual inversion, putting the most important first and the insignificant afterwards: 'Your Excellency', a German can write, 'am reporting or dedicating hereby.' Modern ages are allowed (perhaps as one of the fruits of the Revolution) to write directly: 'Your Excellency, *I* report, *I* dedicate.' Thus generally a weak but clear '*I*' is allowed in the middle of a letter or speech, but very reluctantly at the beginning and end.

This peculiarity now makes it uncommonly easy for us to be more comic than any other people. In humorous parody we poetically represent ourselves as fools and must therefore conceive ourselves to be such. By this very omission of the self, we can make the humorous self-reference not only, as said above, clearer, but also more ridiculous. For we are familiar with such an omission only in serious, polite cases.

This humour of the self extends even to small parts of speech. 'Je *m*'étonne, je *me* tais', for example, means more than 'I am surprised' or 'I am silent.' Bode[43] often therefore translates 'myself' and 'himself' into German by 'Ich *selber*' or 'er *selber*'. Since in Latin the first person is hidden in the verb, it can only be emphasized by participles, as Doctor Arbuthnot did in concluding his *Virgilius Restauratus* directed against Bentley: '*majora moliturus*' [about to undertake greater things].[44]

This function and implication of the parodic first person refutes the delusion that humour must be unconscious and involuntary. Home[45] ranks Addison and Arbuthnot above Swift and La Fontaine in humorous talent, because he believes the latter two possessed only an innate unconscious humour. But if humour is not the product of free intention, it cannot give as much aesthetic pleasure to the author in creating as to the reader; a writer who was such an innate anomaly would necessarily imagine all rational men to be humorists, and, although captain, would be the craziest passenger on his own ship of fools. Is it not clear from Sterne's earlier, youthful essays or from his latest ones, which are sketches for greater works, and from his colder letters, a form into which usually the stream of nature is first to flow, that his wonderful creations did not spring from the accidental flow and dissolution of lead into the ink, but that he sharpened and rounded them off intentionally in casting pits and forms? In the comic enthusiasm of Aristophanes we do not perceive his industrious research and his toil at night, which like that of Demosthenes even became proverbial.[P] Certainly much that is voluntary about humour can eventually become instinctive, just as the pianist's thoroughbass eventually comes not from his mind but his fingers, which really improvise while their owner skims through a book.⁹ The enjoyment of the highest form of the ridiculous conceals the smaller form, to which then the writer becomes accustomed half in jest, half in earnest. In the poet foolishness is as much the result of free will as is cynicism. Swift was known for a cleanliness so great that he once put nothing in the hand of a beggarwoman because it was unwashed, and still better known for his more than Platonic celibacy, which for him and for Newton at last passed into the impotence of sinners, according to biographers. Nevertheless he wrote Swift's *Works*, including both the 'Lady's Dressing-room' and 'Strephon and Chloe'. Aristophanes, Rabelais, Fischart,⁴⁶ and in general the old German comic writers also come to mind; their immortality on paper did not derive from any in life and did not lead to any. In genuine comic presentation there is as little *seductive* indecency as in anatomy. Is not comedy also dissection, only keener and more spiritual? Just as the bolt of lightning passes along the iron rod through gunpowder without igniting it, the comic flame, as mere wit, darts harmlessly down the comic rod through flammable sensuality. So much the worse, when the degeneracy of an age takes offence at harmless comic cynicism at the same time and to the same degree that it feasts on decorative, poisonous, erotic pictures. According to Bechstein⁴⁷ the porcupine (image of the satirist) likes to eat 'Spanish flies', yet is not poisoned by them like other animals. The sybarite, as we know, seeks these cantharides for more than one kind of poison and builds Spanish castles in the air on Spanish flies. We return.

A humorous character is an entity quite different from a humorous poet. The character is completely unconscious. He is ridiculous and serious, but he does not make others ridiculous; he can easily be the target, but not the rival of the poet. It is wholly false to attribute the Germans' lack of humorous poets to their lack of humorous fools; this would be explaining the rarity of wisemen through the rarity of simpletons. The true reason is the poverty and slavery of the true comic poetic spirit exhibited by the creating writers as well as the reading public, who know neither how to catch nor how to relish (enjoy) the privileged comic game which has been loosed and runs down from the Swiss mountains onto the Belgian plains. For the comic spirit thrives only on the open heath. One finds it wherever there is either inner freedom, among the young at universities or among old people, for example, or outer freedom, as in the very largest cities and in immense deserts, in manorial seats and in village parsonages, in free towns, among the rich, and in Holland. In private most men are originals; their wives know this. A passively humorous character is not in itself a satiric subject, for who would elaborate a satire or caricature about a single deformity? The deviation of the small human needle must be aligned with and indicate the deviation of the great earth-magnet. Thus old Shandy, however much he seems a portrait, is only the gaily painted plaster cast of all learned and philosophical pedantry;ʳ the same is true in other ways for Falstaff, Pistol, et al.

§35. *Humorous Sensuousness*

Since without sensuousness the comic cannot exist, the material element, as the exponent of applied finitude in humour, can never become too colourful. The representation should overflow with images and with witty and imaginative contrasts, both in grouping and in colouring. It should fill the soul with sensuousness and inflame it with that dithyramb⁵ which opposes the idea to the material world, distorted and distended in art's concave mirror into a long and angular shape. While the understanding can dwell only in a properly ordered world-building, reason, like God, is not enclosed even in the greatest temple. Insofar as such a Day of Judgment precipitates the material world into a second chaos, simply in order to hold divine judgment, humour would conceivably seem to approach madness, which naturally renounces the senses and common sense, as the philosopher does artificially, and yet like the philosopher retains reason; humour is a raving Socrates, as the ancients called Diogenes.

Let us analyse further the metamorphic sensuous style of humour. First, it individualizes to the smallest detail, even the parts of a subject already individualized. Shakespeare is never more individual, i.e. sensuous, than in comic scenes. Aristophanes is more individual and sensuous than any other ancient.

As has been shown above, the serious always emphasizes the general and so spiritualizes things that we think, for example, of a poetic heart at the sight of an anatomic one rather than the reverse. The comic writer, however, fastens our minds narrowly upon physical detail, and does not fall on his knee, for example, but on both kneepans; he can even use the knee hough. Take the sentence, 'Modern man does not love well, although he is not stupid but rather quite enlightened.' The comic writer or I must translate the man into sensuous life: into a European, still more specifically, into a man of the nineteenth century – and limit this again to a country or to a city. In Paris or Berlin he must find a street and plant the man there. He or I must then also organically animate the second part of the sentence (most quickly accomplished by an allegory). He may be lucky enough to hit upon a man from Friedrichstadt writing by lamplight in a diving bell without any roommate or bellfellow in the cold sea and tied to the world on the ship only by the lengthened air-pipe of his windpipe. 'And so', the comic writer may conclude, 'the man from Friedrichstadt sheds light on himself alone and on his paper, scorning the monsters and fish around him completely.' This scene is our translation of the sentence above.

Comic individuation could be pursued into minutiae. For example: The English love the hangman and being hanged; we Germans prefer the devil, but only as the comparative of the hangman. 'He is for the hangman,' may be expressed more strongly as 'He is gone to the devil.' There is the same difference between 'Be hanged!' and 'To the devil!' To peers one might write, 'May the devil take him', but to superiors this would have to be moderated by the hangman. Among the French the devil and dog stand higher. 'Le chien d'esprit que j'ai', writes the splendid Sévigné[49] (the French grandmother of Sterne, as Rabelais was his grandfather); like all French women she loves to use this animal. Similar sensuous details are: always to choose active verbs of motion, in figurative and literal presentation – to preface and conclude every action as Sterne and others do, even an internal one, with a brief physical action – always to give definite quantities in allusions to money, numbers, and all magnitudes, where one expects the indefinite: 'A chapter as long as my arm', or 'not worthy a curved farthing', etc. Comic sensuousness gains by the monosyllabic compression of the English language, as when Sterne says (*Tristram Shandy*, bk 11, chap. 10) that a French postilion has hardly mounted when he must dismount again, because there is always something missing about his coach: 'a tag, a rag, a jag, a strap'. These syllables, particularly their assonances, are not so easy to translate into German as the Horatian *ridiculus mus* [ridiculous mouse]. Assonances forged in the comic fire occur not only in Sterne (e.g., bk 7, chap. 31, 'all the frusts, crusts, and rusts of antiquity') but also in Rabelais, Fischart, and others, like next-door neighbours to rhymes.

The comic writer should also take advantage of proper names and technical terms. No German perceives the want of a national or capital city more sadly than one who laughs; for it hinders his individualization. 'Bedlam', 'Grubstreet', etc. pass current through all Great Britain and over the sea; we Germans on the contrary must substitute for these the general expressions 'madhouse', 'dirty writing-street', because without a national capital the proper names in the scattered cities are both too little known and less interesting. Thus it is fortunate for an individualizing humorist that Leipzig has a blackboard, an Auerbach's cellar, its Leipzig larks and fairs,[t] which are sufficiently well known abroad to be used with success. But the same familiarity would be desirable in more things and cities.

The paraphrase also belongs to humorous materiality, or the subdivision of subject and predicate, which can often be carried on endlessly. It is most easily copied from Sterne, who in turn most easily imitated Rabelais. When, for example, Rabelais' wants to say that Gargantua played, he begins (1, 22):

> La jouoit
> au flux
> à la prime
> à la vole
> à la pille
> à la triumphe
> à la picardie
> au cent –
> etc. etc.

He names two hundred and sixteen games. Fischart[u] even adduces five hundred and eighty-six games of children and society, which I counted up with much haste and boredom. This humorous paraphrase, which Fischart most often follows to the extreme, Sterne continues in his allegories, whose abundance of sensuous details ranks next to the luxuriant painting of Homeric similes and oriental metaphors. A similar colourful border or margin of alien details surrounds even his witty metaphors; the imitation of this boldness is *that* part, which Hippel[50] selected *particularly* and reserved for himself to improve on (for everyone has spied out in Sterne a side to copy: Wieland took over the paraphrase of subject and predicate, others Sterne's unsurpassable periods, many his eternal 'said he', more took nothing at all, and no one recaptured his airy grace). If one wanted to discuss in the manner of Hippel this idea that the imitators are mere transcendent translators, he would have to say, 'They are the origenic Tetra-, Hexa-, and Octapla of Sterne.' An even clearer example is the description of animals as a Carlsruhe and Viennese copy[51] of men on blotting paper. The mind is uncommonly refreshed when it is forced to contemplate in the particular nothing but the general or the light in the colour black.

Presentation of movement, particularly quick motion, or of rest beside movement, helps heighten the comic effect of humorous sensuousness. Presentation of a mass has a similar effect; through the predominance of the sensuous and the physical, it also produces the ridiculous appearance of the mechanical. Because of the mass of heads, we authors appear really ridiculous in all reviews in Meusel's *Learned Germany*.[52] Hence every reviewer jokes a little.

On Wit

§42. *Definitions*

Each of us may say without vanity that he is intelligent or rational, that he has imagination, feeling, or taste; but no one may say he has wit. Similarly, he can claim to have strength, health, and nimbleness, but not beauty. Each for the same two reasons: First, wit and beauty confer superiority, whatever their degree; but reason, imagination, physical strength, etc., are distinguished only in a person who possesses them to an *unusual* degree; secondly, wit and beauty are *social* powers and triumphs (for what advantage is wit to a hermit or beauty to a hermitess?). One cannot report one's own victories in the art of pleasing without suffering defeat on the way.

What then is wit? Certainly not a faculty which can describe itself. There are some objections to the old definition of wit as an ability to find remote similarities. 'Remote' is vague and 'similarity' is false. Translate 'remote' similarity out of the figurative, and you have a 'dissimilar' similarity, i.e., a contradiction. If the figure is supposed to mean a 'weak' or 'apparent' one, then it is false, since similarity as such is always true equality, although only one of *fewer* parts, and equality as such admits of no degree or deceptive appearance. The converse is true of dissimilarity.

If, however, 'weak' or 'remote' similarity is not supposed to mean anything more than partial equality, wit shares this quality with all other mental powers and their products; for every other comparison produces only partial equality; a complete one would be identity. There is also a kind of wit besides punning which I shall call the witty circle (by analogy to the logical circle), which runs into itself and in which the equated parts are equal. The logical and the witty circles are often drawn and used *concentrically* by modern philosophers of identity.[53] (The definition I have just given makes me one of them.) When the *Greek Anthology* in differentiating object and subject says 'perfume the perfume'[54] or when Lessing says 'spice the spice',[55] there is wit without any remote similarity; on the contrary, two equals are made dissimilar. The same is true of the common French retroactive wit: 'the pleasure of taking or giving some', 'the girl friend of one's own', etc. Puns also lack 'remoteness', as in 'an exchange of letters by letters of exchange'.

The second part of the definition separates wit, as the discovery of similarities, from acumen, as the discovery of dissimilarities. But the comparisons of wit often produce dissimilarities, as when I say, 'Aegisilaus lived in temples in order to reveal his life, but the hypocrite to hide his', or, 'To the arts of speech belongs that of silence', or the figure of antithesis in general. Conversely, the comparisons of acumen often produce similarities; an example would be a good proof of its similarity to wit. The two are a single power of comparisons differing more in direction and objects than in effects. Acumen like that of Seneca, Bayle,[56] Lessing, or Bacon is as striking as the full lightning flash of wit, because of its conciseness. It is hard to say whether sustained antithesis, which often produces a psalmodic parallelism in the philosophic prose of Reinhold[57] and Schiller, is wit or acumen, or rather both.

§43. *Wit, Acumen, and Profundity*

Before we define aesthetic wit, or wit in its narrower sense, we must consider its broadest sense as comparison in general.

On the lowest level of human thought the first, easiest comparison of two ideas, whether their objects be perceptions, ideas, or a mixture of the two, is already wit in the broadest sense. The third idea, as the exponent of their relationship, is not the logical child of the two ideas (or else it would be part and parcel of them, not their child), but the miraculous birth of our creative self. This idea is both freely created through our will and determination and necessary, for otherwise the creator would have seen the creation before he made it, that is, before he saw it. To pass from the fire to the firewood beside it requires the same leap – beyond the reach of the ape's feet – as the leap which connects the sparks of a cat's fur and the sparks of a storm cloud. Wit alone invents, and it does so directly. Friedrich Schlegel is therefore right to call it fragmentary genius.[58] The etymological derivation of the word 'wit' connects it with 'wisdom' and 'to have one's wits about one'. It used to mean the entire genius; accordingly in several languages its synonyms are *Geist*, *esprit*, 'spirit', or *ingeniosus.* A comparison like that of wit, but more intense, is made by *acumen* in order to find dissimilarity and by *profundity* to establish equality. In each case the holy spirit, the third idea, which springs as the third person from the relationship between two ideas, is equally a miraculous child.

Each of the three activities has a distinct object. Wit in the narrower sense discovers a relationship of similarity, i.e., partial equality, hidden in greater inequality. Acumen discovers a relationship of dissimilarity, i.e., of partial inequality, hidden in greater equality. Profundity despite appearances finds complete equality. (Complete inequality is a contradiction and thus unthinkable.) Surprise, which used to be considered a sign and gift of wit, does little to distinguish the activity of wit from that of other faculties such as acumen, profundity, or imagination. Each surprises in its own way, wit more so, because its colourful winged dwarfs leap more lightly and quickly before the eye. But does wit reread lose its value along with its surprise?

First wit must be further defined. In the narrower sense wit discovers rather the similarities between *incommensurable* magnitudes, between physical and spiritual worlds (e.g., sun and truth), in other words, the equation of self and other, of two perceptions. A natural instinct enforces this similarity, and it is therefore more obvious and always instantaneous. The witty relationship is contemplated; acumen, on the contrary, which discovers and distinguishes new relationships between the established relationships of commensurable and similar magnitudes, obliges us to carry through a long series of ideas the light which in wit flashes by itself from the cloud. The reader of a passage produced by acumen must imitate the inventor's whole effort of invention, which wit spares him.

As wit raised to the second power, acumen must in accord with its name (for acuity separates) distinguish and sift anew established similarities.

Now the third power, or rather one and the same, rises above the horizon: profundity. This power is connected with reason, as wit is with imagination. It strives for the equality and unity of all that wit has joined together in *perception* and that acumen has separated through *understanding*. But profundity is a capacity of the whole man rather than a particular power; it is the whole tendency toward the invisible and the highest. It can never stop equating. Just as wit demanded and compared objects, but acumen only comparisons, profundity, as a higher divine wit, after it has abolished one difference after another, must finally arrive at the final essence of essences; and just as acumen loses itself in the highest *knowledge*, *profundity* must lose itself in the highest *being*.

§44. *Nonfigurative Wit*

Aesthetic wit, wit in the narrowest sense, the disguised priest who joins every couple, uses various marriage vows. The oldest, purest formula is that of *nonfigurative* wit, which acts through the understanding. When Samuel Butler compares the reddening dawn after the night to a red cooked lobster,[59] or when

I say 'to number houses and bass notes', or 'women and elephants are afraid of mice', the root of comparison is not figurative but literal. Such relationships do not form the rank and file of antecedent and consequent clauses like those of economic wit, but stand alone and idle like statues. To this class belong Spartan and Attic wit like Cato's comment, 'It is better for a youth to redden than to pale', or 'Soldiers who move their hands on the march and their feet in battle and who snore louder than they shout', or the witticism of that Spartan mother: 'Come back either with or on your shield.' What is the source of pleasure in this illumination? Not the juxtaposition, such as that of women and elephants in the example above, for the two are often neighbours for other reasons in natural history. And not merely assigning one predicate of a phobia in common to two separate subjects; for in natural history an article about mice could mention both subjects extensively without arousing a thought. What heterogeneous ideas are not often conjoined under the banner of a single word in a dictionary, such as town- and war- and other ships? Shall we call the lexicographer Adelung witty? On the contrary, the aesthetic illusion arises even from a nonfigurative point of comparison simply through the juggling, punning rapidity of the language, which makes half, third, or quarter similarities into equalities by finding for two things a single predicative sign. Through this verbal equation in the predicate, species will be sold for subspecies, the whole for a part, cause for effect, or the reverse, thereby giving the aesthetic illusion of a *new* relationship while our feeling for truth maintains the *old*. This division between two appearances will sustain that sweet tickle of the aroused understanding, which in the comic rises to a physical sensation. This produces the proximity of wit to Comus. 'I sharpen ear and quill', says an author who finds a single word for completely different kinds of sharpening; ear and feather themselves are often enough juxtaposed without being witty. If a Frenchman says, 'Many maidens but few wives have men', he establishes his antithesis through the single word 'have', which as predicate of both genus and species is attributed at once to both in inverse relationship.

In his letters to Frederick II Voltaire cannot help reminding the King that His Majesty has made both verses and war upon the world. In this moment I have exemplified what I discuss. But I remark on it only because of the word-order: 'Make verses' comes first as the less common expression; when the audience has accepted this, the common 'make war' is more acceptable. If I had reversed the order, the audience would have believed (and rightly), that I had laboriously strained the first 'make' for the sake of the second. . . . Now if Voltaire said merely, 'Frederick II was a warrior and poet', he would not say anything special. But the following would mean still less: 'You composed various poems in French during the Seven Years' War.' Better, but less correct would be: 'He wars and writes'; 'writes' as the more definite idea contains less than 'wars'. Even better is 'He *civilizes* those he *combats*', for 'combats' includes cities, horses, grainfields, etc., but 'civilizes' only minds; the whole in the first case is equated to the part in the second. This can be extended indefinitely, if one wants to measure syllables and soldiers or make the English jockey's leap from Bucephalus to Pegasus. In these examples the brevity, deception, and twist increase. From two less different wholes (the arts of war and poetry, which coincide in a general notion of force or even of imagination) parts of parts (syllables and soldiers), thus the most dissimilar dissimilarities, are emphasized as exponents and representative of the two wholes. Although only the parts are referred to, both these dissimilar parts and their wholes are then made equal in a single predicate (measure), which is understood both geometrically and arithmetically or acoustically. The understanding now comes to survey such a series of relationships in the easiest and shortest way at the same time that it darkly perceives another true series. Could not this wit, as such a manifold and easy play, be called the perceived or aesthetic understanding, just as the sublime is called the perceived idea of reason and the comic perceived nonsense? I would not ask if we could, if we did not have to. Or we could also call wit sensuous acumen and acumen abstract wit.

§45. Concise Style

Before we follow nonfigurative to figurative wit, *brevity* merits more particular notice. Brevity, i.e., the reduction of signs, affects us agreeably, but not through the increase of thoughts, for since one is always thinking, the number is always the same, and even repetition of the same thought produces a number and every superfluous sign a thought. Rather it heightens thoughts in two ways: First, it presents us at once the more important thought instead of the grammatically empty one[v] and hits us with a downpour instead of a drizzle; second, it confronts sharply the individual objects and points of comparison in a bright light by clearing away all dissimilar incidental circumstances which weaken and hide the comparison. Every dissimilarity awakens activity; the amble along the smooth garden path becomes a jump on the abrupt cliff path. Readers always hope as they doze that they have grasped the minor premise in the major one, and thus may pass the time which they should spend reading it in pleasant recreation. How they startle (but it invigorates them) when they see that they guessed wrong and must rethink from comma to comma!

Brevity is the body and soul of wit, indeed, wit itself; it alone isolates enough to produce contrasts; for pleonasms do not imply any distinctions. Hence the poem made to sheathe wit has the fewest lines and words: the epigram. Tacitus, the Spartans, and many proverbs became witty only because they were always brief, following their *lex minimi* [law of the minimum]. So too Cato, Hamann, Gibbon, Bacon, Lessing, Rousseau, and Seneca. Wit allows so little pleonasm of signs – though easily that of thoughts, as in Seneca – that the English italicize in order to distinguish related words for the inner eye through the outer one. For example, Young says 'Her *Learning* and her *Genius* too decays, / And *dark* and *cold* are her declining days.'[60] Without the print, darkness and coldness would have merged with one another as easily in the imagination as in every night.

The French owe their *nonfigurative* or reflective wit to their precision of language and the latter to the former. What superior possibilities for witty relationship their simple particle *en* provides! English and German prose, which have not yet broken the chain of classic periods into single rings as much as the French has, combine with *chains* rather than *rings*.ʷ When a certain Roman emperor asked a stranger, mocking their family resemblance, 'Was your mother not in Rome?' and the latter replied, 'No, but my father was', then the spark of wit in the answer springs from a collision less of the remotest similarities than of the closest. Translate this into a plain statement and you annihilate the entire witticism. But where then does wit lie? In brevity; the first chain of thought in the question and the suddenly reversing chain in the answer are run through in a few forceful words. If I said here (for the sake of the example rather than for the joke) that in ancient Rome temples preserved the libraries, but now libraries the temples,ˣ I would be forcing the understanding in a few words and moments to the rapid reversal and retracing of the same mental sequence.

French conciseness conquers in prose, in so far as it is in the service of pure philosophy. Whereas imagination seeks living figures, conception seeks only relationships, in which no brevity is too brief;ʸ for this is clarity. Most German – and English – philosophers should translate themselves into French, as Fichte's stylistic precision is manifestly modelled on Rousseau. Thus, while antithesis is not suitable to poetic presentation, it is through its abbreviation that much the more favourable to philosophic production; Lessing and Rousseau experienced this advantage. Kant and still more the Kantians become obscure by repeating themselves, as the transparent body becomes opaque when doubled. Many Germans say no word without adding an echo and re-echo, so that as in *resonating* churches the preacher's voice resounds completely muddled. Only in rare brevity do they write as follows: 'un tel reçu à St. Come, oculiste pour les yeux'. One gets to know a region through a telescope, not a microscope. People read nothing so swiftly as diffuseness; this author is reluctant to admit how quickly he flies through philosophical pages to get to the point or how much he abstracts or extracts anew from abstract works, in order to reflect just a little. He might offend writers whose rind must be peeled to reach the kernel. Why then don't philosophers want to write the way Klopstock painted?

But why didn't Klopstock paint more often the way they write? Philosophical brevity in poetry is but a pygmy. If the understanding deducts (distills) from all forms only invisible relations, the imagination spreads them out alive. For poetry there is no absolute brevity, and a very short day in poetry is little different from a night. Klopstock, especially in his later odes, is the less poetic the more he abridges for the understanding. He gives us a cell full of rose honey instead of the rosebush itself, and instead of the bank of violets a medicine spoon full of violet syrup. To prove this, I ask whether he ever wrote many odes (particularly among the later ones) in which the comparative degree so peculiar to him – this prosaic offshoot of reflection – did not extend its dry twig. The epigrammatic sublimity or sublime points with which he often closes command an incomparably higher rank, as well as his recollection of the unconscious brevity of simplicity. In order not to forget brevity because of it, we will leave it and come to the circle of wit.

§46. *Circular Wit*

In this form of nonfigurative or reflective wit an idea first opposes itself then makes a peace of similarity, but not of equality, with its non-self. I am not speaking of philosophy, but of the circle of wit, this true *causa sui*. It is so easy that it needs only be willed: 'to file the critical file', 'to recover from a recovery', 'to imprison the Bastille', 'to set a thief to catch a thief'. Aside from its brevity this form pleases, because the mind, which must always move on, sees the same idea, such as 'recover', appear before it the second time as its own contrary and is forced by the equality to discover some similarity between them. The show of war forces a show of peace. More compressed, more like a colourful polygon is that circle of Mme du Deffand, who said when she found the great machinist Vaucanson very boring and wooden, 'I have a great idea about him; I bet he made himself.'[61]

§47. *Antithesis*

Reflective wit includes antithesis if it is purely nonfigurative. Among the French it is mostly half nonfigurative, but half – for the imagination carries it thither – figurative in one or the other term, as in 'Que ses arbres réunis soient de nos feux purs et l'asyle et l'*image*' [May these trees thus reunited be the refuge and the image of our pure love]. In antithesis two propositions are opposed, mostly the cause to the effect or the reverse. A subject receives contradictory predicates, just as in our discussion above a single predicate was allotted to contradictory subjects. This aesthetic illusion also arises from the somersaults of language. When Young says wittily of someone playing the role of an absentminded man that he 'takes a memorandum to forget',[63] he means literally 'he writes himself one to remember that he wanted to assume the appearance of forgetting something'. Often the falsehood of the antithesis is hidden subtly in the language: 'The French must become either Robespierre's *judges* or his *subjects*.' For only the judged party is opposed to the judges, the subjects only to the ruler, but not the judge to the subjects.

To give an antithesis existence, brilliance, and force, the French will often start with a quite common thesis. 'I don't know', said a Frenchman in an expression as old as the world, 'what the Greeks would have said of Eleanor; but they would have been silent about Helen.' Voltaire extended this flat locution to the point of absurdity and recklessness, when he said of Fénelon at the time of the Jansenist affair, 'I don't know if Fénelon is a heretic for asserting that the deity is to be loved for its own sake, but I know that Fénelon deserved to be loved for his own sake.' D'Alembert cites this sentence in his eulogy of Fénelon as a fine tribute by Voltaire.[64] Cato the Younger said, 'I would rather be asked why I had been honored by *no* statute than why by *any*.' Cato (and the other example) would shine and triumph less without the *castling* of the clauses. In my opinion he would have produced a less striking effect with his witticism upon posterity and their posterity if he had used the lightning after the thunder and given the phrase this turn: 'It is more disagreeable to me to be asked why I am honored by *one* statue.' 'Naturally,' posterity would have interrupted him, 'but we don't understand why you say anything like that in the first place.' Whereupon he would continue with the second, better clause, now weakened. So much does mere position determine the victory, whether of soldiers or their sentences.

Antithesis is finest and noblest when it becomes almost invisible. 'It takes a long time', says Gibbon, 'for a world to decline, but that is all it takes.'[65] In the first, not infertile thesis, time was presented as mere attendant to an unknown World-Parca; suddenly she appears as the Parca herself. This leap of ideas evinces a freedom which will later be more closely considered as the finest gift of wit.

§48. *Subtlety*

Subtlety I also count as a form of nonfigurative wit. It could indeed be called flattery *incognito*, the poetic *reservatio mentalis* of praise or the enthymeme of censure, all correctly. But this chapter calls it the sign of signs. 'Quand on est assez puissant pour la *grâce* de son ami, il ne faut demander que son *jugement*' [when one is powerful enough for the grace of a friend, all one can ask of him is his judgment]. The term *jugement* includes the idea and possibility of 'damnation' as well as *grâce*; here the imagination is forced to take *jugement* and *grâce* as the same, the genus for the species. It is the same when La Motte defines a great choice between virtue and vice: 'Hésiter, ce seroit choisir' [To hesitate is to make a choice].[66] The fact that the choice is understood as bad, *hésiter*, in turn, the choice, the sign of the sign, gives pleasure through brevity and the appearance of one-sided necessity. As a Gascon politely applauded a story incredible to him, he added merely, 'Mais je ne répéterai votre histoire à cause de mon *accent*' [But I would not repeat your story because of my accent].[67] The dialect signifies the Gascon, the latter in turn mendacity, and this the case at hand, these are almost signs of signs of signs.

Now if a man is to speak subtly, he must have not only talent but also a subject which forces one's understanding. Hence subtle points which turn on ambiguities of sex are so easy; for everyone knows that the moment he cannot extract information from an ambiguous sentence he must seek a simple sense hidden in it, the most definite within the general. Each century the European imagination is degenerating to such a degree that it will ultimately be impossible not to be infinitely subtle, provided one does not know what one is saying.

In the same way one can bestow *subtle* praise only on those who have already been praised *decisively*; the decisive praise is the sign, while the refined praise is the sign of the sign; one then can give instead of the praising sign merely *its* bare sign. The greatest subtlety most easily becomes its opposite when the assumption is not made because of self-consciousness or delicacy. Whereas French dedications are the best in all Europe, the German are the worst, i.e., the coarsest, the most obvious. For the German likes to cast a little light on everything, even on light itself; and for subtlety, this brevity of politeness, he lacks the courage.

The author of this book may hope without immodesty that he has always been more subtle in his dedications than most Frenchmen, which indeed proves real merit, even if not his own.

§49. *Figurative Wit, Its Source*

As the understanding preponderates in nonfigurative wit, so does imagination in figurative wit; the deception of swiftness and of the language helps the former, while the latter depends on a magic of a completely different kind. The same unknown power which in its flames melted into a single life two such heterogeneous beings as body and spirit repeats this ennobling and fusing process within and without us. Meanwhile without deduction or transition it forces us to free the light fire of the spirit from the weight of matter, thought from sound, the powers and movements of a spirit from the parts and features of the face, and thus generally to infer inner movement from outer.

As the interior of our body copies our innermost mind, its anger and love, and the passions become sicknesses, so the physical exterior mirrors the spiritual exterior. No people shakes its head to say yes. The metaphors of all peoples (these linguistic incarnations of nature into humanity) are alike: No one calls error light or truth darkness. As there is no absolute sign – for each sign is also a thing – there is in the finite realm no absolute thing, but each has meaning and signifies something; as in man the divine image, so in nature the human. Man dwells here on an island of spirits, where nothing is lifeless or meaningless; formless voices, voiceless forms perhaps belong together; and we should have presentiments, for everything points beyond the island of spirits across a strange sea.

We owe this girdle of Venus and this arm of love which binds spirit to nature like an unborn child to its mother not only to God but to that small poetic flower, the metaphor. Even the name of metaphor is a miniature proof. Strange! (Allow me this digression.) The physical sense of taste and the spiritual sense of smell like connected images of matter and spirit are also located equally close and far from one another. Kant calls smell a remote taste;[68] but in my opinion he was misled by the perpetually simultaneous effect of the two senses. The chewed flower retains its fragrance in dissolution. If, however, one withdraws from the tongue the cooperation of the nose by breathing just through the mouth, the tongue (exactly as in catarrh) will seem impoverished and dead in the solitary enjoyment, while the smell is independent of the tongue. (Again a model of the interrelationship of a pure realist and a pure idealist!) Scent with its imaginative breadth is more like music, while taste with its prosaic precision is like sight and passes with the former often over to the latter, as in touch the *temperature* of the bodies to their *form*. How unpoetic and unmusical we are compared to the Indians is proved by our degradation of the nose itself, which turns up at its name, as if it were the pillory of the face. A better proof is our poverty in words for smell next to our richness for the *tongue*. For Germans have only the repellent pole, *Gestank* (stink), not the attracting one; *Duft* (aroma) is too optical, *Geruch* (odour) too ambiguous, and *Wohlgeruch* (pleasant odour) too unambiguous. Whole German circles do not smell flowers at all but 'taste' of them and (in Nürnberg and Vienna) call a nosegay a 'tasty bit'. Now back to the beautiful distinction between taste and smell, which is similar to the relationship between body and spirit and which locates taste in water[z] and smell in ether, allocating fruit to the one, flower to the other. Hence a change of language makes either the invisible objects of smell or their nearby invisible element, both as different as scent and air, precisely into heraldic images of the spirit or the reverse, e.g., *Pneuma, animus, spiritus*, smelling spirits, sour spirits, *spiritus rector*, spirits of salt, sal ammoniac, etc. How lovely it is that one now discovers how metaphors, these transsubstantiations of the spirit, resemble flowers, which so beautifully adorn the body and the spirit, like spiritual colours, blossoming spirits!

§50.　*Two Forms of Figurative Wit*

Figurative wit can either *animate* the body or *embody* the spirit.

Originally, when man still bloomed as if grafted with the world on a single stem, this double trope did not yet exist; man did not compare dissimilar elements but proclaimed equality; metaphors, like those of children, were only involuntary synonyms of the body and spirit. As hieroglyphs preceded letters in writing, in speech the metaphor, in so far as it signifies relationships and not objects, was the earlier word which slowly had to fade into denotative expression.[aa] The figurative animation and embodiment still coincided, because self and world were still fused. For this reason every language in its spiritual relationships is a dictionary of faded metaphors.

As man distinguishes himself from the word and invisibility from visibility, his wit must *animate*, although not yet *embody*. He lends his self to the universe and his life to the matter about him. Since, however, his own self appears to him only in the form of a moving body, he has nothing else, nothing more spiritual to lend the external world besides limbs, eyes, arms, or feet. Yet these are alive and animated. *Personification* is the first poetic figure which the savage makes, whereupon the *metaphor* appears as the abridged personification. But with neither trope does he wish to appear as if he were adopting a special style according to Adelung and Batteux[69] any more than an angry man cites his curse as exclamation point or a lover his kiss as a dash. Every image here is a miraculous icon full of divinity; his words are image-statues, his statues are men, and men are himself. The North American Indian believes that the soul of the dead man draws the soul of his arrow after it.

If I suppose animation of the physical to be the earlier form of figurative comparison, I do so because the mental form as the more general is easier to uncover in the physical (as the particular) than the reverse, just as the moral is easier to deduce from the fable than the fable from the moral. For this reason and for others, I should therefore say the moral precedes the fable. Bacon could easily fabricate an allegorical meaning for mythology; but inversely to produce a myth to fit the meaning would have been ten times as hard. This leads me to the second activity of figurative wit, the embodiment of the abstract. Bodies are always harder for the imagination to create than spirits. Bodies require sharper individuation; figures are more definite than powers and consequently more diverse. We know only one self but millions of bodies. As a result it is harder to find in the capricious and playful variation of definite forms one which with its definiteness will express a spirit in its individuality. It was much easier to animate the physical and to say 'the storm rages' than to embody an idea: 'Rage is a storm wind.'

If a writer goes walking through a field of ripe grain, the upright and empty ears of grain easily suggest the simile of an empty head raised that way. (This is one of several comparisons Montaigne took from Plutarch, just as he took maxims from Seneca.) But if he wishes to embody the notion of a man both *insignificant* and *proud*, he will have some trouble hitting upon the exact impression of that image among the innumerable possibilities. The way to a simile is found mostly through a metaphor; here, for example, we substitute 'empty' for insignificant and 'upright' for proud. Instead of 'empty' we could have taken narrow, sick, flat, crippled, dark, crooked, poisonous, dwarfed, hollow, faded, etc., and countless diverging paths would open up. Thus a long circumnavigation might lead past the goal which, as described above, we brushed against on a pleasure walk through a field of grain.

Hence in a simile the idea should precede the physical image if only to avoid the hidden pleonasm of its being half-anticipated in the physical, the converse of which is impossible. The good Caroline Pichler is almost boring with her similes just because of their pleonastic organization.[70] In only *one* case may the image come before the idea: when the image is so unfamiliar and far-fetched that the reader must become acquainted with it literally, in order to prepare him for the figurative meaning and its playful use. Klopstock's similes, taken from mental states, were easier to make than Homer's physical ones, because one can easily tailor the mental circumstance according to need. A particular kind of wit raised to the height of genius by Hippel is that of soldering several general clauses into similes or allegories of a single clause. Thus Hippel[71] expresses his desire to give only hints, not lengthy descriptions, by describing for almost a page and a half the error of a long description and the advantage of a short one, with the following similes: 'Women would rather catch cold than part with any of their finery. Gourmets put aside everything foreign to the business at hand, even a distant view, table music, or entertaining conversation. Everything colossal is weak. He who deifies men makes them even less than they might be according to God and nature', and so on at length. The omission of 'as' or 'as it were', the leap not between images but between ideas, and the independent content of each new observation make it difficult not to plunge into the particulars with pleasure, instead of using them as mere colours condemned to the passive role of images for the chief picture. But the path of taste on this fluid ground, indeed on these waves, is almost too difficult for the author. Can anyone educated by the ancients sanction such luxury in similes? Hardly, except perhaps in Pindar, who like a pre-Hippel had the same habit of fusing a series of general propositions without any riveting words into a single simile and thereby made himself almost unintelligible to his editors.

The path of figurative wit diverges widely from that of figurative imagination. The imagination wants to paint, wit only to colour. Through all similarities the former aims to animate and decorate epically only the figure; wit, cold toward the two elements of the comparison, dissolves both into the spiritual extract of their relationship. Homer makes even the simile not simply a means but endows this subservient member with a characteristic life of its own. The witty simile, more independent and less lyric than metaphor, is better suited to epic irony, especially when introduced by Swift's artistic hand. Metaphor and allegory, on the contrary, are better for lyric whimsy. The ancients had little figurative wit, because as more objective writers they were more inclined to creation than gifted for intellectual analysis. Poetry would rather *animate* the dead, while wit prefers to *disembody* life. The figurative imagination is strictly bound to unified images, because they must live, which a being composed of conflicting members cannot do. Since figurative wit, on the contrary, undertakes only a lifeless mosaic, it can force the reader to jump at every comma. On the pretext of a self-comparison it can arbitrarily and without scruple change its Roman candles, carillons, cosmetic lotions, carvings, or dressing-tables within a single period. But critics often give little consideration to this when judging Courses for an Aesthetic accompanied by Leipzig Lectures.

The English and the Germans have incomparably more figurative wit, the French more reflective wit. The latter is more social; to reach the former the imagination must first spread broad sails, which takes too long and is too difficult inside a drawing room. What a mutually reflecting chain of similarities a single simile of Young or Musäus often encloses! What pale pearls of the third water are the French, against the English gems of the first fire! Mme de Necker cites as an example of happy boldness the fact that the ardent Buffon did not hesitate to combine the metaphorically strong adjective *vive* [animated] with *volonté* [will].[72] While the whole of proper France applauded and accepted this poetic image embodying the will, philosophical Germany sees in it only a literal expression, indeed a pleonasm; for the individual will is truly alive.

The French treasure of images contains, besides its mythological household store, little more than the common tragic military baggage and poetic service: throne, scepter, dagger, flower, temple, sacrificial victim and a few flames, gold, no silver, a bloody scaffold, and their own principal limbs. Because they always have this poetic set of tools at hand, especially the hands, feet, lips, and head, they use them as often and as boldly as Orientals and savages, who like the French materialists today construct the self out of physical members. 'Le sommeil caressé des *mains* de la nature' [sleep caressed by the hands of nature], said Voltaire. 'Ses mains cueillent des fleurs et ses *pas* les font naître' [his hands gather the flowers and his steps bring them forth], said another less badly. Thus with oriental boldness they assign and attach hands with splints to hope, time, or love, so long as the hands can in turn be opposed or attached to feet, lips, lap, or heart.

The poor heart! Among the brave Germans it is still at least the synonym of courage, but in French poetry, as in anatomy, it is the strongest muscle, although it has the smallest nerves. A comic writer might not scruple to call the compressed heart a 'globe de compression', the 'globulus hystericus' of the French muse,[73] or the steam chamber for the blast pipe, the firewheel of its works, its cylinder for playing music and for speech, its savings bank, the smelt, or anything else. But one needs little or no taste to find anything like that incompatible with the tone required for aesthetic courses.

§51. Allegory

Often allegory is less a prolonged metaphor than a modified and arbitrary one. It is the easiest kind of figurative wit as well as the most dangerous form of figurative imagination. Allegory is easy, because through personification it can use whatever is too close and naked for a simile or whatever is too distant (for it constrains the mind through bold juxtaposition); because it elaborates and improves the second term of comparison to fit the first; and third because it always changes metaphors underhandedly. True allegory ties figurative wit into nonfigurative; Möser thus calls the opera a pillory to which one affixes one's ears to display one's head.[74] On the contrary the following allegory by Young is poor: 'Each friend by Fate snatch'd from us, is a Plume / Pluckt from the Wing of human Vanity, / Which makes us stoop from our aëreal Heights. . . . On *drooping* Pinions of Ambition *lowered*' (how tautological) '*Just* skim earth's Surface' (without the 'just' he would not have been able to continue) 'ere we break it up, / O'er putrid Earth to scratch a little Dust' (now he passes from the metaphor of sinking into that of stinking) 'And save the world a nuisance.'[75]

The cold Fontenelle once applied allegorically two tautologous metaphors to two different ideas; thus he said: nothing at all. After comparing philosophy to blindman's buff (in which the blindfolded children must name the person they have caught on penalty of running again) he adds, 'At times we philosophers may catch the truth, although we are properly blindfolded, but we cannot claim that it is she we have caught and in that moment she escapes us again.'[76] For a truth can designate not the thought of a sentence, but our belief and assertion of it, or its appellation. We pass off as true and give a name to what we believe to be truth; how then can she escape us?

Because all good things come in threes, we shall cite still another, indeed very erroneous, example from the third nation, Germany, in fact from Lessing himself. After he has said that he is writing *about* painters and poets, not *for* them, he continues: 'I unwind the web of the silkworms, not to teach the silkworms how to spin' (this already sounds like 'I shear the sheep, but not to teach them how to bear wool') 'but to make purses from the silk for myself and others' (why purses and not stockings, etc., and why silken?), 'purses, to continue the simile' (actually the allegory) 'in which I can keep the *small change* of individual perceptions' (is there a natural transition here from silkworms to coins, which spills over into a third allegory of smallness?) 'until I can exchange them for good weighty *pieces of gold* of general remarks' (very tortured; he wants to boost himself along as far as possible with the help of the synonyms *good, weighty*, and *golden*) 'and coin these into *capital* of *independent truths*' (here I see the fourth allegory, but where did the silkworm go?).[77]

. . .

On the Novel

§69. *Its Poetic Value*

The development of a pure novel form suffers from its breadth, in which almost all forms have room to lie and rattle about. Originally it is epic, but at times the hero or all the characters narrate, instead of the author. The epistolary novel, which is either simply a prolonged monologue or a dialogue, borders on the dramatic form or even on the lyric, as in the *Sorrows of Werther*. In one narrative the action moves with the confined limbs of the drama, as in Schiller's *Ghostseer*; in another it plays and dances over the entire surface of the earth as in the fairy tale. The freedom of prose is also detrimental, because its facility spares the artist an initial effort and discourages the reader from close study. Even its extent – for the novel surpasses all other artistic works in amount of paper – helps worsen it; the connoisseur readily studies and measures a drama of half a quire, but who can deal with one twenty times that size? Aristotle recommends that an epic be capable of being read within a day;[78] Richardson and the present author fulfil this rule in their novels, which are limited to a day's reading, except that since they live further north than Aristotle, it is the usual polar day, consisting of ninety and one-quarter nights. But critics do not sufficiently consider how hard it is for a single inspiration, spirit, and view of the whole and of a single hero to extend and be sustained through ten volumes. They do not consider how a good work must be created in the enveloping warmth and air of an entire climate, not in the narrow confines of a hothouse pot which might produce an ode.[bb] Artists themselves do not reckon on it and, as a result, begin well, continue in a mediocre fashion, and then end miserably. People want only to study the smallest form, which actually requires less study.

Yet in the right hands the novel, the only permissible poetic prose, can flourish instead of wasting away. Why should there not be a poetic encyclopedia, a poetic license to use every poetic license? Let poetry come to us how and where she will, let her dress herself in some prosaic thin, poor body like the devil of hermits or the Jupiter of the heathens; if she is really present, we will welcome her masked ball. If a spirit is there, it may assume any form in the world, like the world-spirit, which it alone can use and wear. When Dante's spirit wanted to appear on earth, the epic, lyric and, dramatic eggshells and skulls were too narrow for him; he then dressed himself in vast night and in flame and in heaven's ether all at once and thus hovered only half-embodied among the strongest, sturdiest critics.

The most indispensable element in the novel is the romantic, into whatever form it may be hammered or cast. Up to now, however, the stylistics have demanded from a novel not the romantic spirit but its exorcism; the novel was supposed to repress and expel what little romanticism still glimmers in reality. The stylistic novel, an unversified didactic poem, became a thick almanac for theologians, philosophers, and housewives. The spirit became an agreeable dressing for the body. As the students in the old school-dramas of the Jesuits used to disguise themselves and act as verbs and their inflections, vocatives, datives, etc., so the stylistics' human characters presented paragraphs and moral applications and exegetic hints, words in season, and heterodox leisure hours. The poet gave his readers, as Basedow[79] gave children, cakes in the form of letters to eat.

Certainly poetry teaches and should teach, and the novel should do so as well, but only as a blossoming flower which through its opening and closing and even through its fragrance announces the weather and the times of day. Its tender stem will never be cut, carpentered, and confined to the wooden teacher's desk or preacher's pulpit; the wooden frame and the person standing therein do not replace the living breath of spring. And what does it mean to give lessons? Simply to give signs. But the whole world and all time are full of signs already. Yet these letters are not read; we need a dictionary and a grammar of the signs. Poetry teaches us to read, while the mere teacher belongs among the ciphers rather than among the deciphering chancery-clerks.

A man who expresses a judgment about the world gives us his world, a miniature fragment of world instead of the living extended one, a sum without the reckoning. Poetry is indispensable, because it renders to the spirit only the spiritually reborn world and does not impose any casual conclusion. In the poet humanity alone speaks to humanity alone, not this man to that man.

§70. *The Epic Novel*

While such degrees are somewhat arbitrary, the novel in its range around the two focuses of the poetic ellipse must approach either the *epic* or the *drama*. The common unpoetic class of novel produces mere biographies lacking the unity and necessity of nature and the romantic freedom of the epic, yet borrowing the limitations of nature and the caprice of the epic. These biographies ring all the changes of times and places in a common course of world and life until they run out of paper. I am almost ashamed to acknowledge that I found more in *Fortunatus' Wishing Hat*,[80] which I have just read, that is, more poetic spirit, than in the most famous novels of the stylists. If the common copyists were to grasp at ether by reaching through earthly clouds, they would draw back a hand full of vapour; it is the enemies of romanticism who elevate on the far side of their earthly and vaporous sphere the most monstrous shapes and inorganic grotesques, even wilder than the true genius could ever produce, as it marches behind the flag of nature.

The *romantic-epic* form, or that spirit which resided in the Old French and Middle High German romances, was called back by Goethe's *Meister* with his magic wand as if out of collapsed ruins into fresh new pleasure palaces. True to the epic character, this resurrected spirit of a more romantic time allows a light, bright, high cloud to pass over which reflects or carries the world and the past rather than a single hero. The similarity between the dream and the novel in which Herder sees the essence of the novel[81] is true and subtle, also the similarity required now between fairy tale and novel. The fairy tale is the freer epic, the dream the freer fairy tale. Goethe's *Meister* has set the example for such better works as the novels of Novalis, Tieck, Ernst Wagner, La Motte Fouqué, and Arnim.[82] Of course, many of these novels, such as those of Arnim, despite all their brilliance have a form more like a divergent than a convergent lens, which does not sufficiently condense the warmth of interest.

§71. *The Dramatic Novel*

But the moderns want to forget that the novel can just as well assume a romantic dramatic form and that it has done so. I prefer this more precise form for the same reason that Aristotle recommends an approach to dramatic terseness in the epic;[83] certainly the freedom of prose makes a certain strictness of form necessary and wholesome for the novel. Richardson, Thümmel, Wieland, Schiller, Jacobi, Fielding, Engel, etc., and the present author have taken this path, which does not open into the playground of history so much as it contracts to the race track of the characters. This form produces scenes of emotional climax, words of the moment, intense expectation, precision of characters and motivations, strong knots, etc. The romantic spirit must be able to wear this more tightly laced body as easily as in the past it has born the heavy cothurnus and raised the tragic dagger.

Part 7

A. W. Schlegel

August Wilhelm von Schlegel

(1767–1845)

A. W. Schlegel was probably the most prominent critic of his time, being acquainted personally with the leading literary figures of Germany, including Schiller (to whose *Musen-Almanach* he frequently contributed), Goethe, and Tieck; he was also the close friend and tutor of Madame de Staël, whom he first met in 1805. He is probably best known to English readers for his Shakespeare criticism, but he also lectured and wrote extensively on contemporary German literature and its background, and also translated for publication many of Shakespeare's plays into German between 1797 and 1810. While lecturing on literature at Jena, he founded with his brother Friedrich the *Athenäum*, the journal which was to become the major vehicle of romantic criticism. Schlegel also wrote poems and plays, but his greatest success came as translator and critic; his translations include works from Spanish, Italian, and Portuguese. Toward the end of his life he became a well-known scholar of the Sanskrit language and literature, publishing the *Ramayana* (1825) and the *Bhagavad-Gita* (1829). He won considerable fame for his 1808 lectures on dramatic art and literature, and in 1827 he gave a successful series of lectures entitled 'Theory and History of the Fine Arts'.

Through his Shakespeare criticism and his founding of the *Athenäum* with his brother Friedrich, A. W. Schlegel was from the outset closely associated with the new romantic movement; indeed, he was seen as one of the original founders of it. But his relation to the theoretical aesthetics of, for example, tragedy and irony is more peripheral and even perhaps tenuous. Indeed, Karl Solger was some years later to discredit A. W. Schlegel's role in articulating the concept of romantic irony and theory of tragedy as misguided; his efforts to explain these theories to his audiences Solger saw as a watered down and even false account (see Solger's 'Resenzion von A. W. Schlegel's *Vorlesungen*', in *Erwin*, edited W. Henckmann (München, 1970), 394–471, and see Oskar Walzel, 'Methode? Ironie bei Friedrich Schlegel und bei Solger', *Helicon*, I (1938), 33–50). Hegel's rejection of romantic irony and his admiration for Solger's aesthetics may best be understood as a consequence of taking A. W. Schlegel as the main representative, and remaining (determinedly?) ignorant of the large difference between this simplistic version, designed for large audiences, and the sophisticated theory of his brother Friedrich.

The selection here is from the 'Lectures on Dramatic Art and Literature', given first in Vienna, in 1808, a mature account of the romantic principles of the 1790s which constituted the most powerful attack upon Neo-classicist criticism to be levelled since Herder. Herder's influence, particularly, as well as that of Lessing and Schiller, is evident both in the principles that inform them and in the lectures themselves. But the lectures also reveal the marked influence of English critics of Shakespeare, and it might be closer to the mark to suggest that Coleridge was indebted in his Shakespeare criticism less to his famous contemporary than to their common heritage, particularly that of Herder, Lessing, and Schiller.

The English text of the *Lectures on Dramatic Art and Literature* is from *Course of Lectures on*

Dramatic Art and Literature, translated J. Black; revised A. J. W. Morrison (London, 1846), 17–29, 368–71, 404–7, 518–21.

Lectures on Dramatic Art and Literature
Vorlesungen über dramatische Kunst und Literatur (1808)

Ancient and Modern, Classical and Romantic

The object of the present series of Lectures will be to combine the theory of Dramatic Art with its history, and to bring before my auditors at once its principles and its models.

It belongs to the general philosophical theory of poetry, and the other fine arts, to establish the fundamental laws of the beautiful. Every art, on the other hand, has its own special theory, designed to teach the limits, the difficulties, and the means by which it must be regulated in its attempt to realize those laws. For this purpose, certain scientific investigations are indispensable to the artist, although they have but little attraction for those whose admiration of art is confined to the enjoyment of the actual productions of distinguished minds. The general theory, on the other hand, seeks to analyse that essential faculty of human nature – the sense of the beautiful, which at once calls the fine arts into existence, and accounts for the satisfaction which arises from the contemplation of them; and also points out the relation which subsists between this and all other sentient and cognizant faculties of man. To the man of thought and speculation, therefore, it is of the highest importance, but by itself alone it is quite inadequate to guide and direct the essays and practice of art.

Now, the history of the fine arts informs us what has been, and the theory teaches what ought to be accomplished by them. But without some intermediate and connecting link, both would remain independent and separate from one and other, and each by itself, inadequate and defective. This connecting link is furnished by criticism, which both elucidates the history of the arts, and makes the theory fruitful. The comparing together, and judging of the existing productions of the human mind, necessarily throws light upon the conditions which are indispensable to the creation of original and masterly works of art.

Ordinarily, indeed, men entertain a very erroneous notion of criticism, and understand by it nothing more than a certain shrewdness in detecting and exposing the faults of a work of art. As I have devoted the greater part of my life to this pursuit, I may be excused if, by way of preface, I seek to lay before my auditors my own ideas of the true genius of criticism.

We see numbers of men, and even whole nations, so fettered by the conventions of education and habits of life, that, even in the appreciation of the fine arts, they cannot shake them off. Nothing to them appears natural, appropriate, or beautiful, which is alien to their own language, manners, and social relations. With this exclusive mode of seeing and feeling, it is no doubt possible to attain, by means of cultivation, to great nicety of discrimination within the narrow circle to which it limits and circumscribes them. But no man can be a true critic or connoisseur without universality of mind, without that flexibility which enables him, by renouncing all personal predilections and blind habits, to adapt himself to the peculiarities of other ages and nations – to feel them, as it were, from their proper central point, and, what ennobles human nature, to recognize and duly appreciate whatever is beautiful and grand under the external accessories which were necessary to its embodying, even though occasionally they may seem to disguise and distort it. There is no monopoly of poetry for particular ages and nations; and consequently that despotism in taste, which would seek to invest with universal authority the rules which at first, perhaps, were but arbitrarily advanced, is but a vain and empty pretension. Poetry, taken in its widest acceptation, as the power of creating what is beautiful, and representing it to the eye or the ear, is a universal gift of Heaven, being shared to a certain extent even by those whom we call barbarians and savages. Internal excellence is alone decisive, and where this exists, we must not allow ourselves to be repelled by the external appearance. Everything must be traced up to the root of human nature: if it has sprung from thence, it has an undoubted worth of its own; but if, without possessing a living germ, it is merely externally attached thereto, it will never thrive nor acquire a proper growth. Many productions which appear at first sight dazzling phenomena in the province of the fine arts, and which as a whole have been honoured with the appellation of works of a golden age, resemble the mimic gardens of children: impatient to witness the work of their hands, they break off here and there branches and flowers, and plant them in the earth; everything at first assumes a noble appearance: the childish gardener struts proudly up and down among his showy beds, till the rootless plants begin to droop, and hang their withered leaves and blossoms, and nothing soon remains but the bare twigs, while the dark forest, on which no art or care was ever bestowed, and which towered up towards heaven long before human remembrance, bears every blast unshaken, and fills the solitary beholder with religious awe.

Let us now apply the idea which we have been developing, of the universality of true criticism, to the history of poetry and the fine arts. This, like the so-called universal history, we generally limit (even though beyond this range there may be much that is both remarkable and worth knowing) to whatever has had a nearer or more remote influence on the present civilization of Europe: consequently, to the works of the Greeks and Romans, and of those of the modern European nations, who first and chiefly distinguished themselves in art and literature. It is well known that, three centuries and a half ago, the study of ancient literature received a new life, by the diffusion of the Grecian language (for the Latin never became extinct); the classical authors were brought to light, and rendered universally accessible by means of the press; and the monuments of ancient art were diligently disinterred and preserved. All this powerfully excited the human mind, and formed a decided epoch in the history of human civilization; its manifold effects have extended to our times, and will yet extend to an incalculable series of ages. But the study of the ancients was forthwith most fatally perverted. The learned, who were chiefly in the possession of this knowledge, and who were incapable of distinguishing themselves by works of their own, claimed for the ancients an unlimited authority, and with great appearance of reason, since they are models in their kind. Maintaining that nothing could be hoped for the human mind but from an imitation of antiquity, in the works of the moderns they only valued what resembled, or seemed to bear a resemblance to, those of the ancients. Everything else they rejected as barbarous and unnatural. With the great poets and artists it was quite otherwise. However strong their enthusiasm for the ancients, and however determined their purpose of entering into competition with them, they were compelled by their independence and originality of mind, to strike out a path of their own, and to impress upon their productions the stamp of their own genius. Such was the case with Dante among the Italians, the father of modern poetry; acknowledging Virgil for his master, he has produced a work which, of all others, most differs from the Aeneid, and in our opinion far excels its pretended model in power, truth, compass, and profundity. It was the same afterwards with Ariosto, who has most unaccountably been compared to Homer, for nothing can be more unlike. So in art with Michael Angelo and Raphael, who had no doubt deeply studied the antique. When we ground our judgment of modern painters merely on their greater or less resemblance to the ancients, we must necessarily be unjust towards them, as Winckelmann undoubtedly has in the case of Raphael.[1] As the poets for the most part had their share of scholarship, it gave rise to a curious struggle between their natural inclination and their imaginary duty. When they sacrificed to the latter, they were praised by the learned; but by yielding to the former, they became the favourites of the people. What preserves the heroic poems of a Tasso and a Camoëns to this day alive in the hearts and on the lips of their countrymen, is by no means their imperfect resemblance to Virgil, or even to Homer, but in Tasso the tender feeling of chivalrous love and honour, and in Camoëns the glowing inspiration of heroic patriotism.

Those very ages, nations, and ranks, who felt least the want of a poetry of their own, were the most assiduous in their imitation of the ancients; accordingly, its results are but dull school exercises, which at best excite a frigid admiration. But in the fine arts, mere imitation is always fruitless; even what we borrow from others, to assume a true poetical shape, must, as it were, be born again within us. Of what avail is all foreign imitation? Art cannot exist without nature, and man can give nothing to his fellow-men but himself.

Genuine successors and true rivals of the ancients, who, by virtue of congenial talents and cultivation have walked in their path and worked in their spirit, have ever been as rare as their mechanical spiritless copyists are common. Seduced by the form, the great body of critics have been but too indulgent to these servile imitators. These were held up as correct modern classics, while the great truly living and popular poets, whose reputation was a part of their nations' glory, and to whose sublimity it was impossible to be altogether blind, were at best but tolerated as rude and wild natural geniuses. But the unqualified separation of genius and taste on which such a judgment proceeds, is altogether untenable. Genius is the almost unconscious choice of the highest degree of excellence, and, consequently, it is taste in its highest activity.

In this state, nearly, matters continued till a period not far back, when several inquiring minds, chiefly Germans, endeavoured to clear up the misconception, and to give the ancients their due, without being insensible to the merits of the moderns, although of a totally different kind. The apparent contradiction did not intimidate them. The groundwork of human nature is no doubt everywhere the same; but in all our investigations, we may observe that, throughout the whole range of nature, there is no elementary power so simple, but that it is capable of dividing and diverging into opposite directions. The whole play of vital motion hinges on harmony and contrast. Why, then, should not this phenomenon recur on a grander scale in the history of man? In this idea we have perhaps discovered the true key to the ancient and modern history of poetry and the fine arts. Those who adopted it, gave to the peculiar spirit of *modern* art, as contrasted with the *antique* or *classical*, the name of *romantic*. The term is certainly not inappropriate; the word is derived from *romance* – the name originally given to the languages which were formed from the mixture of the Latin and the old Teutonic dialects, in the same manner as modern civilization is the fruit of the heterogeneous union of the peculiarities of the northern nations and the fragments of antiquity; whereas the civilization of the ancients was much more of a piece.[2]

The distinction which we have just stated can hardly fail to appear well founded, if it can be shown, so far as our knowledge of antiquity extends, that the same contrast in the labours of the ancients and moderns runs symmetrically, I might almost say systematically, throughout every branch of art – that it is as evident in music and the plastic arts as in poetry. This is a problem which, in its full extent, still remains to be demonstrated, though, on particular portions of it, many excellent observations have been advanced already.

Among the foreign authors who wrote before this school can be said to have been formed in Germany, we may mention Rousseau, who acknowledged the contrast in music, and showed that rhythm and melody were the prevailing principles of ancient, as harmony is that of modern music. In his prejudices against harmony, however, we cannot at all concur. On the subject of the arts of design an ingenious observation was made by Hemsterhuys,[3] that the ancient painters were perhaps too much of sculptors, and the modern sculptors too much of painters. This is the exact point of difference; for, as I shall distinctly show in the sequel, the spirit of ancient art and poetry is *plastic*, but that of the moderns *picturesque*.

By an example taken from another art, that of architecture, I shall endeavour to illustrate what I mean by this contrast. Throughout the Middle Ages there prevailed, and in the latter centuries of that æra was carried to perfection, a style of architecture, which has been called Gothic, but ought really to have been termed old German. When, on the general revival of classical antiquity, the imitation of Grecian architecture became prevalent, and but too frequently without a due regard to the difference of climate and manners or to the purpose of the building, the zealots of this new taste, passing a sweeping sentence of condemnation on the Gothic, reprobated it as tasteless, gloomy, and barbarous. This was in some degree pardonable in the Italians, among whom a love for ancient architecture, cherished by hereditary remains of classical edifices, and the similarity of their climate to that of the Greeks and Romans, might, in some sort, be said to be innate. But we Northerns are not so easily to be talked out of the powerful, solemn impressions which seize upon the mind at entering a Gothic cathedral. We feel, on the contrary, a strong desire to investigate and to justify the source of this impression. A very slight attention will convince us, that the Gothic architecture displays not only an extraordinary degree of mechanical skill, but also a marvellous power of invention; and, on a closer examination, we recognize its profound significance, and perceive that as well as the Grecian it constitutes in itself a complete and finished system.

To the application – The Pantheon is not more different from Westminster Abbey or the church of St. Stephen at Vienna, than the structure of a tragedy of Sophocles from a drama of Shakespeare. The comparison between these wonderful productions of poetry and architecture might be carried still farther. But does our admiration of the one compel us to depreciate the other? May we not admit that each is great and admirable in its kind, although the one is, and is meant to be, different from the other? The experiment is worth attempting. We will quarrel with no man for his predilection either for the Grecian or the Gothic. The world is wide, and affords room for a great diversity of objects. Narrow and blindly adopted prepossessions will never constitute a genuine critic or connoisseur, who ought, on the contrary, to possess the power of dwelling with liberal impartiality on the most discrepant views, renouncing the while all personal inclinations.

For our present object, the justification, namely, of the grand division which we lay down in the history of art, and according to which we conceive ourselves equally warranted in establishing the same division in dramatic literature, it might be sufficient merely to have stated this contrast between the ancient, or classical, and the romantic. But as there are exclusive admirers of the ancients, who never cease asserting that all deviation from them is merely the whim of a new school of critics, who, expressing themselves in language full of mystery, cautiously avoid conveying their sentiments in a tangible shape, I shall endeavour to explain the origin and spirit of the *romantic*, and then leave the world to judge if the use of the word, and of the idea which it is intended to convey, be thereby justified.

The mental culture of the Greeks was a finished education in the school of Nature. Of a beautiful and noble race, endowed with susceptible senses and a cheerful spirit under a mild sky, they lived and bloomed in the full health of existence; and, favoured by a rare combination of circumstances, accomplished all that the finite nature of man is capable of. The whole of their art and poetry is the expression of a consciousness of this harmony of all their faculties. They invented the poetry of joy.

Their religion was the deification of the powers of nature and of the earthly life: but this worship, which, among other nations, clouded the imagination with hideous shapes, and hardened the heart to cruelty, assumed, among the Greeks, a mild, a grand, and a dignified form. Superstition, too often the tyrant of the human faculties, seemed to have here contributed to their freest development. It cherished the arts by which it was adorned, and its idols became the models of ideal beauty.

But however highly the Greeks may have succeeded in the Beautiful, and even in the Moral, we cannot concede any higher character to their civilization than that of a refined and ennobled sensuality. Of course this must be understood generally. The conjectures of a few philosophers, and the irradiations of poetical inspiration, constitute an occasional exception. Man can never altogether turn aside his thoughts from infinity, and some obscure recollections will always remind him of the home he has lost; but we are now speaking of the predominant tendency of his endeavours.

Religion is the root of human existence. Were it possible for man to renounce all religion, including that which is unconscious, independent of the will, he would become a mere surface without any internal substance. When this centre is disturbed, the whole system of the mental faculties and feelings takes a new shape.

And this is what has actually taken place in modern Europe through the introduction of Christianity. This sublime and beneficent religion has regenerated the ancient world from its state of exhaustion and debasement; it is the guiding principle in the history of modern nations, and even at this day, when many suppose they have shaken off its authority, they still find themselves much more influenced by it in their views of human affairs than they themselves are aware.

After Christianity, the character of Europe has, since the commencement of the Middle Ages, been chiefly influenced by the Germanic race of northern conquerors, who infused new life and vigour into a degenerated people. The stern nature of the North drives man back within himself; and what is lost in the free sportive development of the senses, must, in noble dispositions, be compensated by earnestness of mind. Hence the honest cordiality with which Christianity was welcomed by all the Teutonic tribes, so that among no other race of men has it penetrated more deeply into the inner man, displayed more powerful effects, or become more interwoven with all human feelings and sensibilities.

The rough, but honest heroism of the northern conquerors, by its admixture with the sentiments of Christianity, gave rise to chivalry, of which the object was, by vows which should be looked upon as sacred, to guard the practice of arms from every rude and ungenerous abuse of force into which it was so likely to sink.

With the virtues of chivalry was associated a new and purer spirit of love, an inspired homage for genuine female worth, which was now revered as the acmè of human excellence, and, maintained by religion itself under the image of a virgin mother, infused into all hearts a mysterious sense of the purity of love.

As Christianity did not, like the heathen worship, rest satisfied with certain external acts, but claimed an authority over the whole inward man and the most hidden movements of the heart; the feeling of moral independence took refuge in the domain of honour, a worldly morality, as it were, which subsisting alongside of, was often at variance with that of religion, but yet in so far resembling it that it never calculated consequences, but consecrated un-conditionally certain principles of action, which like the articles of faith, were elevated far beyond the investigation of a casuistical reasoning.

Chivalry, love, and honour, together with religion itself, are the subjects of that poetry of nature which poured itself out in the Middle Ages with incredible fullness, and preceded the more artistic cultivation of the romantic spirit. This age had also its mythology, consisting of chivalrous tales and legends; but its wonders and its heroism were the very reverse of those of the ancient mythology.

Several enquirers who, in other respects, entertain the same conception of the peculiarities of the moderns, and trace them to the same source that we do, have placed the essence of the northern poetry in melancholy; and to this, when properly understood, we have nothing to object.

Among the Greeks human nature was in itself all-sufficient; it was conscious of no defects, and aspired to no higher perfection than that which it could actually attain by the exercise of its own energies. We, however, are taught by superior wisdom that man, through a grievous transgression, forfeited the place for which he was originally destined; and that the sole destination of his earthly existence is to struggle to regain his lost position, which, if left to his own strength, he can never accomplish. The old religion of the senses sought no higher possession than outward and perishable blessings; and immortality, so far as it was believed, stood shadow-like in the obscure distance, a faint dream of this sunny waking life. The very reverse of all this is the case with the Christian view: every thing finite and mortal is lost in the contemplation of infinity; life has become shadow and darkness, and the first day of our real existence dawns in the world beyond the grave. Such a religion must waken the vague foreboding, which slumbers in every feeling heart, into a distinct consciousness that the happiness after which we are here striving is unattainable; that no external object can ever entirely fill our souls; and that all earthly enjoyment is but a fleeting and momentary illusion. When the soul, resting as it were under the willows of exile, breathes out its longing for its distant home, what else but melancholy can be the key-note of its songs? Hence the poetry of the ancients was the poetry of enjoyment, and ours is that of desire: the former has its foundation in the scene which is present, while the latter hovers betwixt recollection and hope. Let me not be understood as affirming that everything flows in one unvarying strain of wailing and complaint, and that the voice of melancholy is always loudly heard. As the austerity of tragedy was not incompatible with the joyous views of the Greeks, so that romantic poetry, whose origin I have been describing, can assume every tone, even that of the liveliest joy; but still it will always, in some indescribable way, bear traces of the source from which it originated. The feeling of the moderns is, upon the whole, more inward, their fancy more incorporeal, and their thoughts more contemplative. In nature, it is true, the boundaries of objects run more into one another, and things are not so distinctly separated as we must exhibit them in order to convey distinct notions of them.

The Grecian ideal of human nature was perfect unison and proportion between all the powers – a natural harmony. The moderns, on the contrary, have arrived at the consciousness of an internal discord which renders such an ideal impossible; and hence the endeavour of their poetry is to reconcile these two worlds between which we find ourselves divided, and to blend them indissolubly together. The impressions of the senses are to be hallowed, as it were, by a mysterious connexion with higher feelings; and the soul, on the other hand, embodies its forebodings, or indescribable intuitions of infinity, in types and symbols borrowed from the visible world.

In Grecian art and poetry we find an original and unconscious unity of form and matter; in the modern, so far as it has remained true to its own spirit, we observe a keen struggle to unite the two, as being naturally in opposition to each other. The Grecian executed what it proposed in the utmost perfection; but the modern can only do justice to its endeavours after what is infinite by approximation; and, from a certain appearance of imperfection, is in greater danger of not being duly appreciated.

It would lead us too far, if in the separate arts of architecture, music, and painting (for the moderns have never had a sculpture of their own), we should endeavour to point out the distinctions which we have here announced, to show the contrast observable in the character of the same arts among the ancients and moderns, and at the same time to demonstrate the kindred aim of both.

Neither can we here enter into a more particular consideration of the different kinds and forms of romantic poetry in general, but must return to our more immediate subject, which is dramatic art and literature. The division of this, as of the other departments of art, into the antique and the romantic, at once points out to us the course which we have to pursue.

We shall begin with the ancients; then proceed to their imitators, their genuine or supposed successors among the moderns; and lastly, we shall consider those poets of later times, who, either disregarding the classical models, or purposely deviating from them, have struck out a path for themselves.

Of the ancient dramatists, the Greeks alone are of any importance. In this branch of art the Romans were at first mere translators of the Greeks, and afterwards imitators, and not always very successful ones. Besides, of their dramatic labours very little has been preserved. Among modern nations an endeavour to restore the ancient stage, and, where possible, to improve it, has been shown in a very lively manner by the Italians and the French. In other nations, also, attempts of the same kind, more or less earnest, have at times, especially of late, been made in tragedy; for in comedy, the form under which it appears in Plautus and Terence has certainly been more generally prevalent. Of all studied imitations of the ancient tragedy the French is the most brilliant essay, has acquired the greatest renown, and consequently deserves the most attentive consideration. After the French come the modern Italians; viz., Metastasio and Alfieri.[4] The romantic drama, which, strictly speaking, can neither be called tragedy nor comedy in the sense of the ancients, is indigenous only to England and Spain. In both it began to flourish at the same time, somewhat more than two hundred years ago, being brought to perfection by Shakespeare in the former country, and in the latter by Lope de Vega.

The German stage is the last of all, and has been influenced in the greatest variety of ways by all those which preceded it. It will be most appropriate, therefore, to enter upon its consideration last of all. By this course we shall be better enabled to judge of the directions which it has hitherto taken, and to point out the prospects which are still open to it.

When I promise to go through the history of the Greek and Roman, of the Italian and French, and of the English and Spanish theatres, in the few hours which are dedicated to these lectures, I wish it to be understood that I can only enter into such an account of them as will comprehend their most essential peculiarities under general points of view. Although I confine myself to a single domain of poetry, still the mass of materials comprehended within it is too extensive to be taken in by the eye at once, and this would be the case were I even to limit myself to one of its subordinate departments. We might read ourselves to death with farces. In the ordinary histories of literature the poets of one language, and one description, are enumerated in succession, without any further discrimination, like the Assyrian and Egyptian kings in the old universal histories. There are persons who have an unconquerable passion for the titles of books, and we willingly concede to them the privilege of increasing their number by books on the titles of books. It is much the same thing, however, as in the history of a war to give the name of every soldier who fought in the ranks of the hostile armies. It is usual, however, to speak only of the generals, and those who may have performed actions of distinction. In like manner the battles of the human mind, if I may use the expression, have been won by a few intellectual heroes. The history of the development of art and its various forms may be therefore exhibited in the characters of a number, by no means considerable, of elevated and creative minds.

. . .

Shakespeare's Irony

If the delineation of all his characters, separately considered, is inimitably bold and correct, he surpasses even himself in so combining and contrasting them, that they serve to bring out each other's peculiarities. This is the very perfection of dramatic characterization: for we can never estimate a man's true worth if we consider him altogether abstractedly by himself; we must see him in his relations with others; and it is here that most dramatic poets are deficient. Shakespeare makes each of his principal characters the glass in which the others are reflected, and by like means enables us to discover what could not be immediately revealed to us. What in others is most profound, is with him but surface. Ill-advised should we be were we always to take men's declarations respecting themselves and others for sterling coin. Ambiguity of design with much propriety he makes to overflow with the most praiseworthy principles; and sage maxims are not unfrequently put in the mouth of stupidity, to show how easily such commonplace truisms may be acquired. Nobody ever painted so truthfully as he has done the facility of self-deception, the half self-conscious hypocrisy towards ourselves, with which even noble minds attempt to disguise the almost inevitable influence of selfish motives in human nature. This secret irony of the characterization commands admiration as the profound abyss of acuteness and sagacity; but it is the grave of enthusiasm. We arrive at it only after we have had the misfortune to see human nature through and through; and when no choice remains but to adopt the melancholy truth, that 'no virtue or greatness is altogether pure and genuine', or the dangerous error that 'the highest perfection is attainable'. Here we therefore may perceive in the poet himself, notwithstanding his power to excite the most fervent emotions, a certain cool indifference, but still the indifference of a superior mind, which has run through the whole sphere of human existence and survived feeling.

The irony in Shakespeare has not merely a reference to the separate characters, but frequently to the whole of the action. Most poets who portray human events in a narrative or dramatic form take themselves a part; and exact from their readers a blind approbation or condemnation of whatever side they choose to support or oppose. The more zealous this rhetoric is, the more certainly it fails of its effect. In every case we are conscious that the subject itself is not brought immediately before us, but that we view it through the medium of a different way of thinking. When, however, by a dexterous manœuvre, the poet allows us an occasional glance at the less brilliant reverse of the medal, then he makes, as it were, a sort of secret understanding with the select circle of the more intelligent of his readers or spectators; he shows them that he had previously seen and admitted the validity of their tacit objections; that he himself is not tied down to the represented subject, but soars freely above it; and that, if he chose, he could unrelentingly annihilate the beautiful and irresistibly attractive scenes which his magic pen has produced. No doubt, wherever the proper tragic enters every thing like irony immediately ceases,[5] but from the avowed raillery of Comedy, to the point where the subjection of mortal beings to an inevitable destiny demands the highest degree of seriousness, there are a multitude of human relations which unquestionably may be considered in an ironical view, without confounding the eternal line of separation between good and evil. This purpose is answered by the comic characters and scenes which are interwoven with the serious parts in most of those pieces of Shakespeare where romantic fables or historical events are made the subject of a noble and elevating exhibition. Frequently an intentional parody of the serious part is not to be mistaken in them; at other times the connection is more arbitrary and loose, and the more so the more marvellous the invention of the whole, and the more entirely it is become a light revelling of the fancy. The comic intervals everywhere serve to prevent the pastime from being converted into a business, to preserve the mind in the possession of its serenity, and to keep off that gloomy and inert seriousness which so easily steals upon the sentimental, but not tragical, drama. Most assuredly Shakespeare did not intend thereby, in defiance to his own better judgment, to humour the taste of the multitude: for in various pieces, and throughout considerable portions of others, and especially when the catastrophe is approaching, and the mind consequently is more on the stretch and no longer likely to give heed to any amusement which would distract their attention, he has abstained from all such comic intermixtures. It was also an object with him, that the clowns or buffoons should not occupy a more important place than that which he had assigned them: he expressly condemns the extemporizing with which they loved to enlarge their parts.[6] Johnson founds the justification of the species of drama in which seriousness and mirth are mixed, on this, that in real life the vulgar is found close to the sublime, that the merry and the sad usually accompany and succeed one another.[7] But i does not follow that because both are found together, therefore they must not be separable in the compositions of art. The observation is in other respects just, and this circumstance invests the poet with a power to adopt this procedure, because every thing in the drama must be regulated by the conditions of theatrical probability; but the mixture of such dissimilar, and apparently contradictory, ingredients, in the same works, can only be justifiable on principles reconcilable with the views of art, which I have already described. In the dramas of Shakespeare the comic scenes are the antechamber of the poetry, where the servants remain; these prosaic attendants must not raise their voices so high as to deafen the speakers in the presence-chamber; however, in those intervals when the ideal society has retired they deserve to be listened to; their bold raillery, their presumption of mockery, may afford many an insight into the situation and circumstances of their masters.[8]

. . .

Shakespeare

Hamlet is singular in its kind: a tragedy of thought inspired by continual and never-satisfied meditation on human destiny and the dark perplexity of the events of this world, and calculated to call forth the very same meditation in the minds of the spectators. This enigmatical work resembles those irrational equations in which a fraction of unknown magnitude always remains, that will in no way admit of solution. Much has been said, much written, on this piece, and yet no thinking head who anew expresses himself on it, will (in his view of the connection and the signification of all the parts) entirely coincide with his predecessors. What naturally most astonishes us, is the fact that with such hidden purposes, with a foundation laid in such unfathomable depth, the whole should, at a first view, exhibit an extremely popular appearance. The dread appearance of the Ghost takes possession of the mind and the imagination almost at the very commencement; then the play within the play, in which, as in a glass, we see reflected the crime, whose fruitlessly attempted punishment constitutes the subject-matter of the piece; the alarm with which it fills the King; Hamlet's pretended and Ophelia's real madness; her death and burial; the meeting of Hamlet and Laertes at her grave; their combat, and the grand determination; lastly, the appearance of the young hero Fortinbras, who, with warlike pomp, pays the last honours to an extinct family of kings; the interspersion of comic characteristic scenes with Polonius, the courtiers, and the grave-diggers, which have all of them their signification, – all this fills the stage with an animated and varied movement. The only circumstance from which this piece might be judged to be less theatrical than other tragedies of Shakespeare is, that in the last scenes the main action either stands still or appears to retrograde. This, however, was inevitable, and lay in the nature of the subject. The whole is intended to show that a calculating consideration, which exhausts all the relations and possible consequences of a deed, must cripple the power of acting; as Hamlet himself expresses it:

> And thus the native hue of resolution
> Is sicklied o'er with the pale cast of thought;
> And enterprises of great pith and moment,
> With this regard, their currents turn awry,
> And lose the name of action.

With respect to Hamlet's character: I cannot, as I understand the poet's views, pronounce altogether so favourable a sentence upon it as Goethe does.[9] He is, it is true, of a highly cultivated mind, a prince of royal manners, endowed with the finest sense of propriety, susceptible of noble ambition, and open in the highest degree to an enthusiastic admiration of that excellence in others of which he himself is deficient. He acts the part of madness with unrivalled power, convincing the persons who are sent to examine into his supposed loss of reason, merely by telling them unwelcome truths, and rallying them with the most caustic wit. But in the resolutions which he so often embraces and always leaves unexecuted, his weakness is too apparent: he does himself only justice when he implies that there is no greater dissimilarity than between himself and Hercules. He is not solely impelled by necessity to artifice and dissimulation, he has a natural inclination for crooked ways; he is a hypocrite towards himself; his far-fetched scruples are often mere pretexts to cover his want of determination: thoughts, as he says on a different occasion, which have

> but one part wisdom
> And ever three parts coward.

He has been chiefly condemned both for his harshness in repulsing the love of Ophelia, which he himself had cherished, and for his insensibility at her death. But he is too much overwhelmed with his own sorrow to have any compassion to spare for others; besides his outward indifference gives us by no means the measure of his internal perturbation. On the other hand, we evidently perceive in him a malicious joy, when he has succeeded in getting rid of his enemies, more through necessity and accident, which alone are able to impel him to quick and decisive measures, than by the merit of his own courage, as he himself confesses after the murder of Polonius, and with respect to Rosencrantz and Guilden-stern. Hamlet has no firm belief either in himself or in anything else: from expressions of religious confidence he passes over to sceptical doubts; he believes in the Ghost of his father as long as he sees it, but as soon as it has disappeared, it appears to him almost in the light of a deception. He has even gone so far as to say, 'there is nothing either good or bad, but thinking makes it so'; with him the poet loses himself here in labyrinths of thought, in which neither end nor beginning is discoverable. The stars themselves, from the course of events, afford no answer to the question so urgently proposed to them. A voice from another world, commissioned, it would appear, by heaven, demands vengeance for a monstrous enormity, and the demand remains without effect; the criminals are at last punished, but, as it were, by an accidental blow, and not in the solemn way requisite to convey to the world a warning example of justice; irresolute foresight, cunning treachery, and impetuous rage, hurry on to a common destruction; the less guilty and the innocent are equally involved in the general ruin. The destiny of humanity is there exhibited as a gigantic Sphinx, which threatens to precipitate into the abyss of scepticism all who are unable to solve her dreadful enigmas.

As one example of the many niceties of Shakespeare which have never been understood, I may allude to the style in which the player's speech about Hecuba is conceived.[10] It has been the subject of much controversy among the commentators, whether this was borrowed by Shakespeare from himself or from another, and whether, in the praise of the piece of which it is supposed to be a part, he was speaking seriously, or merely meant to ridicule the tragical bombast of his contemporaries. It seems never to have occurred to them that this speech must not be judged of by itself, but in connection with the place where it is introduced. To distinguish it in the play itself as dramatic poetry, it was necessary that it should rise above the dignified poetry of the former in the same proportion that generally theatrical elevation soars above simple nature. Hence Shakespeare has composed the play in Hamlet altogether in sententious rhymes full of antitheses. But this solemn and measured tone did not suit a speech in which violent emotion ought to prevail, and the poet had no other expedient than the one of which he made choice: overcharging the pathos. The language of the speech in question is certainly falsely emphatical; but yet this fault is so mixed up with true grandeur, that a player practised in artificially calling forth in himself the emotion he is imitating, may certainly be carried away by it. Besides, it will hardly be believed that Shakespeare knew so little of his art, as not to be aware that a tragedy in which Aeneas had to make a lengthy epic relation of a transaction that happened so long before as the destruction of Troy, could neither be dramatical nor theatrical.

. . .

Goethe and Schiller

All must allow that Goethe possesses dramatic talent in a very high degree, but not indeed much theatrical talent. He is much more anxious to effect his object by tender development than by rapid external motion; even the mild grace of his harmonious mind prevented him from aiming at strong demagogic effect. *Iphigenia in Taurus* possesses, it is true, more affinity of the Greek spirit than perhaps any other work of the moderns composed before Goethe's; but is not so much an ancient tragedy as a reflected image of one, a musical echo: the violent catastrophes of the latter appear here in the distance only as recollections, and all is softly dissolved within the mind. The deepest and most moving pathos is to be found in *Egmont*, but in the conclusion this tragedy also is removed from the external world into the domain of an ideal soul-music.

That with this direction of his poetic career to the purest expression of his inspired imagining, without regard to any other object, and with the universality of his artistic studies, Goethe should not have had that decided influence on the shape of our theatre which, if he had chosen to dedicate himself exclusively and immediately to it, he might have exercised, is easily conceivable.

In the mean time, shortly after Goethe's first appearance, the attempt had been made to bring Shakespeare on our stage. The effort was a great and extraordinary one. Actors still alive acquired their first laurels in this wholly novel kind of exhibition, and Schröder,[11] perhaps, in some of the most celebrated tragic and comic parts, attained to the same perfection for which Garrick had been idolized. As a whole, however, no one piece appeared in a very perfect shape; most of them were in heavy prose translations, and frequently mere extracts, with disfiguring alterations, were exhibited. The separate characters and situations had been hit to a certain degree of success, but the sense of his composition was often missed.

In this state of things Schiller made his appearance, a man endowed with all the qualifications necessary to produce at once a strong effect on the multitude, and on nobler minds. He composed his earliest works while very young, and unacquainted with that world which he attempted to paint; and although a genius independent and boldly daring, he was nevertheless influenced in various ways by the models which he saw in the already mentioned pieces of Lessing, by the earlier labours of Goethe, and in Shakespeare, so far as he could understand him without an acquaintance with the original.

In this way were produced the works of his youth: *Die Raüber, Cabale und Liebe*, and *Fiesco*. The first, wild and horrible as it was, produced so powerful an effect as even to turn the heads of youthful enthusiasts. The defective imitation here of Shakespeare is not to be mistaken: Francis Moor is a prosaical Richard III, ennobled by none of the properties which in the latter mingle admiration with aversion. *Cabale und Liebe* can hardly affect us by its extravagant sentimentality, but it tortures us by the most painful impressions. *Fiesco* is in design the most perverted, in effect the feeblest.

So noble a mind could not long persevere in such mistaken courses, though they gained him applauses which might have rendered the continuance of his blindness excusable. He had in his own case experienced the dangers of an undisciplined spirit and an ungovernable defiance of all constraining authority, and therefore, with incredible diligence and a sort of passion, he gave himself up to artistic discipline. The work which marks this new epoch is *Don Carlos*. In parts we observe a greater depth in the delineation of character; yet the old and tumid extravagance is not altogether lost, but merely clothed with choicer forms. In the situations there is much of pathetic power, the plot is complicated even to epigrammatic subtlety; but of such value in the eyes of the poet were his dearly purchased reflections on human nature and social institutions, that, instead of expressing them by the progress of the action, he exhibited them with circumstantial fullness, and made his characters philosophize more or less on themselves and others, and by that means swelled his work to a size quite incompatible with theatrical limits.

Historical and philosophical studies seemed now, to the ultimate profit of his art, to have seduced the poet for a time from his poetical career, to which he returned with a riper mind, enriched with varied knowledge, and truly enlightened at last with respect to his own aims and means. He now applied himself exclusively to Historical Tragedy, and endeavoured, by divesting himself of his personality, to rise to a truly objective representation. In *Wallenstein* he has adhered so conscientiously to historical truth, that he could not wholly master his materials, an event of no great historical extent is spun out into two plays, with prologue in some degree didactical. In form he has closely followed Shakespeare; only that he might not make too large a demand on the imagination of the spectators, he has endeavoured to confine the changes of place and time within narrower limits. He also tied himself down to a more sustained observance of tragical dignity, and has brought forward no persons of mean condition, or at least did not allow them to speak in their natural tone, and banished into the prelude the mere people, here represented by the army, though Shakespeare introduced them with such vividness and truth into the very midst of the great public events. The loves of Thekla and Max Piccolomini form, it is true, properly an episode, and bear the stamp of an age very different from that depicted in the rest of the work; but it affords an opportunity for the most affecting scenes, and is conceived with equal tenderness and dignity.

Maria Stuart is planned and executed with more artistic skill, and also with greater depth and breadth. All is wisely weighed; we may censure particular parts as offensive: the quarrel for instance, between the two Queens, the wild fury of Mortimer's passion, &c.; but it is hardly possible to take any thing away without involving the whole in confusion. The piece cannot fail of effect; the last moments of Mary are truly worthy of a queen; religious impressions are employed with becoming earnestness; only from the care, perhaps superfluous, to exercise, after Mary's death, poetical justice on Elizabeth, the spectator is dismissed rather cooled and indifferent.

With such a wonderful subject as the *Maid of Orleans*, Schiller thought himself entitled to take greater liberties. The plot is looser; the scene with Montgomery, an epic intermixture, is at variance with the general tone; in the singular and inconceivable appearance of the black knight, the object of the poet is ambiguous; in the character of Talbot, and many other parts, Schiller has entered into an unsuccessful competition with Shakespeare; and I know not but the colouring employed, which is not so brilliant as might be imagined, is an equivalent for the severer pathos which has been sacrificed to it. The history of the *Maid of Orleans*, even to its details, is generally known; her high mission was believed by herself and generally by her contemporaries, and produced the most extraordinary effects. The marvel might, therefore, have been represented by the poet, even though the sceptical spirit of his contemporaries should have deterred him from giving it out for real; and the real ignominious martyrdom of this betrayed and abandoned heroine would have agitated us more deeply than the gaudy and rose-coloured one which, in contradiction to history, Schiller has invented for her. Shakespeare's picture, though partial from national prejudice, still possesses much more historical truth and profundity.[12] However, the German piece will ever remain as a generous attempt to vindicate the honour of a name deformed by impudent ridicule; and its dazzling effect, strengthened by the rich ornateness of the language, deservedly gained for it on the stage the most eminent success.

Part 8

Goethe

Johann Wolfgang von Goethe

1749–1832

Goethe, poet, playwright, novelist, and scientist, can hardly be said to have been connected with the romantic ironists included in this volume, or with Jean Paul Richter, except as an object of their admiration for being the foremost example of a contemporary artist achieving in practice the aesthetic principles expounded by the ironists (however much Goethe himself might have taken exception to this view). Their controversial view of Goethe as a source of inspiration for breaking down the Neo-classical stranglehold upon modern creative literature, and the allegedly false criticism generated from a too strict reliance upon classical forms, is testified to by the numerous occasions upon which Goethe figured as the subject for expounding Romantic principles and even manifestos of the new criticism. Goethe's criticism, scattered over a wide range, particularly of contemporary literature, was probably most influential (at least to an English audience) in the area of his writing on Shakespeare, about which it is sometimes exaggeratedly claimed that romantic criticism gained its original impulse from the *Hamlet* selections in *Wilhelm Meisters Lehrjahre* (1796). Romantic criticism certainly had centred upon Shakespeare as the model and standard of modern literature in distinction from classical models. While the comparative approach of Lessing was transformed by Herder into a historical relativism, Goethe's own attitude to Shakespeare (and to Romanticism generally) was less stable, undergoing considerable transformation as he went from eager youthful admiration, to restrained criticism, and finally to a harsher and more general hostility toward Shakespeare's fundamental principles of structure and design. His attitude is charted in three essays and one translation: (1) 'Zum Shakespeares Tag' (1771); (2) the *Wilhelm Meister* sections (1796); (3) his translation of *Romeo and Juliet*, which substantially alters the play to fit his classicist theory; and, finally, (4) 'Shakespeare und kein Ende' (1815), where Goethe argues against, for example, Tieck, that Shakespeare is no dramatic poet.

As a critic, Goethe evolved a theory of literature that deviated in most major respects from his Romantic contemporaries; but the selection chosen here, 'Aphorisms', still reveals numerous surprising similarities in spite of his classical principles. Whether the 'Aphorisms', written over a long period of his life, can be taken as representative of Goethe's critical principles is, however, arguable. Goethe's basic principles on art and criticism during the Romantic period are to be found in his correspondence with Schiller and his essay on Winckelmann, for example. Nevertheless, 'Aphorisms' still expresses Goethe's classical conception of art and his rejection of, for example, naturalism and patriotic art. Many of Goethe's maxims are directed in answer to J. G. Schadow, sculptor to the court of Prussia, who had in 1801 attacked the Weimar artists and supported Berlin naturalism and patriotic art.

A short collection of some of Goethe's other criticism can be found in *Schriften zur Literatur*, ed. E. Nahler (Berlin, 1970), 2 vols., which contains some central critical works. Other essays can be found, for example, in volume XVIII of the *Berliner Ausgabe* (1972).

The text of the 'Aphorisms' follows the German of the *Berliner Ausgabe* (Berlin und Weimar, 1972), XVIII, 632–42. The English text of the *Wilhelm Meister* selections is from *Wilhelm Meister's Apprenticeship*, translated by Thomas Carlyle, 3 vols. (Edinburgh and London, 1824), II, 26–8, 71–5, 176–81.

'Aphorisms on Art and Art History'
'Aphorisms über Kunst und Kunstgeschichte' (from literary remains)

In translating, we must go up to the brink of the Untranslatable; it is only then that we really become aware of the foreignness of the nation and the language.

If you would write, and certainly if you would dispute, about art today, you should at least have some inkling of the continuing achievements of philosophy in our time.

If you would reproach an author with obscurity, look first into yourself, to see if all is lucid there: in twilight, even the clearest writing is unreadable.

If you would dispute, have a care upon this occasion not to say things which no one would quarrel with.

If you would dispute certain principles, you should first be able to set them out very clearly, and in this clarity contend with them. Then you will not fall into the trap of fencing with phantoms of your own making.

The obscurity of certain maxims is only relative. Not everything which is illuminating to the man who practises them can be made clear to the listener.

An artist skilled in producing estimable works is not always capable of giving an account of them – either his own, or others.

Nature and idea are not to be separated without destroying both art and life.

When artists discuss nature, they always assume the idea, without being clearly conscious of it.

And so it is with those who praise experience only; they do not consider that experience is only the half of experience.

First they tell us of nature, and the imitation of nature; then there is supposed to be such a thing as beautiful nature. We are to choose. But only the best, of course. But by what marks are we to recognize the best? What norm should guide our choice? And where are we to find the norm? Surely not in nature too?

And let us assume the object were given: the most beautiful tree in the forest, which even the forester acknowledged to be a perfect specimen. Now, to transform that tree into a picture, I walk all round it and seek out its most beautiful aspect. I step back far enough to survey it in full. I wait for a favourable light – and then they tell me that of that tree in nature a great deal will still have been transferred to paper!

The layman may believe that; the artist, behind the scenes of his craft, should know better.

The very quality in a work of art which strikes the uncultivated as natural, is not nature (from without), but man (nature from within).[1]

We know of no world but with relation to man; we desire no art but the art which is the imprint of this relation.

The first artist to capture on the horizon in his picture the points of destination of the horizontal lines in all their variety and multiplicity, invented the principle of perspective.

The first artist to develop the colour scale out of the contraction and expansion to which the retina is adapted – or syncrisis [unifying] and diacrisis [separating], to use Plato's terms – discovered the principle of colouring.

Seek within yourselves, and you will find all; and rejoice if outside you, whatever you may call it, there is a nature which sayeth yea and amen to everything you have found within yourselves!

Many things long ago invented and discovered have not made any impact on the world; they can function, and yet go unnoticed, function and not rouse a general response. This is why any history of invention has the strangest riddles to grapple with.

It is as difficult to learn from models as from nature.

The form needs to be as well-digested as the material – indeed, it is much more difficult to digest.

Many have studied in accordance with ancient art, yet not made its nature entirely their own. Are they to be chided on that account?

Higher demands, even when not fulfilled, are intrinsically more estimable than lower, though they be fulfilled entirely.

Dry and naive, sturdy and stiff, timid and correct – all the characteristics we ascribe to early German art belong to every older, simpler artistic style. The early Venetians, Florentines etc. possess them all too.

And we Germans are supposed to think ourselves original only when we cannot rise above our beginnings!

Because Albrecht Dürer, for all his incomparable talent, could never rise to an idea of harmony and proportion in beauty, nor yet to the thought of a seemly purposiveness, does that mean we shall have to cling to the earth for ever?

Albrecht Dürer's talent was helped by his close realistic perception and an admirable human sympathy in tune with his immediate world; it was harmed by a dark imagination, excessive and without form.

It would be interesting to show how Martin Schön[2] compares with him, and how limited the German achievement is in this case; and useful to show that it is early days yet.

In each of the Italian schools, after all, the butterfly did break forth from the chrysalis!

And are we to crawl around for ever as caterpillars because a few Northern artists found their measure doing so?

Now that Klopstock has delivered us from rhyme,[3] and Voss[4] has given us new models of prosody, are we to go back to writing doggerel like Hans Sachs?[5]

Come, let us be many-sided! Brandenburg turnips are good, at their best eaten with chestnuts, and these two noble fruits grow very far apart.

As well as occidental and Northern forms, allow us to include in our multifarious writings forms from the Orient and the South!

We are many-sided only when we strive for the highest because we must (in earnest) and when we descend to the lesser just because we will (for fun).

Do not grudge German poets the pious wish to count as Homer's successors too! German sculptors, it will do you no harm to aim for the fame of the last followers of Praxiteles![6]

How much must a painter study before he can see a peach as Huysum[7] does, and are we not to try whether we can possibly see a man as a Greek saw him?

We should not hate the artist who must take his proportions (the measurable) from the art of the ancients, just because we want to take the Immeasurable from them.

It is quite enough that art-lovers agree in acknowledging and esteeming what is perfect; disputes about the mediocre will never end.

All the richness and concentration which is the sole excellence in a work of art goes unrecognized; everything fruitful and stimulating gets pushed aside; a deep and all-embracing synthesis is readily grasped by no one.

You choose yourselves a model, and with it you adulterate your individuality: that is the sum of your art. No thought for any principles, any school, any successors; all is arbitrary, random, and just as it happens to strike you. To cast off laws which are merely hallowed by tradition – there is no objection to that; but not to realize that after all there have to be laws arising from the nature of every art – that is something nobody thinks about.

Every work of art, good and bad, belongs to nature the moment it comes into being. The art of the ancients belongs to nature; indeed, when it pleases, it belongs to nature at its most natural. And instead of this noble nature, we are to study a base and common one!

For the common is really what nature means to these gentlemen! To create out of one's own being might well mean to give up the very thing that comes easy.

Art: a different kind of nature, mysterious too, but more intelligible, for art springs from the intelligence.

Nature works according to laws which she laid down for herself in concord with the Creator; art works according to rules which she has agreed upon with the genius.

Art rests upon a kind of religious sense, upon a profound, unshakeable seriousness. This is why art unites so readily with religion. Religion does not need an aesthetic sense, for it rests upon its own seriousness; nor does it bestow any, just as it cannot impart taste.

Reality at its *highest* degree of usefulness (purposiveness) will also be beautiful.

Perfection is already present if the necessary has been accomplished; beauty is there if the necessary has been accomplished, but is hidden.

Perfection is compatible with disproportion; beauty is compatible only with proportion.

Works of art are destroyed the moment the artistic sense disappears.

Allegory transforms the appearance into a concept, the concept into an image, but in such a way that the concept may be captured definite and complete in the image, and may be expressed by it.

Symbolism transforms the appearance into an idea, the idea into an image, and in such a way that the idea remains infinitely powerful and unattainable in the image, and even if expressed in every language, would remain unattainable.

In Rembrandt's excellent etching of Christ driving the money-changers from the temple,[8] the halo which usually surrounds Our Lord's head has shifted, as it were on to the forward movement of the hand, raised in a sturdy blow, but now transfigured with light in a divine act. The head, like the face, is in darkness.

Every great artist sweeps us off our feet, sets us afire. Everything in us which shares that particular faculty comes alive. And since we have an idea of greatness, and some disposition towards it, it is very easy for us to imagine that its seed lies in us too.

Everyone has a heart, some have a temperament, artistic principles are rare.

In all the arts a certain level can be attained by means of natural talent alone. At the same time, it is impossible to transcend that level unless art comes to our aid.

'It all comes from within himself!', they declare – thinking to praise the artist. Oh! that I might never hear such things again! Properly understood, the products of this kind of original genius are mostly reminiscences; anyone with experience will be able to point them out in detail.

This so-called original creation usually turns out false originals and mannerists.

Why else should we rail so much at mannerism in art, than because we believe it to be impossible to turn away from it to the right path?

Art should not represent what is embarrassing.

What the last hand can do, the first must state decisively. That is the stage which must determine what shall follow.

'You must not sniff around at my pictures. The colours are bad for you.' Rembrandt.

Not even the finest artist always succeeds in turning a number of sketches into a whole.

Even a moderate talent shows a mind at work in the presence of nature. That is why there is a pleasure to be derived from any tolerable drawing of that kind.

The cause of dilettantism: flight from style, ignorance of method, always the crazy effort to achieve the very thing that is impossible – which would require the highest art even to get near it.

The error of the dilettante: wanting to make a direct connection between imagination and technique.

There is a tradition that Daedelus,[9] the first sculptor, envied the potter the invention of his wheel. Doubtless nothing would have come of envy, but the great man probably anticipated that technology would ultimately be ruinous to art.

Technology in alliance with bad taste is the enemy of art most to be feared.

A propos the Berlin *Manufacturers' Pattern-Book* the question was raised whether so much elaboration in the finish of the pages was necessary. It emerged that the very thing that most attracted the young craftsman-artist was the finish of the design; and only observing and imitating this enabled him to grasp the whole and appreciate the value of the forms.

Chodowiecki[10] is a very respectable, and, according to us, an *ideal* artist. His *good* works are an excellent witness to his *intellect* and his *taste*. Any ideal quality beyond this was not to be expected from the circles in which he worked.

The most terrible thing for the apprentice is that in the end he still has to assert his own individuality against his master. The more powerful the master's teaching, the greater the distress, the despair even, of the recipient.

A noble philosopher once spoke of architecture as *frozen music*[11] – and had to face a great deal of head-shaking at the remark. We believe that the best way of re-introducing this beautiful idea is to call architecture *silent music*.

Think of Orpheus, who was confronted by a vast empty building-site, and so wisely sat down on the most beautiful spot, and with the life-giving sounds of his lyre conjured forth a spacious market-place. Torn from their massy beds, the blocks of stones were deeply stirred by the imperious, yet friendly coaxing sounds, and moved enraptured, compelled to shape themselves as the craftsman would have them, and then pile themselves up in due order in rhythmical layers and walls. And in this way street may add itself to street. And there will be no lack of protective outer walls. The sounds die away, but the harmony remains. The citizens of such a town live and move in the midst of eternal melodies. The spirit cannot sink, activity cannot flag, the eye takes over the function, charge and duty of the ear, and on the most ordinary day, the citizens feel that they dwell in an ideal condition. Without reflecting on or questioning its source, they will partake of the highest moral and religious pleasure. Make it your custom to walk to and fro in St Peter's, and you will perceive something analogous to what we have ventured to express.

On the other hand, the citizen of a badly built town, where the houses have been swept together haphazardly by a fretful broom, lives all unawares in a dark and desert condition. A stranger entering it feels as if he were listening to a cacophony of bagpipe, penny-whistle and tambourine, and would have to steel himself to behold the inescapable spectacle of dancing bears and leaping apes.

The temples of the ancients concentrate the God in man; medieval churches aspire towards God in the heavens.

From *Wilhelm Meister's Apprenticeship*
Wilhelm Meisters Lehrjahre (1796)

Hamlet Analysis

'You all know Shakespeare's incomparable Hamlet: our public reading of it at the Castle yielded every one of us the greatest satisfaction. On that occasion, we proposed to act the piece; and I, not knowing what I undertook, engaged to play the Prince's part. This I conceived that I was studying, while I began to get by heart the strongest passages, the soliloquies, and those scenes in which force of soul, vehemence and elevation of feeling have the freest scope; where the agitated heart is allowed to display itself with touching expressiveness.

'I farther conceived that I was penetrating quite into the spirit of the character, while I endeavoured as it were to take upon myself the load of deep melancholy, under which my prototype was labouring, and in this humour to pursue him through the strange labyrinths of his caprices and his singularities. Thus learning, thus practising, I did not doubt that I should by and by become one person with my hero.

'But the farther I advanced, the more difficult did it become for me to form any image of the whole, in its general bearings; till at last this seemed to me almost impossible. I next went through the piece entirely, and all at once; but here also I found much that I could not away with. At one time the characters, at another time the manner of displaying them, seemed inconsistent; and I almost despaired of finding any general tint, in which I might present my whole part with all its shadings and variations. In such devious paths I toiled, and wandered long in vain; till at length a hope arose that I might reach my aim in quite a new way.

'I set about investigating every trace of Hamlet's character, as it had shewn itself before his father's death: I endeavoured to distinguish what in it was independent of this mournful event; independent of the terrible events that followed; and what most probably the young man would have been, had no such things occurred.

'Soft, and from a noble stem, this royal flower had sprung up under the immediate influences of majesty: the idea of moral rectitude with that of princely elevation, the feeling of the good and dignified with the consciousness of high birth, had in him been unfolded simultaneously. He was a prince, by birth a prince; and he wished to reign, only that good men might be good without obstruction. Pleasing in form, polished by nature, courteous from the heart, he was meant to be the pattern of youth and the joy of the world.

'Without any prominent passion, his love for Ophelia was a still presentiment of sweet wants. His zeal in knightly accomplishments was not entirely his own; it needed to be quickened and inflamed by praise bestowed on others for excelling in them. Pure in sentiment, he knew the honourable-minded, and could prize the rest which an upright spirit tastes on the bosom of a friend. To a certain degree, he had learned to discern and value the good and the beautiful in arts and sciences; the mean, the vulgar was offensive to him; and if hatred could take root in his tender soul, it was only so far as to make him properly despise the false and changeful insects of a court, and play with them in easy scorn. He was calm in his temper, artless in his conduct, neither pleased with idleness, nor too violently eager for employment. The routine of a university he seemed to continue when at court. He possessed more mirth of humour than of heart; he was a good companion, pliant, courteous, discreet, and able to forget and forgive an injury; yet never able to unite himself with those who overstept the limits of the right, the good, and the becoming.'

. . .

Loving Shakespeare as our friend did, he failed not to lead round the conversation to the merits of that dramatist. Expressing, as he entertained, the liveliest hopes of the new epoch which these exquisite productions must form in Germany, he ere long introduced his Hamlet, who had busied him so much of late.

Serlo declared that he would long ago have played the piece, had this been possible, and that he himself would willingly engage to act Polonius. He added, with a smile: 'An Ophelia, too, will certainly cast up, if we had but a Prince.'

Wilhelm did not notice that Aurelia seemed a little hurt at her brother's sarcasm. Our friend was in his proper vein, becoming copious and didactic, expounding how he would have Hamlet played. He circumstantially delivered to his hearers the opinions we before saw him busied with; taking all the trouble possible to make his notion of the matter acceptable, sceptical as Serlo shewed himself regarding it. 'Well then,' said the latter, finally, 'suppose we grant you all this, what will you explain by it?'

'Much; every thing,' said Wilhelm. 'Conceive a prince such as I have painted him, and that his father suddenly dies. Ambition, and the love of rule, are not the passions that inspire him. As a king's son, he would have been contented; but now he is first constrained to consider the difference which separates a sovereign from a subject. The crown was not hereditary; yet a longer possession of it by his father would have strengthened the pretensions of an only son, and secured his hopes of the succession. In place of this, he now beholds himself excluded by his uncle, in spite of specious promises, most probably for ever. He is now poor in goods and favour, and a stranger in the scene which from youth he had looked upon as his inheritance. His temper here assumes its first mournful tinge. He feels that now he is not more, that he is less, than a private nobleman; he offers himself as the servant of every one; he is not courteous and condescending, he is needy and degraded.

'His past condition he remembers as a vanished dream. It is in vain that his uncle strives to cheer him, to present his situation in another point of view. The feeling of his nothingness will not forsake him.

'The second stroke that came upon him wounded deeper, bowed still more. It was the marriage of his mother. The faithful tender son had yet a mother, when his father passed away. He hoped, in the company of his surviving noble-minded parent, to reverence the heroic form of the departed; but his mother too he loses, and it is something worse than death that robs him of her. The trustful image, which a good child loves to form of its parents, is gone. With the dead there is no help, on the living no hold. She also is a woman, and her name is Frailty, like that of all her sex.

'Now first does he feel himself completely bent and orphaned; and no happiness of life can repay what he has lost. Not reflective or sorrowful by nature, reflection and sorrow have become for him a heavy obligation. It is thus that we see him first enter on the scene. I do not think that I have mixed aught foreign with the piece, or overcharged a single feature of it.'

Serlo looked at his sister, and said, 'Did I give thee a false picture of our friend? He begins well; he has still many things to tell us, many to persuade us of.' Wilhelm asseverated loudly, that he meant not to persuade, but to convince: he begged for another moment's patience.

'Figure to yourselves this youth,' cried he, 'this son of princes; conceive him vividly, bring his state before your eyes, and then observe him when he learns that his father's spirit walks; stand by him in the terrors of the night, when the venerable ghost itself appears before him. A horrid shudder passes over him; he speaks to the mysterious form; he sees it beckon him; he follows it, and hears. The fearful accusation of his uncle rings in his ears; the summons to revenge, and the piercing oft-repeated prayer, Remember me!

'And when the ghost has vanished, who is it that stands before us? A young hero panting for vengeance? A prince by birth, rejoicing to be called to punish the usurper of his crown? No! trouble and astonishment take hold of the solitary young man: he grows bitter against smiling villains, swears that he will not forget the spirit, and concludes with the expressive ejaculation:

> The time is out of joint: O! cursed spite,
> That ever I was born to set it right!

'In these words, I imagine, will be found the key to Hamlet's whole procedure. To me it is clear that Shakespeare meant, in the present case, to represent the effects of a great action laid upon a soul unfit for the performance of it. In this view the whole piece seems to me to be composed. There is an oak-tree planted in a costly jar, which should have borne only pleasant flowers in its bosom; the roots expand, the jar is shivered.

'A lovely, pure, noble, and most moral nature, without the strength of nerve which forms a hero, sinks beneath a burden which it cannot bear, and must not cast away. All duties are holy for him; the present is too hard. Impossibilities have been required of him; not in themselves impossibilities, but such for him. He winds, and turns, and torments himself; he advances and recoils; is ever put in mind, ever puts himself in mind; at last does all but lose his purpose from his thoughts; yet still without recovering his peace of mind.'

On the Novel and Drama

One evening a dispute arose among our friends about the novel and the drama, and which of them deserved the preference. Serlo said it was a fruitless and misunderstood debate; both might be superior in their kinds, only each must keep within the limits proper to it.

'About their limits and their kinds,' said Wilhelm, 'I confess myself not altogether clear.'

'Who *is* so?' said the other; 'and yet perhaps it were worth while to come a little closer to the business.'

They conversed together long upon the matter; and in fine, the following was nearly the result of their discussion:

'In the novel as well as in the drama, it is human nature and human action that we see. The difference between these sorts of fiction lies not merely in their outward form; not merely in the circumstance that the personages of the one are made to speak, while those of the other have commonly their history narrated. Unfortunately many dramas are but novels, which proceed by dialogue; and it would not be impossible to write a drama in the shape of letters.

'But in the novel, it is chiefly *sentiments* and *events* that are exhibited; in the drama, it is *characters* and *deeds*. The novel must go slowly forward; and the sentiments of the hero, by some means or another, must restrain the tendency of the whole to unfold itself and to conclude. The drama on the other hand must hasten, and the character of the hero must press forward to the end; it does not restrain, but is restrained. The novel hero must be suffering, at least he must not in a high degree be active; in the dramatic one, we look for activity and deeds. Grandison, Clarissa, Pamela, The Vicar of Wakefield, Tom Jones himself, are, if not suffering, at least retarding personages; and the incidents are all in some sort modelled by their sentiments. In the drama the hero models nothing by himself; all things withstand him, and he clears and casts away the hindrances from off his path, or else sinks under them.'

Our friends were also of opinion, that in the novel some degree of scope may be allowed to Chance; but that it must always be led and guided by the sentiments of the personages; on the other hand, that Fate, which, by means of outward unconnected circumstances, carries forward men, without their own concurrence, to an unforeseen catastrophe, can have place only in the drama; that Chance may produce pathetic situations, but never tragic ones; Fate on the other hand ought always to be terrible; and is in the highest sense tragic, when it brings into a ruinous concatenation the guilty man, and the guiltless that was unconcerned with him.

These considerations led them to back the play of Hamlet, and the peculiarities of its composition. The hero in this case, it was observed, is endowed more properly with sentiments than with a character; it is events alone that push him on; and accordingly the piece has in some measure the expansion of a novel. But as it is Fate that draws the plan; as the story issues from a deed of terror, and the hero is continually driven forward to a deed of terror, the work is tragic in the highest sense, and admits of no other than a tragic end.

They were now to study and peruse the piece in common; to commence what are called the book-rehearsals. These Wilhelm had looked forward to as to a festival. Having formerly collated all the parts, no obstacle on this side could oppose him. The whole of the actors were acquainted with the piece; he endeavoured to impress their minds with the importance of these book-rehearsals. 'As you require', said he, 'of every musical performer that, in some degree, he shall be able to play from the book; so every actor, every educated man, should train himself to recite from the book, to catch immediately the character of any drama, any poem, any tale he may be reading, and exhibit it with grace and readiness. No committing of the piece to memory will be of service, if the actor have not in the first place penetrated into the sense and spirit of his author; the mere letter will avail him nothing.'

Serlo declared, that he would overlook all subsequent rehearsals, the last rehearsal itself, if justice were but done to these rehearsals from the book. 'For commonly,' said he, 'there is nothing more amusing than to hear an actor speak of study: it is as if freemasons were to talk of building.'

The rehearsal passed according to their wishes; and we may assert, that the fame and favour which our company acquired afterwards, had their foundation in these few but well-spent hours.

'You did right, my friend,' said Serlo, when they were alone, 'in speaking to our fellow-labourers so earnestly; and yet I am afraid that they will scarce fulfil your wishes.'

'How so?' asked Wilhelm.

'I have noticed', answered Serlo, 'that as easily as you may set in motion the imaginations of men, gladly as they listen to your tales and fictions, it is yet very rarely that you find among them any touch of an imagination you can call productive. In actors this remark is strikingly exemplified. Any one of them is well content to undertake a beautiful, praiseworthy, brilliant part; and seldom will any one of them do more than self-complacently transport himself into his hero's place, without in the smallest troubling his head, whether other people view him so or not. But to seize with vivacity what the author's feeling was in writing; what portion of your individual qualities you must cast off, in order to do justice to a part; how by your own conviction that you are become another man, you may carry with you the convictions of the audience; how by the inward truth of your conceptive power, you can change these boards into a temple, this pasteboard into woods; to seize and execute all this is given to very few. That internal strength of soul, by which alone deception can be brought about; that lying truth, without which nothing will affect us rightly, have by most men never even been imagined.

'Let us not then press too hard for spirit and feeling in our friends! The surest way is first coolly to instruct them in the sense and letter of the piece; if possible to open up their understandings. Whoever has the talent will then, of his own accord, eagerly adopt the spirited feeling and manner of expression; and those who have it not, will at least be prevented from acting or reciting altogether falsely. And among actors, as indeed in all cases, there is no worse arrangement than for any one to make pretensions to the spirit of a thing, while the sense and letter of it are not ready and clear to him.'

Notes

The references to *Critical* and *Athenäum Fragments*, as well as to Novalis' *Miscellaneous Writings*, are to paragraph numbers, not to pages.

Friedrich Schlegel

'On Incomprehensibility'

1. Christian Garve (1742–98), German popularizer of philosophy.
2. Immanuel Kant (1724–68); the 'table of categories' refers to section 3, chapter 1 of Book 1 of the 'Transcendental Analytic' under the first main section, 'Transcendental Doctrine of Elements' (p. 113 of Kemp-Smith's translation).
3. 'Critical Age', parodying the name given to Kant's Critical Philosophy.
4. Christoph Girtanner (1760–1800), German physician whose publications included research into medicine and chemistry.
5. This is Fragment 216 of the *Athenäum* collection.
6. Johann Dyk (1750–1813), Leipzig bookseller and translator of French popular comedies.
7. Karl Leonard Reinhold (1758–1823), German philosopher and follower of Kant. See *Critical Fragment* 66 on Reinhold.
8. 'Götzen' in the German, probably referring to Goethe's play *Götz von Berlichingen*.
9. *Critical Fragment* 108.
10. *Critical Fragment* 48.
11. Stanislas, Chevalier de Boufflers (1738–1815), French poet.
12. *Genoveva*: Tieck's play, *Leben und Tod der Heiligen Genoveva* (1799), based on a medieval legend.
13. A. W. Schlegel's didactic 'Elegies' in *Sämtliche Werke* (1846–7), vols. 1–2.
14. Critical Fragment 20.
15. Schlegel's gloss takes off from the last stanza of Goethe's poem 'Beherzigung'.

Critical Fragments

16. *Nathan der Weise* (1779), by Gotthold Ephraim Lessing.
17. François Hemsterhuis (1721–90), Dutch aesthetician and moral philosopher influenced by the Neoplatonic tradition.
18. August Ludwig Hülsen (1765–1810), German philosopher and educator, friend of Fichte and the Schlegels.

Athenäum Fragments

19. The last two sentences of this fragment are by Schleiermacher.
20. On the importance of the 'intellectual point of view' see 'On Goethe's *Meister*', p. 65.
21. Lessing's play, *Nathan der Weise* (1779).
22. Birthplace and residence of Kant throughout his life.
23. This is probably the most famous, most frequently quoted of all Schlegel's fragments.
24. Johann Joachim Winckelmann (1717–68), German aesthetician and archaeologist, famous for his work, *Die Geschichte der Kunst im Altertum* (1762), which had a profound impact upon the development of aesthetics in Germany over the next several decades.
25. See the foregoing essay, 'On Incomprehensibility', for a discussion of this fragment.
26. See Novalis, *Miscellaneous Writings*, 73 on the idea of the mediator.
27. Gottfried August Bürger (1748–94), poet of ballads, the most famous of which was 'Lenore'.
28. *Wilhelm Lovell* (1793–6), and *Franz Sternbalds Wanderungen* (1798), novels by Ludwig Tieck. *Herzensergiessungen eines kunstliebenden Klosterbruder* (1797) was written with Wilhelm Wackenroder, as a mixed genre of the historical, religious and aesthetic.
29. Leibgaber was a character in Jean Paul's novel *Siebenkäs*.

Ideas

30. Friedrich Schleiermacher's *Reden über Religion* (1799).
31. This fragment, from the manuscript of the *Ideas*, was not printed in the *Athenäum*.
32. Decii, a Roman family noted for sacrificing their lives for the sake of Rome's glory.
33. See *Ideas* 8 above, and note 30.

'On Goethe's Meister'

34. The section of Goethe's *Meister* is contained in this anthology (pp. 231–4).

'Letter about the Novel'

35. Friedrich Richter is Jean Paul.
36. Jean de la Fontaine (1621–95), French author famous for his *Fables*.
37. Denis Diderot (1713–84), author of *Jacques le Fataliste*, French philosopher, novelist, and critic, whose novels and *Encyclopédie* brought him international repute.
38. *Die Allgemeine Zeitung*, a contemporary newspaper published by Cotta. 'Jack Pudding' – a literal rendering of the German 'Hanswurst', the traditional name for the clown in comedy. The clown was formally banished from the German stage of Leipzig in the 1730s by Gottsched, in an attempt to raise the tone of the drama; the Viennese, on the other hand, obstinately clung to the Hanswurst right into the following century.
39. *Emilia Galotti*, a tragedy by Lessing.
40. *Cecilia Beverley*, a novel by Fanny Burney, Mme d'Arblay (1752–1840).
41. Oliver Goldsmith's sentimental novel, written in 1766.

Novalis

Miscellaneous Writings

1. Lines enclosed in angled brackets were crossed out by Novalis while reworking the MS.
2. Richard Samuel draws attention to a passage in Schelling's treatise 'Vom Ich als Prinzip der Philosophie oder über das Unbedingte im Menschlichen Wissen' (1795), section 2–3, which Novalis almost certainly had in mind.
3. Cf. *Dialogue* 5.
4. This fragment was emended editorially by F. Schlegel. Samuel notes a similar turn of phrase in Schiller's 'On the Aesthetic Education of Man': 'Every individual man, one can say, carries, according to his natural tendency and destiny, a pure ideal man in himself; the greatest mission of his Being is to be in harmony with the inalterable unity of that ideal man in all his variations.' Schiller then refers to Fichte's publication, *Vorlesungen über die Bestimmung des Gelehrten*.
5. *Lyceum* (that is, *Critical*) *Fragment* 108.
6. The German word is 'Progredibilitaet'.
7. Gottfried August Bürger (1748–94), poet.

Dialogues

8. 'Omarists': a reference to those who share the sentiments of the Caliph Omar, who, in the early stages of the Mohammedan expansion, ordered the burning of the books in the great library at Alexandria.
9. Cf. *Miscellaneous Writings*, 1, p. 84 above.
10. See *Critical Fragment* 8 and Friedrich Schlegel's article 'Über Lessing', where he refers to Lessing as one of the revolutionary spirits.

'On Goethe'

11. Novalis refers to 'Beiträge zur Optik' (1791–4), 'Die Metamorphose der Pflanzen' (1790), and 'Die Metamorphose der Insekten' (1796–8).
12. Cf. Friedrich Schlegel's 'On Goethe's *Meister*', above, p. 60.
13. J. W. Ritter (1776–1810), German physicist, who made discoveries in galvanism, electrochemical properties of elements, and the effects of light on chemical reactions.
14. Theophrastus (c. 372–287 B.C.), Greek philosopher.
15. F. W. A. Murhard, *Geschichte der Physik* (1798–9).

'Studies in the Visual Arts'

16. Cf. Novalis to Caroline Schlegel, 9 September 1798: 'The letter about antiquity is completely altered.'
17. Probably a reference to John Brown (1735–88), medical doctor of Edinburgh and author of *Elementa Medicinae* (1780), in which Brown describes the concept of excitability and stimulation.
18. J. G. Herder, *Plastik. Einige Wahrnehmungen über Form und Gestalt aus Pygmalions bildendem Traum* (Riga, 1779; Suphan edn, VIII, 1–87).
19. *Ibid.*, VIII, 15f.

Ludwig Tieck

Tony *review*

1. Menaechmi: William Warner's translation (1595) of the *Menaechmi* of Plautus (c. 254–c. 184 B.C.) may have given Shakespeare the inspiration for *The Comedy of Errors*.
2. Boccaccio (1313–75), Italian novelist and poet.
3. Mateo Bandello (1485–1561), Bishop of Agen (1550–61), Italian writer of tragic tales and novellas, published in 1554 and in 1574. Of his 214 tales and novellas, several provided the sources for Shakespeare's *Much Ado about Nothing*, *Twelfth Night*, and *Romeo and Juliet*, as well as for Webster's *Duchess of Malfi*.
4. Miquel de Cervantes Saavedra (1547–1616).
5. Charlotte Lennox, author of *Shakespeare Illustrated: or, the Novels and Histories on which the plays of Shakespeare are founded* . . . 3 vols. (London, 1753–4).

'The Old English Theatre'

6. *Amadis de Gaule*, a novel known by its French name, but of Spanish or Portuguese origin, published by Montalvo in Spanish about 1508, in four books. The 'successors' probably refers to the expansions of the original four books by Herberay des Essarts into eight books in 1527, and the German expansion into thirteen books, published by S. Feyerabend (1569–95). C. M. Wieland (1733–1813) completed his long poem *Der Neue Amadis* in 1771, and Goethe wrote a short poem of the same title.
7. Thomas Middleton (1570–1627). In its time, *The Witch* was a flop, but material from *The Witch* was incorporated into a revival of Shakespeare's *Macbeth* around 1616, perhaps supervised by Middleton.
8. John Heywood (?–c. 1572), English dramatist and epigrammatist, and friend of Sir Thomas More.

Preface to Wilhelm Lovell

9. G. W. Rabener (1714–71), eighteenth-century German prose satirist whose works were published initially in 1745–8.
10. For Friedrich Schleiermacher's translation of Plato, see the modern edition, *Sämtliche Werke Platon*, ed. W. F. Otto, E. Grassi, and G. Plamböcke, 6 vols. (Hamburg, 1974–6).

'Final Conclusion' to Puss-in-Boots

11. Socrates is satirized by Aristophanes in his play, *Clouds*.

Karl Solger

Erwin

1. Compare Coleridge's definition of the symbol, in the *Statesman's Manual*, almost exactly contemporary with Solger's *Erwin* publication.
2. Henckmann compares Goethe, 'Maxims and Reflections', numbers 279, 1112, 1113; in 314 Goethe writes: 'This is the truly symbolic, where the particular

represents the universal, not as dream or shadow, but as the living, momentary revelation of the inscrutable.' And compare Schelling, *Philosophie der Kunst* (Darmstadt, 1960), section 39. For a brief discussion of the relation between Schelling and Solger's aesthetics, see Ingrid Strohschneider-Kohrs, *Romantische Ironie in Theorie und Gestaltung* (*Hermaea*, 6, Tübingen, 1960), under the section on Solger. Hegel's relation to Solger is discussed by B. A. Kahlert, *System der Aesthetik* (Leipzig, 1846).

3. These comments and the continuation of the passage show that Solger is distinguishing allegory from symbol in a way quite different from that familiar to English readers. That is, he defines 'allegory' differently from, say, Coleridge; his distinction between allegory and symbol implies then either a different valuation of allegory or a quality that falls within our category of the symbol usually not distinguished by us. In the *Vorlesungen*, for example, Solger speaks of the necessity of seeing beauty from two points of view depending upon whether the linguistic expression charts movement from appearance to reality (as allegory does) or from reality to appearance (as symbol does); instead, the distinction might be better understood by English readers as between 'allegorical symbol' and 'plastic (tending toward concrete) symbol'. See below, n. 4, and the correspondence excerpts on symbol and allegory, pp. 154 and 157–8.

4. One might risk suggesting that for Solger 'mere allegory' was 'mere' only because its symbolical energy had suffered 'semantic entropy', and had become inaccessible to later cultures. His discussion here of the Greek gods as symbols bears out this view, and also shows that Solger was aware of the difference between 'what is commonly thought of as allegory' – that is, general concepts or forms or abstractions represented by persons or images – and what *he* defined true allegory to be. The relation between allegory and symbol as basic forms of art is discussed in the Tieck-Solger letters on art and mysticism, pp. 154–8.

5. Hegel continues the problem of symbolical versus allegorical art in his discussion of the three world-historical stages of the development of art: symbolical art he links to the Orient, while art developed its highest revelation of essence in the classical art of the Greeks; finally, with romantic, Christian art the plasticity of sensuous appearance is achieved in an internalized, spiritualized fullness.

6. Solger refers presumably to Jonson's *Every Man* plays.

7. See section 31 below, 'Concept of Humour', in the *School for Aesthetics*, Course VII.

8. Jean Paul's *Siebenkäs* (1796–7), one of Solger's favourite works.

9. *School for Aesthetics*, Course VII, section 32.

10. Compare Course IX of the *School* and *Athenäum Fragment* 116.

11. See above, p. 133–4.

12. Anselm and Bernhard are two of the interlocutors of the dialogues, though they participate only occasionally.

13. Solger probably refers to C. M. Wieland, translator of Lucian.

14. Compare *Athenäum Fragment* 42 on Schlegel's distinction between 'kunstlerisch' and 'rhetorisch-polemisch Ironie'.

15. This is one of the most striking instances of Solger's reliance upon Plato as model. See the slave-boy demonstration in the *Meno*; Socrates' comments are translated almost verbatim.

Tieck–Solger Correspondence

1. 'Titurel' probably refers to the Arthurian hero in Wolfram von Eschenbach's *Parzival*; it is also the title given to an unfinished epic in four-line stanzas by

Wolfram. It was written between 1210 and 1220. Another work, *Der Jüngere Titurel*, probably by Albrecht von Scharfenberg, is a long poem based on Wolfram's fragments, written about 1272. It was one of the most popular works of the Middle Ages.

2. 'Sybil of the Orient', Calderón's (1600–81) 'La Sibila del Oriente y gran Reina de Saba'.

3. Sacramental auto; a type of allegorical sacramental play, of which Calderón is said to have written seventy-three.

4. Lope de Vega (1562–1635), Spanish dramatist.

5. 'die Stelle im gestiefelten Kater', probably a reference to the epilogue; see *Tieck Schriften*, v, 277.

6. On Novalis' relation to Jakob Boehme, see E. Ederheimer, *Jakob Boehme und die Romantiker* (Heidelberg, 1904), II, 57f.

7. Friedrich Gottlieb Klopstock (1724–1803).

8. Christoph Martin Wieland (1733–1813), major critic and creative writer.

9. Solger refers presumably to his letter to Tieck of 22 November 1818, p. 155 above.

10. August von Kotzebue (1761–1819), German dramatist and author of over two hundred plays, many achieving great contemporary popularity.

Jean Paul Richter

School for Aesthetics: *Richter's own notes*

a Only the majority and minority, the minimum and maximum permit this expression. For no man actually differs qualitatively from another. Like the rise and fall of peoples, the transition from servile childhood to morally free adulthood, which clearly demonstrates evolution through degrees, confutes the proud man who prefers to consider himself distinguished by genus rather than by degree.

b Because he wishes to use the usual muscles for walking on the ground and cannot, while in the heavenly air, he feels no need of muscles for flying.

c Since even in ethics the two classes of *moral sense* and *moral strength* can be distinguished, Rousseau should also be classed as passive.

d This is equally true of the philosophical genius, whom I (unlike Kant) cannot specifically distinguish from the poet.[12] See the reasons for this in *The Campan Valley*, p. 51, which have not yet been refuted. The *inventive* philosophers were all poetic, that is, the truly systematic ones. Something different are the *sifting* philosophers, who never create an organic system, but at best clothe, nourish, amputate, etc. The difference in application between related kinds of genius, however, merits a special, difficult investigation.

e For unreflectiveness in action, i.e., the forgetting of personal relations, agrees so well with poetic and philosophic reflectiveness, that reflection and writing poetry often occur in dream and in madness, where such forgetfulness governs most strongly. The genius is in more than one sense a somnambulist: In his bright dream he can do more than he who is awake, and he climbs every dark height of reality. But rob him of the world of dream, and he tumbles in the real world.

f For pure negation or emptiness would exclude every opposed effort, and negative magnitude would have the same effect as positive.

g Prophecy, or the whole of prophecy, omniscience, is, we feel, something higher than mere complete recognition of the cause. With that indeed the conclusion or rather the perception of the effect would be given at once. Still, it would not be an anticipation or destruction of time, but a mere contemplation, i.e., experience, of it.

h The whole of life or being can only be intuited; the parts are subject to proofs based on those larger intuitions.

i As is well known, the vessels in old age become cartilage and the cartilage bones, and earth enters into the body until the body enters the earth.

j Let it-be remembered that I have given above the name of *objective* contrast to the contradiction between the ridiculous effort and the sensuously perceived circumstance, but the name *subjective* to a second contradiction, which we attribute to the ridiculous being when we lend *our* knowledge to *its* action.

k *Empfindselig (sensible)*, a coinage of Hamann's, is better than *empfindelnd (sentimental)*, and not merely for the sake of euphony; the former means simply an excessive luxuriating frequency of feeling according to the analogies *redselig*, *saumselig*, and *friedselig*; but the latter indicates, although incorrectly, a feeling both petty and false.

l But incorrectly, for the comic prepares the pathetic as little as relaxation does tension; rather the reverse is true.

m In this technique he imitated Holberg,[33] Foote, Swift, etc.

n Musäus was later humble enough to introduce his golden vein into the lead galleries of the *Universal German Library* and to give it reviews of novels; it is a shame that today these whimsical reviews are allowed to die along with the books and the Library and that these sunken pearls are not lifted out of the desert and strung together.

o The Persians say, 'Only God can have a self'; the Turks, 'Only the devil says "I"'. *Bibliothèque des Philosophes*, by Gautier.

p *Ad Aristophanis lucernam lucubrare* [To work late at night by Aristophanes' lamp]. See in Welcker's translation of the *Frogs*, preface p. 4. This and the earlier one of the *Clouds* I may perhaps dare to praise for their comic power, their easier introduction of the great Comus to us, for their rich instructive observations, and finally for the high aesthetic perspective, without thereby incurring for myself an accusation of arrogant judgment about a linguistic domain ruled by such powerful philological kings.

q Cicero says: *adeo illum risi, ut pene sim factus ille* [I laughed so much at him that I almost became him].

r Every absurdity in *Tristram Shandy*, although for the most part micrological, is a product of human nature not of accidental individuality. If the general, however, is lacking, as in Peter Pindar,[48] no wit can save a book from death. That for many years Walter Shandy has been resolving every time the door creaks to oil it, etc., is our nature, not his alone.

s The further the reader gets into *Tristram Shandy*, the more lyric Sterne's humour becomes. Thus his marvellous journey in the seventh book, the humorous dithyramb in the eighth book (chaps. 11, 12), etc.

t Therefore, as many named particularities as could be tolerated should be made current for *every* German city (they already have their beers). The prime goal would be to place in the hands of the comic writer over a period of time a dictionary and *cadastre flora* of comic individuation. Such a Swabian league of cities would join the separate cities into the very slips or boards of a comic national theatre. The Comicus would then be able to describe more easily and the reader would understand more easily. The lindens, the Tiergarten, the Charité, the Wilhelmshöhe, the Prater, and the terrace of Brühle fortunately provide arable latitude for every individualizing comic poet. But if, for example, the present author chose the proper names of places and circumstances which should be best for comic individuation, because they are best known and well named, from among the few cities where he has lived (Hof,

Leipzig, Weimar, Meinungen, Coburg, Bayreuth), he would be little understood and as a result poorly appreciated in any other place.

u In philological, figurative, and sensuous fullness Fischart far surpasses Rabelais and he equals Rabelais in erudition and Aristophanic word-coining. He is more Rabelais's regenerator than his translator; his Pactolus deserved to be panned for gold by the investigators of languages and customs. Here are some traits from his picture of a pretty maid, from his *Historical Sketch* (1590), p. 142: 'Her little cheeks bloomed with roses, and illuminated more brightly the circumfluent air with their reflection like a rainbow, like women coming out of a bath in pictures of the ancients; through her swan-white throat tube one might see the red wine slip as through a Moorish glass; she had a truly alabaster little gullet, a porphyry skin, through which all the veins appeared, like the white and black little stones in a clear little fountain; apple-round and sweetly hard breasts of marble, true apples of Paradise and alabaster balls, finely *decorated* near her heart and nicely *elevated*, not too high like the Swiss and Cologner, not too low like the Dutch, but like the French, etc.' His prose frequently rhymes, sometimes, as in chapter 26, p. 351, to fine effect. The fifth chapter about married people is a masterpiece of sensuous description and observation, but chaste and free as the Bible and our ancestors.

v The inscription at the foot of the statue of an idle French king: *Statua statuae*, or the witticism about an empty parterre as *le double de l'autre*.

w I.e., more with a series of figurative similes than with an antithesis, as will be shown further in the discussion of figurative wit.

x For our divine service is now mostly held in books.

y The only exception is Hamann, whose commas at times form planetary systems, whose periods become solar systems, and whose words (like those of primitive languages, according to Herder) are whole sentences. Often brevity is easier to write than to read; the author arrives at the expressed thought by merely eliminating incidental ones; the reader must supply the latter from the former.

z Without solution in water there is no taste.

aa It is symbolically fitting that *trade*, this foe of poetry, caused the transformation of hieroglyphs into letters (cf. Buhle, *History of Philosophy*, vol. 1) because the tradesman likes conciseness.

bb An ode can be created in a single day, but *Clarissa*, despite its flaws, cannot be completed even in one year. The ode reflects a single side of the world or of a spirit, while the true novel reflects every side.

School for Aesthetics: *editor's notes*

On the Poetic Faculties

1. 'Reproductive Imagination' is Hale's rendering of 'Einbildungskraft' in contrast to 'Phantasie', rendered 'imagination', to distinguish active and passive imagination. Jean Paul may be influenced here by the tradition traced by Tom McFarland, in reference to Coleridge's distinction between primary and secondary imagination and fancy, in his article 'The Origin and Significance of Coleridge's Theory of Secondary Imagination', *New Perspectives on Coleridge and Wordsworth*, ed. G. H. Hartman (New York, 1972), 195–246. Jean Paul's interest in eighteenth-century English literature, and particularly the influence of Sterne on his style, in conjunction with many Coleridgean theories, is an important reminder of the flow of ideas between Germany and England at this time, and of the fact that the English

tradition provided both Jean Paul and Coleridge with a heritage of critical ideas, more theoretically systematized no doubt by the German tradition, but nevertheless present in the prose and fiction, as Sterne's writings vividly illustrate.

2. *Clavicula Salomonis* refers to the *Key of Solomon*, a Hebrew manuscript ascribed to King Solomon of Israel (10th century B.C.), supposedly dictated to him by the angels; the treatise is an introduction to the magical arts, full of Greek, Babylonian, Egyptian and other ancient traditions. It is sometimes known as the 'Secret of Secrets'. Jean Paul further refers to the legend of Solomon's seal or ring, an amulet supposed to control and protect from evil spirits.

3. Karl Ramler (1725–98), aesthetician and editor of *Batteux, Cours de Belles Lettres* (1756–8). Christian Wolff (1679–1754), follower of Leibniz's philosophy and an important precursor of Kant.

4. M. Hale notes that Edward Young in *Conjectures on Original Composition* (1759), and Alexander Gerard, in *An Essay on Genius* (1774), set precedents for this 'passive genius' concept.

5. Jean Paul probably read Diderot's *Le Neveu de Rameau* in a German translation by Goethe. Jean Paul's *Levana* (1807) may be taken as a reply to Jean Jacques Rousseau's (1712–78) *Emile* (1762).

6. 'Acumen' is 'Scharfsinn', 'profundity' 'Tiefsinn' in German.

7. Karl Philipp Moritz (1757–93), philosopher, author of *Anton Reiser* and *Andreas Hartknopf*, and friend of Goethe and Jean Paul.

8. Helferich Peter Sturz (1757–79), prose writer.

9. Georg Christian Lichtenberg (1742–80), satirist, known for his description of Hogarth's engravings.

10. Christoph Martin Wieland (1733–1813), major critic and creative writer.

11. J. C. Adelung (1732–1806).

On Genius

12. Kant, *Kritik der Urteilskraft*, section 47.

13. Guido Reni (1575–1642), Italian painter.

14. Vittorio Alfieri (1749–1803), Italian dramatist.

15. Friedrich Heinrich Jacobi (1743–1819), German philosopher and novelist, and friend of Jean Paul, well known especially for his *Über die Lehre des Spinoza* (Breslau, 1789).

16. Daniel Peucer (1699–1756), rhetorician, and Daniel Morhof (1639–91), literary historian.

17. Jakob Boehme (1575–1624), mystical philosopher who greatly influenced Schelling and many other writers such as Ludwig Tieck.

18. Johann Georg Hamann (1730–88), mystical philosopher.

On Humorous Poetry

19. Leibgaber, a character in Jean Paul's novel *Siebenkäs* (1796–7).

20. Gottlieb Wilhelm Rabener (1714–71), satirist.

21. *Athenäum Fragment* 116.

22. K. F. Bahrdt (1741–92); August Cranz (1737–1801); J. K. Wezel (1747–1819); Garlieb Merkel (1769–1850).

23. *Allgemeine Deutsche Bibliothek*, a Berlin Enlightenment journal published by Friedrich Nicolai from 1765 to 1792.

24. Justinus Kerner (1786–1862); J. A. Kanne (1773–1824), pseudonym Walter Bergins; Achim von Arnim (1781–1831); Joseph von Görres (1776–1848); Clemens Brentano (1778–1842), pseudonym Maria; F. C. von Weisser (1761–1836); A. K. Bernhardi (1768–1820); Franz Horn (1781–1837); Stephan Schütze (1771–1839); Ernst Wagner (1769–1812).

25. Claudius Galen (A.D. c. 130–c. 200), Greek physician and writer on medicine. In Wieland's *Der Neue Amadis* and in the *History of the Wise Danischmend*, the footnotes contain numerous scholarly references (signed, e.g., 'Martin Scriblerus' and other fictitious names) to bodily functions of the grosser kind; they include references to, amongst others, Hippocrates and ancient medicine generally.

26. Johann Gottwerth Müller von Itzehoe (1743–93).

27. Echo of the title of Wieland's novel *Der Prozess um des Esels Schaffen – Die Geschichte der Abderifen* (The Republic of Fools: being the history of the state and people of Abdera) satirizing philistinism.

28. *Soccus*, the low shoe worn by comic actors, as the *cothurnus* was worn by tragic actors.

29. Louis Sébastien Mercier (1740–1814), *Tableaux de Paris* (1781–90).

30. August von Kotzebue (1761–1819), German dramatist, author of over two hundred plays, many achieving great contemporary popularity.

31. Friedrich Gotter (1746–97).

32. Moritz August von Thümmel (1738–1817), novelist influenced by Sterne, and author of *Reise in die mittägliche Provinzen von Frankreich* (1791–1805).

33. Ludwig von Holberg (1684–1754), Danish comedian.

34. Justus Möser (1720–94).

35. Refers to Jean Paul's *Dr. Fenks Leichenrede*.

36. Ernst Platner, *Gespräch über den Atheismus* (Leipzig, 1783).

37. Johann Karl Musäus (1735–87), comic novelist.

38. Christian Friedrich Schubart (1739–91), journalist and author of Storm and Stress poetry.

39. Alain René Le Sage (1668–1747), author of the picaresque *Gil Blas de Santillane* (1715).

40. Charles Pigault-Lebrun (1753–1835), French author of comedies.

41. C. P. J. de Crébillon (1707–77), French novelist.

42. Fichte used the term to refer to pure selfhood.

43. J. J. Bode (1730–93), translator of numerous English novelists.

44. John Arbuthnot (1667–1735), friend of Pope and Swift.

45. Henry Home, Lord Kames (1696–1782), in *Elements of Criticism* (1762), a book that was influential in Germany and went through seven editions in England by the end of the century.

46. Johann Fischart (1524–89), humorist.

47. Johann Matthäus Bechstein (1757–1822), expert in birds and forestry.

48. Pseudonym of John Wolcot (1738–1819), physician and author of satires.

49. Marquise Marie de Sévigné (1626–96), whose letters were published in 1726.

50. T. G. von Hippel (1741–96), German humorist.

51. Noted centres of pirated editions; an unauthorized edition of Jean Paul's *School* was published in Vienna in 1815, according to Hale.

52. J. G. Meusel (1743–1820), author of a literary *Who's Who?*

On Wit

53. Schelling's philosophy is alluded to here.

54. *Greek Anthology*, v, 91, roughly translated, 'I send to you a sweet perfume, gracing the

perfume, not you. For you yourself are able to perfume the perfume.'
55. Lessing, in the first of the *Fables* of 1759.
56. Pierre Bayle (1647–1706), French philosopher and critic.
57. K. L. Reinhold (1758–1823), worked with Wieland on the *Deutsche Merker*; also a follower of Kant's.
58. *Critical Fragment* 9.
59. *Hudibras*, Canto 5.
60. Young, *On Fame*, Satire 3.
61. Mme de Necker, *Mélanges*, 2 vols. (Paris, 1798–1801), I, 266.
62. Perhaps a reference to the Baucis and Philemon legend; see Ovid, *Metamorphoses*, Book VIII.
63. Young, *On Fame*, Satire 3.
64. Jean d'Alembert (1717–83), *Eloges* (Paris, 1779), 296.
65. According to Berend, not Edward Gibbon but Fontenelle.
66. Antoine de La Motte-Houdar (1672–1731), *Fables Nouvelles* (Paris, 1719), 9.
67. Mme de Necker, *Mélanges*, I, 267.
68. *Anthropologie in pragmatischer Hinsicht* (1798), section 21.
69. J. C. Adelung (1732–1806); Charles Batteux (1713–80).
70. Caroline Pichler (1769–1843), edited *Gleichnisse* (1808).
71. T. G. von Hippel (1741–96), German humorist influenced by Sterne.
72. *Mélanges*, II, 47.
73. Jean Paul refers to the mine invented by de Belidor in 1756, called 'globe de compression'; 'Globulus hystericus' describes a delusion of suffering (according to Hale).
74. Justus Möser, *Harlekin, or Defence of the Grotesque-Comic* (1777), 53.
75. Young's *Night Thoughts*, Night 3, lines 278–85.
76. Fontenelle, *Réflexions sur la poétique*.
77. Lessing, conclusion to the *Antiquarische Briefen*.

On the Novel

78. *Poetics*, chapter 24.
79. J. B. Basedow (1723–90), *Philalethie* (1764), I, 286.
80. A folk book of 1504.
81. Herder, *Adrastea*, ed. Suphan, XXIII, 295–7.
82. Ernst Wagner (1769–1812), novelist influenced by Jean Paul in, for example, *Wilibalds Ansichten des Lebens* (1804). Friedrich, Baron de la Motte-Fouqué (1777–1843) author of *Undine* (1811) a work that charmed Fouqué's contemporaries from Goethe to Walter Scott, and later Heinrich Heine. Achim von Arnim (1781–1831), novelist noted for his collection of old German folksongs and author of *Aphorismen über die Kunst* (1802).
83. *Poetics*, chapter 23–4.

A. W. Schlegel

Lectures on Dramatic Art and Literature

1. Johann Joachim Winckelmann (1717–68), archaeologist and aesthetician, whose *History of Ancient Art* (1762) powerfully influenced German criticism.
2. Here Schlegel follows closely Herder in his 'Shakespeare' essay in *Von Deutscher Art und Kunst*.

3. François Hemsterhuis (1721–90), Dutch aesthetician and moral philosopher.
4. Pietro Antonio Domenico Buonaventura Metastasio (Pietro Trapassi, 1698–1782), Italian poet. Vittorio Alfieri (1749–1803), Italian dramatist.
5. Schlegel's point is at variance with the views of Friedrich Schlegel and Solger. See O. Walzel, 'Methode? Ironie bei F. Schlegel und bei Solger', *Helicon*, 1 (1938), 33–50, for discussion of this and other of Schlegel's most important deviations from romantic irony theory.
6. As for example in *Hamlet*, Act III, scene ii, in Hamlet's instructions to the actors.
7. Samuel Johnson, *Preface to Shakespeare*, ed. W. K. Wimsatt (Harmondsworth, 1969), 62ff.
8. Here again, Schlegel seems to be in disagreement with Solger, Novalis, F. Schlegel, and Jean Paul. See the Introduction, p. 20, on the relation of earnestness and jest.
9. See Goethe's 'Zum Shakespeares Tag' (1771) and the *Hamlet* discussion from *Wilhelm Meister* included in the anthology; Goethe's own views underwent considerable change between the writing of these two pieces.
10. The player's speech about Hecuba occurs in *Hamlet*, Act III, scene ii, ll. 270–5.
11. Friedrich Ludwig Schröder (1744–1816), German actor, in charge of the Hamburg Theatre for many years at the end of the century, published alterations and translations of plays.
12. For Shakespeare's handling of the Maid of Orleans legend, see *The First Part of King Henry VI*.

Goethe

'*Aphorisms*'

1. See Goethe's essay, 'Simple Imitation of Nature, Manner, Style', in vol. 19 of the Berliner Ausgabe.
2. Martin Schongauer, painter and engraver, whose work had interested Goethe since 1798.
3. Klopstock wrote his famous 'Messias' in hexameters, his 'Odes' in free verse.
4. Johann Heinrich Voss (1751–1826), poet and translator of Homer's *Odyssey* (1781) and *Iliad* (1793).
5. Hans Sachs (1494–1576), German poet.
6. Praxiteles, celebrated Greek sculptor who flourished around 346 B.C. He worked in Parian marble; it is uncertain whether any of his works survive.
7. John van Huysum (1682–1740), illustrious painter and disciple of his father, Justus Van Huysum.
8. Etched in 1635.
9. Daedelus, according to mythology, was a Greek sculptor and master builder banished from Athens to King Minos' Crete.
10. Daniel Chodowiecki, painter considered by some of Goethe's contemporaries as a representative of naturalism.
11. Schelling, *Lectures on the Philosophy of Art*, may be Goethe's source.

Bibliography

Part I: Primary Sources

Friedrich Schlegel

Kritische Friedrich-Schlegel-Ausgabe. General editor, Ernst Behler, with Anstett and Eichner. 22 vols. München, 1958–67.
Prosaische Jugendschriften. Ed. J. Minor. 2 vols. Vienna, 1882.
Kritische Schriften. Ed. W. Rasch. München, 1956.
Lucinde and the Fragments. Trans. and with an introduction by Peter Firchow. Minneapolis, Minn., 1971.
Aesthetic and Miscellaneous Works. Trans. E. J. Millington. London, 1900.
Dialogue on Poetry. Trans. Ernst Behler and R. Struc. Pennsylvania and London, 1968.
Literary Notebooks, 1797–1801. Ed. Hans Eichner. Toronto, 1957.

Novalis (Friedrich von Hardenberg)

Novalis Schriften. Ed. Paul Kluckhorn and Richard Samuel. 4 vols. Stuttgart, 1960–75.

Ludwig Tieck

Schriften. 28 vols. Berlin, 1828–54.
Kritische Schriften. Ed. L. Tieck. Leipzig, 1848–52.
Ausgewählte Kritische Schriften. Ed. E. Ribbat. Tübingen, 1975.
Nachgelassene Schriften. Ed. R. Köpke. 2 vols. Leipzig, 1855.
Erinnerungen aus dem Leben des Dichters . . . Ed. R. Köpke. 2 vols. Leipzig, 1855.
Das Buch Über Shakespeare. Ed. H. Lüdeke. Halle, 1920.
Tieck and Solger. The Complete Correspondence. Ed. Percy Matenko. New York, Berlin, 1933.

Karl Solger

Erwin. Vier Gespräche über das Schöne und die Kunst. Ed. W. Henckmann. München, 1971, after the 1907 Berlin edition.
Philosophische Gespräche. Berlin, 1817.
Vorlesungen über Aesthetik. Ed. K. W. L. Heyse. Leipzig, 1829.
Nachgelassene Schriften und Briefwechsel. Ed. L. Tieck and F. von Raumer. 2 vols. Leipzig, 1826.
Tieck and Solger. The Complete Correspondence. Ed. Percy Matenko. New York, Berlin, 1933.

Jean Paul Richter

Sämtliche Werke. Ed. Eduard Berend. 37 vols. in three parts. Weimar, 1927–44, Berlin, 1952–63.
Horn of Oberon. Jean Paul Richter's School for Aesthetics. Trans. Margaret R. Hale. Detroit, 1973.

A. W. Schlegel

Sämtliche Werke. Ed. E. Böcking. 12 vols. in six parts. Leipzig, 1846–7.
Kritische Schriften. 2 vols. Berlin, 1828.
Vorlesungen über dramatische Kunst und Literatur. Ed. E. Lohner, vols. 5 and 6 of *Kritische Schriften und Briefen.* Stuttgart, 1966–7.
Course of Lectures on Dramatic Art and Literature. Trans. J. Black. London, 1815. Revised J. W. Morrison. London, 1846.
Lectures on German Literature from Gottshed to Goethe. Trans. H. G. Giedler, from notes by G. Toynbee in 1833. Oxford, 1944.

Johann Wolfgang Goethe

Berliner Ausgabe. 22 vols. Berlin and Weimar, 1960–78.
Wilhelm Meisters Lehrjahre. Berliner Ausgabe, vol. 10. Berlin and Weimar, 1962.
Kunsttheoretische Schriften und Übersetzungen. Berliner Ausgabe, vol. 18. Berlin and Weimar, 1972.
Schriften zur Literatur. Ed. E. Naylor. 2 vols. Berlin, 1970.
Wilhelm Meister's Apprenticeship. Trans. Thomas Carlyle. 3 vols. Edinburgh and London, 1824.
Goethe on Art. Trans. John Gage. London, 1980.
Correspondence between Schiller and Goethe, from 1794–1805. Translated with notes by Dora Schmitz, 2 vols. London, 1877–9.

Part II: Secondary reading: selected texts

The following texts have been chosen as points of departure for further reading.

General

Benjamin, Walter. *Der Begriff der Kunstkritik in der deutschen Romantic.* In *Schriften,* II. Frankfurt am Main, 1955.
Ederheimer, E. *Jakob Boehme und die Romantiker.* Heidelberg, 1904.
Lovejoy, A. O. 'Schiller and the Genesis of Romanticism'. *Modern Language Notes,* 35 (1920), 136–46.
'On the Meaning of Romantic in early German Romanticism'. *Modern Language Notes,* 31 (1916), 385–96, and 32 (1917), 65–77.
Strohschneider-Kohrs, Ingrid. *Die Romantische Ironie in Theorie und Gestaltung. Hermaea,* 6, Tübingen, 1960.
Walzel, Oskar. *German Romanticism.* Trans. A. E. Lussky. New York and London, 1932 (original German edition, 1908).

Friedrich Schlegel

Dieckmann, Liselotte. 'Friedrich Schlegel and the Romantic Concepts of the Symbol.' *Germanic Review*, 34 (1959), 276–83.
Eichner, Hans. *Friedrich Schlegel*. New York, 1970.
  'Friedrich Schlegel's Theory of Romantic Poetry.' *PMLA*, 71 (1956), 1018–41.
  'The Supposed Influence of Schiller's "Naive and Sentimental Poetry" on Friedrich Schlegel's "Ueber das Studium der griechischen Poesie".' *Germanic Review*, 30 (1955), 260–4.
Henel, H. 'Friedrich Schlegel und die Grundlagen der moderne literarischen Kritik.' *Germanic Review*, 20 (1945), 81–93.
Immerwahr, R. 'The Subjectivity or Objectivity of Friedrich Schlegel's Poetic Irony.' *Germanic Review*, 26 (1951), 173–91.
  'Friedrich Schlegel's Essay "On Goethe's *Wilhelm Meister*".' *Monatsheft*, 49 (1957), 1–22.
Lange, Victor. 'Friedrich Schlegel's Literary Criticism.' *Comparative Literature*, 7 (1955), 289–305.
Szondi, Peter. 'Friedrich Schlegel und die romantische Ironie: Mit einem Anhang über Ludwig Tieck.' *Euphorion*, 48 (1954), 397–411.

Novalis

Barrack, C. M. 'Novalis's Metaphysic of the Poet.' *Germanic Review*, 46 (1971), 257–84.
Dyck, Martin. *Novalis and Mathematics. A Study of Friedrich von Hardenberg's Fragments on Mathematics and its Relation to Magic, Music, Religion, Philosophy, Language and Literature*. Chapel Hill, 1960.
Fauteck, H. 'Die Sprachtheorie Friedrich von Hardenbergs.' *Neue Forschungen*, 34. Berlin, 1940.
Haering, T. *Novalis als Philosoph*. Stuttgart, 1954.
Lewis, L. J. 'Novalis and the Fichtean Absolute.' *German Quarterly*, 35 (1960), 464–74.
Peacock, Ronald. 'Novalis and Schopenhauer: A critical transition in Romanticism.' *German Studies presented to L. A. Willoughby*. Oxford, 1952, 133–43.
Ritter, H., ed. *Novalis in Zeugnissen seiner Zeitgenossen*. Stuttgart, 1973.
Schaber, S. C. 'Novalis' Theory of the Work of Art and Hieroglyph.' *Germanic Review*, 48 (1973), 35–44.

Ludwig Tieck

Griggs, E. L. 'Ludwig Tieck and Samuel Taylor Coleridge.' *Journal of English and Germanic Philology*, 54 (1955), 262–8.
Günther, H. *Romantische Kritik und Satire bei Tieck*. Leipzig, 1907.
Lussky, A. E. *Tieck's Romantic Irony*. Chapel Hill, 1932.
Matenko, Percy. *Ludwig Tieck and America*. Chapel Hill, 1954.
Wheeler, K. M. 'Coleridge's Friendship with Ludwig Tieck.' *New Approaches to Coleridge*. Ed. D. Sultana. London, 1981, 96–109.
Zeydel, E. H. *Ludwig Tieck and England. A Study of the Literary Relations of Germany and England during the early Nineteenth Century*. Princeton, 1931.
  Ludwig Tieck, the German Romanticist. Princeton, 1935.

Karl Solger

Boucher, Maurice. *K. W. F. Solger, Esthétique et philosophie de la présence*. Paris, 1934.
Goethe, J. W., 'Solgers *Nachgelassene Schriften und Briefwechsel*', *Berliner Ausgabe*. Berlin
    and Weimar, 1972, vol. 17, 685–7.
Hegel, G. W. F. 'Über Solgers *Nachgelassene Schriften und Briefwechsel*.' In *Jahrbücher für
    wissenschaftliche Kritik*, 51–4 (1828), 105–10. And in G. W. F. Hegel. *Vermischte
    Schriften aus der Berliner Zeit*. Ed. H. Blockner. Stuttgart, 1958 (*Jubiläumsausgabe*, vol.
    20).
Heller, Josef. *Solgers Philosophie der ironischen Dialektik*. Berlin, 1928.
Mueller, G. E. 'Solger's Aesthetics – A Key to Hegel'. *Corona: Studies in Celebration of the
    Eightieth Birthday of Samuel Singer*. Ed. A. Schirokauer. Durham, 1941, 212–27.
Walzel, Oskar. 'Methode? Ironie bei Friedrich Schlegel und bei Solger.' *Helicon*, 1
    (1938), 33–50.
    'Tragik bei Solger.' *Helicon*, 3 (1940), 27–49.

Jean Paul Richter

Berend, Eduard. *Jean Pauls Aesthetik*. Berlin, 1909.
Birzniks, Paul. 'Jean Paul's Early Theory of Poetic Communication.' *Germanic Review*, 41
    (1966), 186–201.
Brewer, Eduard V. 'The New England Interest in Jean Paul.' *Modern Philology*, 27
    (1943), 1–25.
Carlyle, Thomas. *Critical and Miscellaneous Essays*. New York, 1900.
Profitlich, Ulrich. *Der seelige Leser: Untersuchungen zur Dichtungstheorie Jean Pauls*. Bonn,
    1968.
Smeed, J. W. 'Carlyles Jean Paul-Uebersetzungen.' *Deutsche Vierteljahrschrift der
    Literatur*, 35 (1961), 262–70.
Unger, Rudolf. 'Jean Paul und Novalis.' *Jean Paul-Jahrbuch 1925*, 134–52.
Wilkending, Gisela. *Jean Pauls Sprachauffassung in ihrem Verhältnis zu seiner Aesthetik*.
    Marburg, 1968.
Jean Paul Bibliographie. Ed. E. Berend, revised J. Krogoll. Stuttgart, 1963.

A. W. Schlegel

Ewton, R. W. *The Literary Theories of August Wilhelm Schlegel*. The Hague, 1972.
Solger, Karl. 'Resenzion von A. W. Schlegel's *Vorlesungen*', in *Erwin*, ed. W.
    Henckmann. München, 1970, 394–471.
Walzel, Oscar, 'Methode? Ironie bei Friedrich Schlegel und bei Solger.' *Helicon*, 1
    (1938), 33–50.

Johann Wolfgang Goethe

Bode, Wilhelm. *Goethes Aesthetik*. Berlin, 1901.
Jurgensen, Manfred. *Symbol als Idee. Studien zu Goethes Aesthetik*. Bern, München, 1968.
Kimura, Naoji. *Goethes Wortgebrauch zur Dichtungstheorie im Briefwechsel mit Schiller und in
    den Gesprächen mit Eckermann*. München, 1965.
Menzer, Paul. *Goethes Aesthetik*. Köln, 1957.

Müller, Curt. *Die geschichtliche Voraussetzungen des Symbolbegriffs in Goethes Kunstanschauung.* Leipzig, 1937.

Oppel, Horst. *Das Shakespeare-Bild Goethes.* Mainz, 1949.

Sengle, Friedrich. *Goethes Verhältnis zum Drama. Die Theoretische Bemerkungen im Zusammenhange mit seinem dramatischen Schaffen.* Berlin, 1937.

Trevelyan, Humphry. *Goethe and the Greeks.* Cambridge, 1941.

Index

Index

Index

Index